Hossein Bidgoli

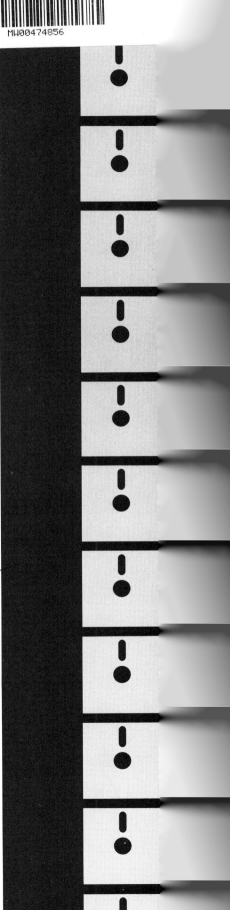

INFORMATION SYSTEMS LITERACY AND SOFTWARE PRODUCTIVITY TOOLS

Introductory Concepts

تقديم محمد حسين فتحي كوش

H. Bidgoli

١٩٩١

Macmillan Publishing Company
New York

Collier Macmillan Canada, Inc.
Toronto

Maxwell Macmillan International Publishing Group
New York   Oxford   Singapore   Sydney

To so many fine memories of my brother, Mohsen, for his uncompromising belief in the power of education.

Cover photo by Jack McWilliams. The Walk-Through Computer is a permanent exhibit of The Computer Museum, Boston, MA.

Editor: Vernon R. Anthony
Production Editor: Rex Davidson
Art Coordinator: Ruth A. Kimpel
Photo Editor: Gail Meese
Text Designer: Anne Daly
Cover Designer: Russ Maselli
Production Buyer: Pamela D. Bennett

This book was set in Baskerville and Helvetica.

Macmillan Publishing Company
866 Third Avenue, New York, New York 10022

Collier Macmillan Canada, Inc.

Library of Congress Cataloging-in-Publication Data
Bidgoli, Hossein.
    Information systems literacy and software productivity tools/Hossein Bidgoli.
        p. cm.
    Includes index.
    Contents: bk. 1. Introductory concepts—bk. 2. DOS—bk. 3. WordPerfect 5.1—bk. 4. dBase III PLUS—bk. 5. WordStar 5.5—bk. 6. Quattro—bk. 7. GoldSpread—bk. 8. IBM BASIC—bk. 9. DOS, WordPerfect 5.1, Lotus 1-2-3, and dBase III PLUS—bk. 10. DOS, WordStar 5.5, Lotus 1-2-3, and dBase III PLUS.
    ISBN 0-02-309474-5 (bk. 1.)
    1. Electronic data processing.   2. Computer software. I. Title.
QA76.B488 1991
005.369—dc20

90-20366
CIP

Printing: 1 2 3 4 5 6 7 8 9   Year: 1 2 3 4

Preface

The first part of the text is devoted to the principles of data processing and information systems. The coverage brings the world of information processing to a first-time computer user. This presentation provides the understanding and appreciation for computers as a problem-solving tool. The appendices provide a detailed glossary of all the important information systems and commonly used terminologies, then provide a succinct presentation of DOS and BASIC programming. Also, answers to selected review questions are provided in Appendix A. The readers can test their understanding by answering these questions.

- Chapter 1 *The World of Computers* provides an overview of computers and information systems and a history of computers.
- Chapter 2 *Hardware and Software Concepts* examines input, output, operating systems, classes of computers, and programming languages.
- Chapter 3 *The World of Microcomputers* takes a comprehensive look at microcomputer hardware, software, and their application. This chapter provides a thorough discussion of the types of application software used today, and provides the foundation for the hands-on section of the text.
- Chapter 4 *Computer-Based Information Systems* outlines a complete conceptual model for a CBIS, classifies CBIS by level, and looks at trends, including artificial intelligence, expert systems, natural language processing, and robotics.
- Chapter 5 *Computer-Based Information Systems in Action* shows how CBISs are used in business to support finance, manufacturing, marketing, personnel, and strategic planning. The types of software used within each of these functional areas are also discussed.
- Chapter 6 *Database and Information Systems* examines the role of database management systems in a CBIS, database design, and trends in DBMS.
- Chapter 7 *Distributed Processing and Information Systems* is a comprehensive view of data communications, networks, and telecommunications.
- Chapter 8 *Systems Analysis and Design* takes a non-technical look at how business systems are built, including the use of CASE tools.
- Chapter 9 *CBIS and Society* explores issues and trends, including career opportunities, computer crime, and the increasing power and variety of applications of computer technology.

The chapters are pedagogically designed with the reader in mind. Features include:

- Introductory sections that explain, in basic terms, what the software is, why it was developed, and how it is used. Too many books "jump right in" without giving the student a sense of context.

- Numerous, real-life examples. This book teaches the use of computers by example, so the computer and its applications are clear and in context.
- Each chapter ends with 15–25 review questions, 10 multiple choice, and 10 true/false questions.
- Each chapter includes a complete summary of key terms.

In any introductory computer class, having an accurate text makes managing the class far easier. The best way to make a text accurate is to use it. In the four years that I took developing this text I have received corrections and suggestions that make this book one you should find both easy to use and reliable.

Ancillaries for instructor's use with this text include:

- An instructor's manual.
- A test bank.
- A computerized test bank.
- Transparency masters.

Acknowledgments

Several colleagues reviewed different versions of this manuscript and made constructive suggestions. Without their help the manuscript could not have been refined. The help and comments of the following reviewers are greatly appreciated: Kirk Arnett, Mississippi State University; Tom Berliner, University of Texas—Dallas; Glen Boswell, San Antonio College; Michael Davis, Texas Technical University; Steve Deam, Milwaukee Area Technical College; Beth Defoor, Eastern New Mexico University—Clovis; Richard Ernst, Sullivan Junior College; Barbara Felty, Harrisburg Area Community College; Pat Fenton, West Valley College; Phyllis Helms, Randolph Community College; Mehdi Khosrow-pour, Pennsylvania State—Harrisburg; Candice Marble, Wentworth Military Academy; John Miller, Williamsport Area Community College; Charles McDonald, East Texas State University; Sylvia Meyer, Community College of Vermont; J. D. Oliver, Prairie View A&M University; Greg Pierce, Penn State University; Eugene Rathswohl, University of San Diego; Herbert Rubhun, University of Houston—Downtown; R. D. Shelton, Loyola College; Sandra Stalker, North Shore Community College; G. W. Willis, Baylor University; and Judy Yeager, Western Michigan University.

Many different groups assisted me in completing this project. I am grateful to over four thousand students who attended by executive seminars and various classes in information systems and software productivity tools. They helped me fine-tune the manuscript during its various stages. My friend Bahram Ahanin helped me to improve many concepts of hardware/software and put them in a non-technical and easy-to-understand format. My colleague and friend Dr. Reza Azarmsa provided support and encouragement. I am grateful for all of his encouragement. My colleague Andrew Prestage assisted me in numerous trouble-spots by running and debugging many of the screens presented in the book. My colleague Robert Grossberg tested the manuscript in several of his classes and assisted me in developing numerous test questions.

Several of my students assisted me in running and testing the accuracy of the screens presented throughout the book. I thank Daryl Dunn, Sandra Retzke, Wendy Kramme, Judy Buchanan, Catherine Begg, and Kathleen Whelan. My friend Dr. Lois Holloway tested all the BASIC programs.

I am indebted to Jacki Lawson, who typed and retyped various versions of this manuscript. Her thoroughness and patience made it easier to complete this project. She deserves special recognition for all this work. David Koeth designed the majority of the charts presented in the first phase of the text development. His help and thoroughness is appreciated.

A team of professionals from Macmillan Publishing Company assisted me from the very beginning of this venture. Charles Stewart had faith in this project's potential from the onset, for which I thank him. The assistance of Vern Anthony, my executive editor, in guiding me throughout the project is greatly appreciated. Rex Davidson, Jo Anna Arnott, Gail Meese, Ruth Kimple, Teresa George, and Michelle Byron, all from Macmillan, assisted me in completing this project. I am grateful and appreciate their work.

Finally, I want to thank my family for their support and encouragement throughout my life. My two sisters, Azam and Akram, deserve my very special thanks and recognition.

Dr. Hossein Bidgoli is professor of Management Information Systems at California State University, Bakersfield. He holds a Ph.D. degree in systems science from Portland State University with a specialization in design and implementation of MIS. His master's degree is in MIS from Colorado State University. Dr. Bidgoli's background includes experience as a systems analyst, information systems consultant, financial analyst, and he was the director of the Microcomputer Center at Portland State University.

Dr. Bidgoli, a two-time winner of the MPPP (Meritorious Performance and Professional Promise) award for outstanding performance in teaching, research and university/community service is the author of fifteen texts and numerous professional papers and articles presented and published throughout the United States on the topics of computers and MIS. Dr. Bidgoli has also designed and implemented over twenty executive seminars on all aspects of information systems and decision support systems.

Contents

Contents

Contents

INFORMATION SYSTEMS LITERACY

The World of Computers:
A Quick Trip

1

1–1

INTRODUCTION

In this chapter we provide an overview of computer and data processing systems. We discuss the different data processing systems that were used before the computer era. General capabilities of computers, their unique power, and their applications are reviewed. We explain the characteristics of successive generations of computers and examine the input-process-output cycle. You will learn the differences between data and information. And finally, we discuss types of processing, including batch and transaction processing.

1–2

COMPUTERS IN OUR LIVES

If automobiles had developed as computers have, today you would be able to buy a Mercedes Benz for less than $2, get over two million miles to a gallon, and park up to three dozen cars in the corner of your office! If airplanes had developed as computers have, today you would be able to go around the globe in less than 20 minutes for just 50 cents! The computer that weighed over 18 tons 50 years ago now weighs less than 5 pounds. It is 100 times more powerful and its cost is less than 1 percent of that of the first computers.

Every day you use computers directly or indirectly. For example, in school your transcripts are prepared by computers. Multiple choice and true/false tests are graded by computers. In grocery stores the inventory system and cash registers are managed by computers. Home appliances, such as TVs, VCRs, and microwaves, use some types of computers.

A cashless and checkless society is just around the corner. Even now, all your financial transactions can take place by using computers. Computers can take money from your account or deposit it automatically.

Executives don't need to leave their offices to attend meetings in different cities, states, or countries. Using computer conferencing, an executive can attend several meetings in different locations without leaving the office. You can prepare reports and transfer them from location to location by using computers. None of the space program could have been achieved without computer help. Computers also have played a significant role in medical research and the treatment of various diseases.

Even the production time of this book has been reduced significantly by using computers. We typed the text using a word processor and prepared various drafts. Editors inserted comments from reviewers and students using the editing features of a word processor. Computerized typesetting equipment was used to typeset the book. Warehousing, inventory control, and shipping were all accomplished with the help of computers. The names and addresses of professors who received examination copies of this book were stored in a computer file, and the mailing labels and letters sent to these individuals were prepared using a computer. The publisher stored the entire text in several computer files. Changes for the future editions easily can be made using editing features of the computer.

1–3

DEFINING A COMPUTER

There are many definitions of computers. In this text, we define a **computer** as a machine that accepts data as input, processes the data without human interference using a set of stored instructions, and outputs information. In this context, instructions are step-by-step directions given to a computer for performing a specific task. **Computer programs** are made up of instructions written in a language understood by a computer.

Any computer system consists of hardware and software. Hardware components are all physical devices, such as a keyboard, monitor, and processor unit. The software component consists of computer programs written in different computer languages.

In the next chapter we tell you more about computer languages. For now, just remember that to be able to communicate with a computer, you must talk to it in its own language. There are several hundred computer languages available.

A language used by many **microcomputers** is called **BASIC** (Beginners All Purpose Symbolic Instruction Code). A simple example of a BASIC program is as follows:

```
10  A=10
20  B=20
30  C=A+B
40  PRINT C
50  END
```

This program instructs the computer to add values A and B, store the result in a location called C, and then print the result. Line 50 tells the computer that this is the end of the program.

Consider the diagram presented in figure 1–1. This diagram illustrates the building blocks of a computer. The input devices are used to send data and information to the computer. The keyboard is an example of an input device. The output devices are used to receive the output generated by the computer.

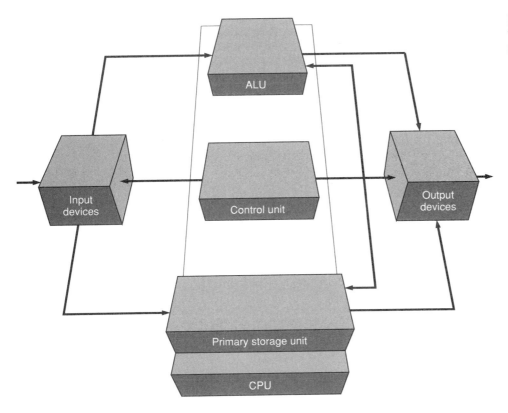

Figure 1–1
The Building Blocks of a Computer

Figure 1–2
Components of a Data Process-ing System

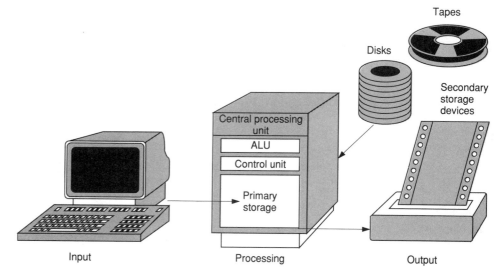

The output may be presented on a display monitor, **CRT** (cathode ray tube), or VDT (video display terminal). This type of output is called **soft copy**. If the output is presented by the printer, it is called **hard copy**.

The main (primary) memory is like the human brain. Memory is the location in which computers store data and instructions. The **CPU** (central processing unit) is the heart of the computer. The CPU is divided into two components: the ALU and the control unit. The **ALU** (arithmetic logic unit) performs **arithmetic operations** (addition, subtraction, multiplication, and division) and **logical operations** (comparing numbers). The **control unit** acts like the captain of a ship. It tells the computer what to do. For example, it tells the computer from which device data is read or to which device to send the output. Figure 1–2 shows the components of a data processing system. We talk about these different devices more in the next chapter.

1–4

TYPES OF COMPUTERS

In general terms, computers can be classified as digital or analog. A **digital computer** works on numbers—discrete processes that are separate and count-able. To the computer, there can be an infinite number of increments between 1 and 2. Every number, character, or special symbol has a numeric value in computer memory. When you compare A and B, a computer knows that character A must come before character B because the numeric value of character A is always smaller than the numeric value of character B.

Analog computers work on continuous processes such as temperature, pressure, and speed. These processes are called continuous because they do not jump from one value to the next. For example, when a speedometer of an automobile goes from 40 to 50 miles per hour, it passes all the values between these two numbers—it does not jump from 40 to 50. Analog computers usually are used in appliances and automobiles. For example, in a gas station, gasoline pumps contain an analog computer that converts fuel flow measurement into quantity and price values.

In this book, we are interested in only digital computers. They enable us to process masses of data to provide meaningful information.

Computers as we currently know them have been around for approximately 50 years. What did we do before computers existed? What do developing nations that do not have access to computers do? In these situations, data is processed with devices other than computers.

      The major classes of data processing systems include manual, mechanical, electromechanical, and electronic (see fig. 1–3).

CLASSES OF DATA PROCESSING SYSTEMS

Manual Data Processing

1–5–1

As you might guess, a **manual data processing system** processes data manually. You might use paper, pencil, and ledgers. Other devices include the Chinese abacus and the slide rule.

Manual data processing

Pencil and paper, files, ledgers, folders

(a)

Mechanical data processing

2345.62
7890.41
9203.82
9833.09
4532.02
4598.56

Adding machines, cash registers, typewriter, credit card imprinter

(b)

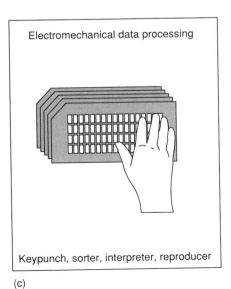

Electromechanical data processing

Keypunch, sorter, interpreter, reproducer

(c)

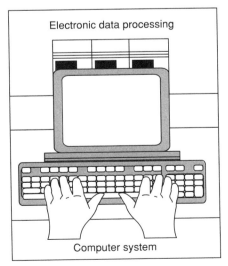

Electronic data processing

Computer system

(d)

Figure 1–3
Data Processing Systems

1–5–2   Mechanical Data Processing

The two major problems associated with any manual data processing system are sufficient speed and accuracy. To improve these two inherent drawbacks of manual data processing, **mechanical data processing** was developed. The credit card imprinter is a mechanical data processing device. Imagine that if every time you used your credit card to purchase gas, the operator in the gas station was required to write down all the information on your card. Purchasing gas would be a tedious process and the accuracy of the information could not be guaranteed.

1–5–3   Electromechanical Data Processing

The significant difference between **electromechanical systems** and earlier systems of data processing is that the data or information must be in machine-readable form. Punch cards, card readers, and sorters were invented to improve the speed and accuracy of data processing systems. By punching holes on a paper card, a punch card machine puts data into a computer-readable format, which can be read very quickly. A sorter machine can sort thousands of cards with a very high degree of speed and accuracy.

1–5–4   Electronic Data Processing

Electronic data processing is the fastest and most accurate system. In this book, you will see many examples of the amazing power of electronic data processing.

1–6

DATA VERSUS INFORMATION

Figure 1–4 shows a simple diagram for a data processing system. The input to a data processing system is raw data. The data is processed by a computer, and the results are called information or processed facts. What is the difference between data and information?

    Data is raw facts. If you have only facts (data), you cannot make a decision. For example, if you say you received an 82 in your computer class, this number is data. By looking at the number 82, you cannot make any statement regarding your performance. Are you a good student? Have you passed the class? But if you know that the class average was 91 and the lowest grade was 80, you can say something about your performance—you now have **information** or

Figure 1–4
A Simple Diagram for a Data Processing System

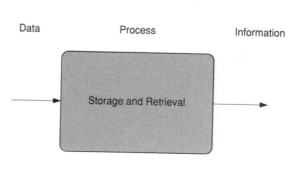

processed facts. At this point, a decision can be made. You may have to decide to work harder to be more competitive with the rest of the class.

The entire field of information systems is concerned with the production of timely, accurate, and useful information. It is said that many organizations are data rich but information poor. The real challenge for practitioners in the dynamic field of information processing is to design computer-based information systems to generate accurate, timely, and useful information.

1-7
DEFINING DATA PROCESSING

When you say that data has been processed to generate information, one or several of the following tasks may have taken place:

1. Arithmetic operations. You might add the volume of sales to generate a value that indicates the total sales of your company in the northwest region.
2. Sort operations. You might sort the total sales of your company for all 50 states from the highest to the lowest volume. You then can choose the best and the worst sales regions.
3. Classification operations. You might classify your sales data into 10 different product groups. Using this information, you can see the total sales generated by product group X. This information will help you choose the best and the worst products in the company on the basis of total sales.

There are many types of data processing that enable you to convert raw data to information. The method you choose depends on the specific situation. You must remember, however, the computer processes only the data it is given. If the data is erroneous, the information provided will be erroneous as well.

Experts in the field call computers error-free machines, given that proper working conditions have been established. By proper working conditions, we mean a room with the proper temperature (not too hot or too cold), that is dust-free, and has the right humidity. Figure 1-5 illustrates data processing functions.

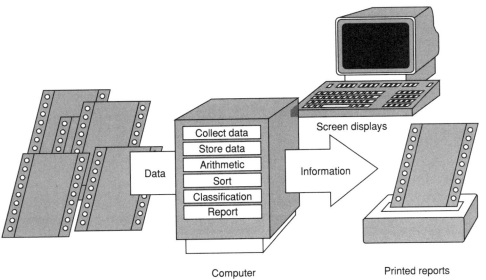

Figure 1-5
Data Processing Functions

Screen displays

Data

Collect data
Store data
Arithmetic
Sort
Classification
Report

Information

Computer

Printed reports

1–8

THE POWER OF COMPUTERS

Generally speaking, computers draw their power from three distinguishing factors that far exceed the capacity of any human being: great speed, great accuracy, and storage and retrieval capability.

1–8–1   Speed

Computers process data with amazing speed. Speed is measured as the number of instructions performed per second as follows:

Millisecond	= 1/1,000 second	= 1 thousandth
Microsecond	= 1/1,000,000 second	= 1 millionth
Nanosecond	= 1/1,000,000,000 second	= 1 billionth
Picosecond	= 1/1,000,000,000,000 second	= 1 trillionth

1–8–2   Accuracy

Computers are error-free machines—they do not make mistakes. To make the accuracy issue more clear, consider the following two numbers:

2.00000000001
2.00000000002

To us, these numbers are so close that we consider them equal. To a computer, these two numbers are very different. When you think about a computer application such as a space mission, this level of accuracy and speed is required to bring the space shuttle back to Earth at a given time and in a specific location.

1–8–3   Storage and Retrieval

Storage means saving data or information into the memory of a computer. Retrieval is the act of bringing the data or information back from memory. Computers can store vast quantities of data and can locate a specific item very quickly.

1–9

COMPUTER OPERATIONS

Computers can perform three basic tasks: arithmetic operations, logical operations, and storage and retrieval operations. All other tasks are accomplished by one or a combination of these tasks. For example, playing games could be a combination of all three functions.

1–9–1   Arithmetic Operations

Computers can add, subtract, multiply, divide, and raise to power. The five basic operations are as follows:

A + B (addition)	5 + 2 = 7
A − B (subtraction)	5 − 2 = 3
A * B (multiplication)	5 * 2 = 10
A/B (division)	5/2 = 2.5
A^B (exponentiation)	5^2 = 25

You should get into the habit of using the symbols used by computers. (The exponentiation symbol may vary from language to language.)

Logical Operations

1-9-2

Computers can perform logical operations by comparing two numbers. For example, a computer can compare A and B to determine which number is larger.

Storage and Retrieval Operations

1-9-3

Computers can store massive amounts of data in a very small place, and they can locate a particular item of information very quickly. It is possible to store several thousand books in a memory device that will fit in the corner of your office.

1-10

COMPUTER APPLICATIONS

Practically speaking, the number of applications performed by computers is unlimited. There is not a single day that we are not affected by the computer. Computers are used in nearly all business organizations. They are used in humanities, and they can even play music. There is no job that you will occupy after graduation that does not use computers either directly or indirectly. Table 1-1 summarizes some of the more practical applications of computer technology. Figure 1-6 illustrates some of these applications.

1-11

COMPUTER GENERATIONS

Over the past four decades, there have been major advancements in hardware. Computers began with **vacuum-tube** technology. In 1946, rudimentary computers were bulky and unreliable. They generated excessive heat and were very difficult to program. The second generation of computers began in 1957. This

Table 1-1
Popular Applications of Computers

Industry	Application
Space program	Launching spaceships
Medicine	Drug testing, in the operating room, dental health, and so forth
Geology	Earthquake analysis, soil and mineral analysis
Government	Tracking IRS information, social security, and so on
Business	Accounting and finance for private and public organizations
Education	Computer-aided instruction (CAI), remote education sites
Manufacturing	Computer-aided design (CAD), robotics
Traffic Control	Provide more effective traffic systems
Appliances	Microwaves, VCRs, TVs, and so on
Music	Control and create sound
Entertainment	Generate three-dimensional pictures and animation in movies and videos
Airlines	Reservation systems

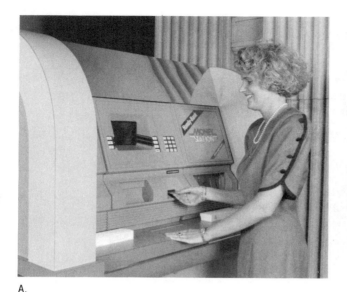

A.

B.

C.

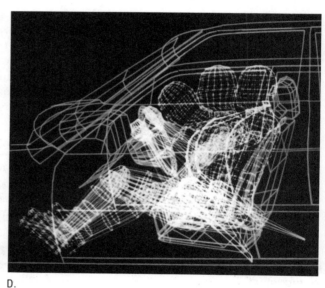

D.

Figure 1–6

Computers in Action. A. ATM in Lobby of Office Building. (Larry Hamill/Macmillan). B. Instrument Panel of Corvette. (Courtesy of General Motors, Milford Proving Grounds). C. Nurse Entering Information from Patients' Charts into Computer. (Larry Hamill/Macmillan). D. Computer Simulation. (Courtesy of Daimler-Benz and Evans & Sutherland). E. Technician Adjusting Robotic Testing Device. (Courtesy of General Motors, Milford Proving Grounds). F. Lexis System for Legal Research. (Larry Hamill/Macmillan). G. Musical Instrument Digital Interface. (Courtesy of Sisapa Record Company, Inc.). H. Mainframe in Medium- to Large-Size Business. (Larry Hamill/Macmillan). I. OSU-CRAY YMP 8 Supercomputer. (Jo Hall/Macmillan). J. Minicomputer for Small- to Medium-Size Business (Apollo 10,000 Workstation). (Larry Hamill/Macmillan).

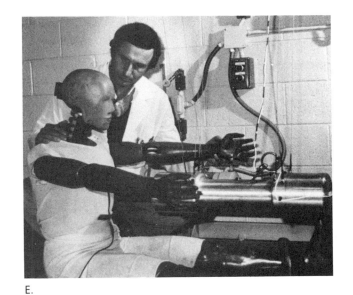

E.

F.

G.

H.

I.

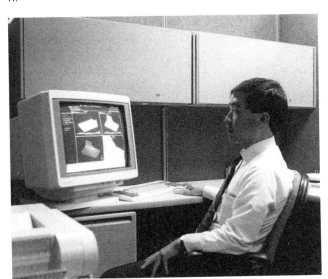

J.

Table 1–2

Hardware Trends

Generation	Date	Major Attribute	Example
First	1946–1956	Vacuum tubes	ENIAC
Second	1957–1963	Transistors	IBM 7094, 1401
Third	1964–1970	Integrated circuits	IBM 360, 370
Fourth	1971–1992	VLSI	Cray XMP
Fifth	1992–?	Gallium arsenide	?

generation, which used **transistors,** was indeed a significant improvement over the first. These computers were faster, more reliable, and easier to program and maintain. The third generation began in 1964 with computers that operated on **integrated circuits** (IC). These circuits enabled computers to be even smaller, faster, more reliable, and more sophisticated. Remote data entry and telecommunications were introduced during this generation. The fourth generation began about 1970. This generation of computers is associated with several attributes: miniaturization, very large scale integration (VLSI) circuits, widespread use of microcomputers, optical disks, and bubble memories.

In the early 1990s, we expect to see the beginning of the so-called fifth generation of computer technology. The major attributes of this generation will include parallel processing, gallium arsenide chips, and optical technologies. A parallel processing computer contains hundreds or thousands of CPUs, which means that the computer is capable of processing data much faster than current computers.

Because silicon technology is not able to emit light and has speed limitations, computer designers have concentrated on **gallium arsenide** technology. Electrons move almost five times faster in gallium arsenide than they do in silicon. Devices made with this synthetic compound can emit light, withstand higher temperatures, and survive much higher doses of radiation than silicon devices.[1]

The major problems associated with gallium arsenide are the difficulties in mass production and working with it. Gallium arsenide is soft and fragile compared to silicon; it breaks more easily during slicing and polishing. At the present time, because of its high cost and difficulty of production, military systems are the major users of this technology. However, research continues to eliminate some of the shortcomings of this impressive technology.

Optical technologies offer at least three unique features not found in earlier technologies: greater speed, parallelism (several thousand independent light beams can pass through an ordinary device), and interconnection (much denser arrays of interconnections are possible because light rays do not affect each other). Optical computing is in its infancy and much more research is needed in order to produce a full-featured optical computer. Presently, the storage devices using this technology are revolutionizing the computer field by enabling massive amounts of data to be stored in a very small space.

The fifth generation will include revolutionary architecture that does not exist in the first four generations of computer technology. Table 1–2 highlights the trends in hardware technology.

---

[1]Posa, John J. Using Silicon and Gallium Arsenide. *High Technology* (March, 1987): 38–41.

1-12
INPUT, PROCESS, AND OUTPUT CONCEPTS

Throughout this text you will be using a computer as a black box. This means that you send data to the computer, the computer performs the processing task, and information is given back to you on some type of output device. According to the black box theory, you don't need to know what goes on inside the "box." You provide the input data, tell the computer how this data should be processed, and leave the rest to the computer.

Although you do not need a deep understanding of how the computer works, some knowledge about the internal operation of a computer will help you better appreciate this powerful device. After all, you don't need to be able to overhaul an engine to be able to drive an automobile. In Appendix A, we provide a general overview of the internal operation of a computer.

1-13
DATA REPRESENTATION

Every character, number, or special symbol that you type from the keyboard is represented as a binary number in the computer's memory. Binary and other number systems are discussed in Appendix A. For now, remember that a **binary system** consists of 0 and 1. The 1 represents on, and the 0 represents off. Figure 1-7 illustrates this system. To represent these different data items, computers use a special format. The two most common formats are **ASCII** (American Standard Code for Information Interchange) (pronounced "as-key") and **EBCDIC** (Extended Binary Coded Decimal Interchange Code) (pronounced "eb-se-dick"). You do not need to be worried about these codes. The computer handles them internally. Table 1-3 presents selected symbols in both ASCII and EBCDIC data formats.

EBCDIC uses an eight-bit presentation. The eight bits are divided into two four-bit groups. The first half is the zone, and the second half is the digit. For example, for presenting numbers (without a sign), all the zone bits are 1s, and the digit bits (except zero) are a combination of 1s and 0s. ASCII uses a seven-bit presentation also divided into zone and digit parts. However, the zone part uses different combinations of 0s and 1s. For numbers, the zone part is always 011 and the digit part is a combination of 0s and 1s, except for zero itself.

On
1

Off
0

Figure 1-7
A Graphic Representation of a Binary System

Table 1–3
Selected Keyboard Symbols
in ASCII and EBCDIC

Symbol	ASCII	EBCDIC
space	0100000	01000000
A	1000001	11000001
B	1000010	11000010
Z	1011010	11101001
a	1100001	10000001
b	1100010	10000010
z	1111010	10101001
*	0101010	01011100
%	0100101	01101100
(	0101000	01001101
0	0110000	11110000
1	0110001	11110001
9	0111001	11111001

1–14
TYPES OF PROCESSING

When using a computer, you can process the data either in batch mode or in an interactive mode. In **batch processing,** data is sent to the computer periodically. For example, every 24 hours, every two weeks, or every month. This type of processing is suitable for applications that don't need an immediate response. Payroll is a good example—you do not need to pay hourly employees each hour.

However, many applications require an immediate response. In these applications, a transaction is processed as soon as it occurs. This type of processing is known as real-time or **transaction processing**. An airline reservation system is a good example of this type of processing. A reservation must be entered into the computer immediately, otherwise the plane may leave with many empty seats or one seat may be sold to many customers.

SUMMARY

This chapter provided an overview of computers and the precomputer era. You learned about different types of data processing, and the differences between data and information. The unique characteristics of computers, different applications and different generations of computers were explained. The chapter concluded with a brief discussion of batch processing and transaction processing systems. The material presented in this chapter should provide you with the necessary background to better understand the rest of this text.

REVIEW QUESTIONS

*These questions are answered in Appendix A.

1. How do you define a computer?

*2. What is a computer program?

3. What is soft copy? Hard copy?

4. What are the major components of a computer system?

5. What is the CPU? ALU? Control unit?

6. What is the difference between analog and digital computers?

7. How many types of data processing systems have we experienced?

*8. What are the two major shortcomings of a manual data processing system?

9. What is the difference between data and information? If you are told that Company XYZ had $12,000,000 of total sales in 1989, is this data or information? Discuss.

10. What does it mean when you say that you have processed data?

11. List three factors from which computers draw their power.

12. What does it mean when people say computers are accurate? How do you measure the accuracy of a computer?

13. What can computers do for you?

*14. What are logical operations?

15. List 10 applications of computers.

*16. How many generations of computers have we seen?

17. How are the fifth generation computers identified?

18. What are the major technologies associated with each computer generation?

*19. Why is the binary system so important to computer operation?

20. What is data representation? ASCII? EBCDIC?

21. Is the data representation the responsibility of the computer user or the computer itself? Discuss.

22. Explain two important types of processing: batch and real time. List two applications of each.

23. Consult a local bank. What are some of the applications of computers?

24. Try to have a tour of a computer center either in your school or in an organization which you are familiar with. What types of computers do they have? Who are some of the vendors of these computers?

25. Computers are being used in hospitals. What are some of their applications?

26. What are some of the applications of computers in running a college or university?

27. Computers of the future may think. Discuss.

KEY TERMS

ALU	CRT	Logical operation
Analog computer	Data	Manual data processing system
Arithmetic operation	Digital computer	Mechanical data processing
ASCII format	EBCDIC format	
BASIC	Electromechanical systems	Microcomputer
Batch processing	Electronic data processing	Soft copy
Binary system	Gallium arsenide	Transaction processing
Computer	Hard copy	Transistors
Computer program	Information	Vacuum tube
Control unit	Integrated circuits	
CPU		

Multiple Choice

ARE YOU READY TO MOVE ON?

1. A computer is a machine that
   a. processes data
   b. uses a set of stored instructions
   c. outputs information

d. all of the above

e. none of the above

2. Which of the following can be used to provide hard copy?

    a. printer

    b. CRT

    c. plotter

    d. a and c

    e. a, b, and c

3. The "heart" of the computer is the

    a. ALU

    b. memory

    c. control unit

    d. program

    e. CPU

4. Which of the following is not one of the classes of data-processing systems?

    a. electronic data processing

    b. mechanical data processing

    c. digital data processing

    d. manual data processing

    e. electromechanical data processing

5. Computer-based information systems must provide information that is

    a. legible and sorted

    b. unique, original, and understandable

    c. accurate, timely, and useful

    d. decoded and processed

    e. none of the above

6. The four generations of computer technology to date can be characterized by

    a. supercomputers, mainframes, minicomputers, microcomputers

    b. manual, mechanical, electromechanical, electronic

    c. abacus, imprinter, punch card, digital

    d. pre-analog, analog, digital, post-digital

    e. vacuum tube, transistor, IC, miniaturization

7. Two commonly known formats used to represent data are

    a. ASCII and EBCDIC

    b. ASCII and FORTRAN

    c. BASIC and FORTRAN

    d. analog and digital

    e. none of the above

8. In batch processing, data is sent to the computer

    a. when the operating system is loaded

    b. on a periodic basis

    c. as soon as it is needed

    d. when the computer is turned on

    e. every 24 hours

9. An example of interactive processing is
   a. an automatic teller machine
   b. a payroll system
   c. a school grade report system
   d. both a and b
   e. none of the above

10. The next generation of computers (the fifth generation) will be characterized by
    a. silicon chips
    b. artificial intelligence technologies
    c. input/output devices
    d. transistors
    e. solid state electronics

True/False

1. For our purposes, a computer is a machine that processes data without human interference.
2. A video display terminal (CRT) is generally used as an output device.
3. The arithmetic logic unit can perform addition, subtraction, multiplication, and division, but it cannot compare one number to another.
4. A digital computer works on numbers, and an analog computer works on a continuous process.
5. Speed and accuracy are two of the most important criteria for a computerized data processing system.
6. Data and information mean the same thing when referring to computer input and output.
7. Computers perform three basic tasks: arithmetic operations, logical operations, and storage/retrieval operations.
8. The "black box" concept of input, process, and output states that you must have a complete understanding about the inner workings of the computer.
9. In the binary system, a zero (0) is represented by a high voltage and a one (1) is represented by a low voltage.
10. Computers use only the decimal system (base 10) because it is the system with which we are most familiar.

Multiple Choice	True/False	ANSWERS
1. d	1. T	
2. d	2. T	
3. e	3. F	
4. c	4. T	
5. c	5. T	
6. e	6. F	
7. a	7. T	
8. b	8. F	
9. a	9. F	
10. b	10. F	

Hardware and Software Concepts

2-1

INTRODUCTION

In this chapter we discuss the different types of hardware and software commonly used in day-to-day operations. The chapter explains input, output, and memory devices. We introduce computer classifications based on size, speed, and sophistication. The chapter concludes with a brief survey of some of the popular computer languages used with micro and mainframe computers.

2-2

INPUT DEVICES

Input devices are used for sending data and information to the computer. Through the years, input devices have been improved to make the data input task easier. Commonly used input devices include a keyboard, mouse, touch screen, light pen, scanner, and data tablet.

2-2-1

Keyboard

Keyboards are the most widely used input device. Originally, keyboards were designed with a configuration very similar to a typewriter. In recent years, there have been several modifications. To make the user's task easier, most keyboards include control keys, arrow keys, function keys, and several special keys. Keyboards are capable of performing the majority of computer input tasks. However, for some special tasks, a scanner or mouse is faster and more accurate. Figure 2–1 shows an IBM PS/2 keyboard.

2-2-2

Touch Screen

Touch screens work with menus and are a combination of several input devices. Some touch screens rely on light detection to determine which item from the menu has been selected. Other screens are pressure-sensitive. Touch screens may be easier to use than keyboards; however, in some cases they may not be as accurate because they can misread the chosen instruction.

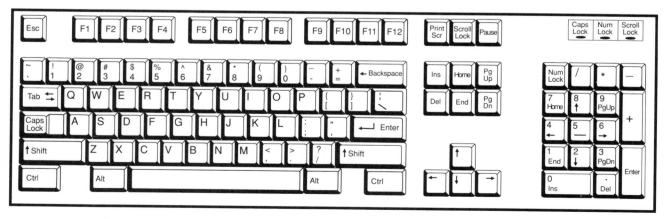

Figure 2–1
IBM PS/2 Keyboard

Light Pen
2–2–3

Light pens are similar to conventional pens and are connected to the terminal with a cable. Light pens are particularly useful to engineers, draftsmen, and designers for graphic applications. When the pen is placed on a location on the CRT, the information in this spot is sent to the system. The data can be characters, lines, or blocks. A light pen is easy to use, inexpensive, and accurate.

Mouse
2–2–4

You use a **mouse** for rapid cursor movement. You move the mouse until the cursor is on the desired item; then you push a button to enter a command or an instruction. The cursor is a special character that indicates your position on the computer screen or acts as an indicator (pointer) to focus attention on a specific point on the monitor.

Data Tablet
2–2–5

A **data tablet** consists of a small pad and a pen. Menus are presented on the tablet, and you make selections with the pen. Currently, the data tablet is most widely used in CAD (computer-aided design) and CAM (computer-aided manufacturing), where the user draws on the tablet with the pen rather than using a CRT or light pen.

Bar Code
2–2–6

Bar code readers are optical scanners that use laser light to read bar codes. These devices are very fast and accurate, and have many applications in inventory systems, data entry, and tracking systems. They are used mostly with UPC (universal product code) systems in grocery stores.

Optical Character Reader
2–2–7

Optical character readers (OCRs) work on the same principle as optical scanners. However, because the OCR must recognize special characters, upper- and lowercase characters, and special spacing, using an OCR is more difficult than using bar code readers. However, these systems have achieved remarkable success and are steadily improving.

Magnetic ink character recognition (MICR) and optical-mark recognition (OMR) are two other scanner devices. A MICR system reads characters printed with magnetic ink. MICRs primarily are used by banks for reading the information on the bottom of checks. An OMR system is sometimes called "mark sensing" because the machine senses marks on a piece of paper. Multiple-choice and true/false tests often are graded by this type of device.

Voice-Recognition System
2–2–8

Voice-recognition systems, the newest type of input device, have attracted much attention in recent years. The principle behind these systems is to enable the user to talk to the system and formulate queries. The integration of voice-recognition systems, NLP (natural language processing), and menu systems would be the ultimate input device for a typical user. Currently, there is no workable full-featured voice-recognition system on the market. Figure 2–2 shows some typical input devices.

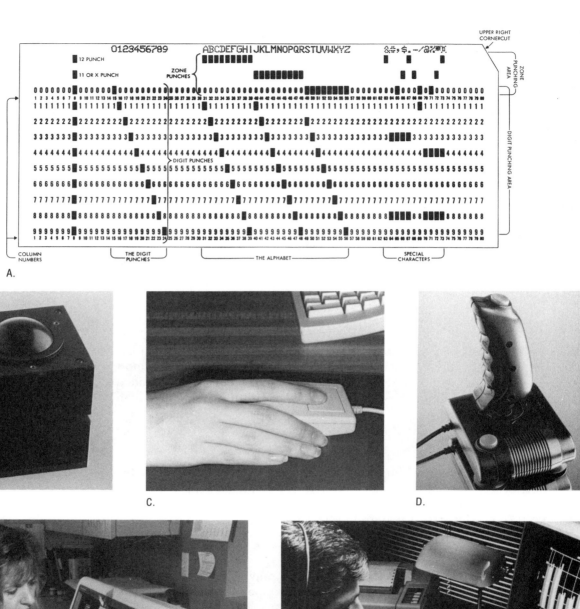

A.

B.

C.

D.

E.

F.

Figure 2–2

Commonly Used Input Devices. A. 80 Column Punch Card. (Courtesy of IBM Corp.). B. Trackball. (Cobalt Productions/Macmillan). C. Electromechanical Mouse. (Larry Hamill/Macmillan). D. Joystick. (Cobalt Productions/Macmillan). E. Magnetic Resonance Imaging Technician Using a Light Pen to Enter Data into a Computer. (Larry Hamill/Macmillan). F. Voice Recognition Data Entry System. (Courtesy of Texas Instruments).

There are many **output devices** available for both mainframe and microcomputers. The most common output devices are the **CRT** (cathode ray tube) or VDT for soft copies and **printers** for hard copies. CRTs are either color or monochrome (one color). Some of them have graphics capabilities, some do not. Printers come in different sizes and shapes. A typical printer is either dot matrix or letter quality.

A dot-matrix printer uses a group of dots to form letters or images. Although the print quality is not particularly high, the cost is relatively low. However, some of the newest dot-matrix printers have improved print quality significantly. Letter-quality, laser, ink jet, thermal, and electrostatic printers deliver a much higher quality of print. These printers are favored for business correspondence. Printer speeds vary from a few hundred to several thousand characters per minute. When selecting a printer, you should consider cost, quality, noise level, and speed.

Other output devices include plotters, for converting the computer output to graphics, and voice synthesizers, for converting the computer output to voice. Voice synthesization is gaining in popularity. When you use telephone directory assistance, the number given to you may be produced by a computer. Voice output also is being used as a marketing device. A computer can dial a long list of phone numbers and leave a message. If the phone is busy, the computer makes a note and dials the number later. (And, if you hang up, the computer's feelings will not be hurt!) Figure 2–3 shows some typical output devices.

There are two types of memories used by any computer: main memory and secondary memory. As the name indicates, the main memory of the computer is a part of the CPU; it stores data and information. This memory is usually volatile, meaning it loses its contents as soon as the electrical source is disconnected. Secondary memory is used mostly as an archival device. Secondary memory is non-volatile.

Main Memory Devices

At the present time, there are two types of main memory devices in existence: semiconductor and bubble memory. Semiconductor memory chips are made of silicon. Silicon is found naturally in quartz; however, the silicon used for chips is manufactured synthetically. A **semiconductor memory** device can be either volatile or non-volatile. When used for volatile memory, it is called random-access memory (RAM). A better name for RAM would be read-write memory. It means you can read from it, and you also can write to it. When used for non-volatile memory it is called ROM (read-only memory). In ROM memory, you can only read from it; you cannot write to it.

Bubble memory is built on a thin crystalline film (mineral garment). By polarizing the bubbles, data is presented on this non-volatile memory. The presence of a bubble represents a one, and the absence of a bubble represents a zero. Two drawbacks of this kind of memory are its high cost and relatively low speed.

A.

B.

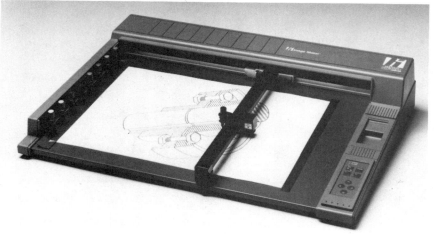

C.

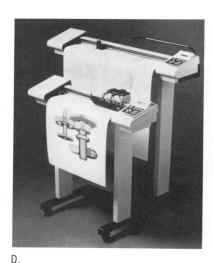

D.

Figure 2–3

Typical Output Devices. A. Desktop Laser Printer. (Courtesy of Texas Instruments). B. Laser-Based Page Printer (HP LaserJet III). (Courtesy of Hewlett-Packard). C. Desktop Plotter (Jetpro 360 Ink Jet Printer/Plotter). (Courtesy of Houston Instrument). D. Large Plotter. (DPM-60, 61, 62 DLs). (Courtesy of Houston Instrument). E. Dot Matrix Printer (4207, 4210, 4224). (Courtesy of IBM Corp.). F. Line Printer (4234, 4248, 5202, 4245). (Courtesy of IBM Corp.). G. Color Graphics Printer (HP PaintJet). (Courtesy of Hewlett-Packard). H. Eight-Pen ColorPro Plotter. (Courtesy of Hewlett-Packard).

2–4–2   Secondary Memory Devices

Secondary memory devices are non-volatile and are used for storing large volumes of data for long periods of time. There are three primary types of secondary memory devices: magnetic tape, magnetic disk, and optical disk.

Magnetic tape is made of plastic material and is similar to a cassette tape. Data is stored sequentially on the tape. Records can be stored in a block or separately, and there is a gap between each record or each block. This space is called the inter-record gap (IRG). Magnetic tape usually is used to store historical data for back up purposes (see fig. 2–4).

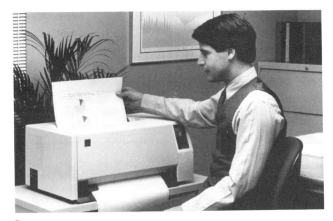

E.

F.

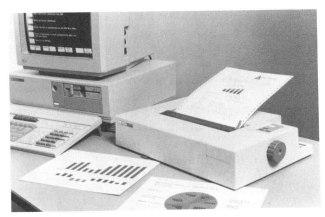

G.

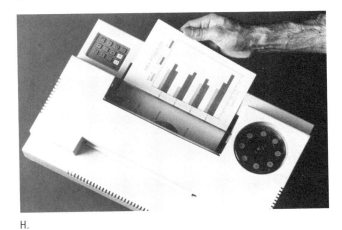

H.

Figure 2–4
Using Magnetic Tape Storage
(Larry Hamill/Macmillan)

Magnetic disk is used for random access processing. The disk is made of mylar or is a metallic platter. Magnetic disks are similar to a phonograph record in that data can be accessed in any order regardless of the order on the surface. Compared with magnetic tape, disk is much faster and more expensive.

Optical disks use laser beams, highly concentrated beams of light, to access and store data. This technology can store vast amounts of data. However, because this optical technology is relatively new, it is expensive.

2–5
CLASSES OF COMPUTERS

There are several ways that computers can be classified. Generally speaking, computers are classified based on cost, memory size, speed, and sophistication (single-tasking versus multi-tasking). A single-tasking computer performs one task at a time. A multi-tasking computer performs several tasks at a time. Using these criteria, computers are classified into micro, mini, mainframe, and super computers.

The applications of these computers include anything from homework (microcomputer) to space shuttle launches (super computer). Because the speed and sophistication of small computers are steadily increasing, it is difficult to draw a clear line between the different classes of computers. A microcomputer of today has more power than a mainframe of the 1970s, and all indications show that this trend will continue.

2–6
DEFINING A COMPUTER PROGRAM

A computer program is simply a series of instructions. It tells a computer what specific steps must be taken in order to solve a problem.

To write a computer program, you first must know what needs to be done, then plan a method to accomplish it. You also must choose the proper language for the task. Many computer languages are available—the language selected depends on the problem under consideration and the type of computer that you are using.

Regardless of the language used, when you write a program the program is called the source code. This source code must be translated into object code, which the computer will be able to understand and use. The object code is always in binary 0s and 1s.

A program that translates your program from source code to object code is called a compiler. If your source code is written in an **assembly language** (see section 2–8), the translator is called an assembler. Some languages use interpreters. An interpreter is similar to a compiler; however, interpreters are slower and less sophisticated. The major difference between a compiler and an interpreter is that compilers offer the user a choice between executing or saving the object code version of a program; interpreters do not. An interpreter converts a program to machine language and executes it statement by statement. It does not wait for the entire program to be entered. Interpreters usually are used when an interactive process is happening between the user and the computer. In such a case, the user receives immediate feedback. Figure 2–5 illustrates the program translation process.

The following is a simple program written in BASIC:

```
10  A=20
20  B=30
30  C=A+B
40  PRINT C
50  END
```

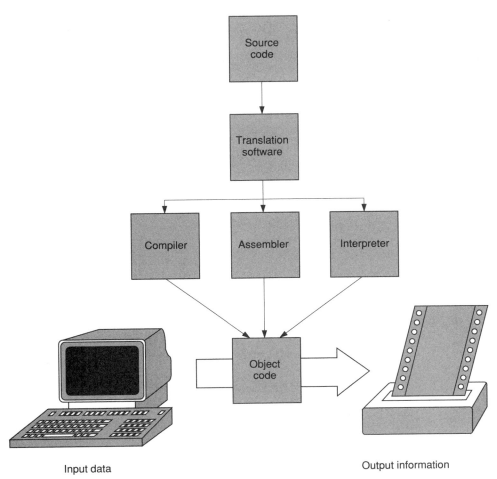

Input data

Output information

In lines 10 and 20, values are assigned to two different addresses: A and B. In line 30, the values are added and the result is stored in a location (address) called C. An address is similar to an empty bucket. It holds one value at a time. A new value replaces the old one. Line 40 tells the computer to print the value in location C. Line 50 tells the computer that it has reached the end of the program.

2−7

OPERATING SYSTEMS

An **operating system** is a set of programs that controls and supervises computer hardware and software. An operating system provides an interface between a computer and the user. It usually resides in the main memory of a computer. An operating system increases computer efficiency by helping users share computer resources and performing repetitive tasks which otherwise would be performed by the users.

A typical operating system consists of two sets of programs: control programs and supervisor programs.

Control programs manage the computer hardware and resources. This may include job management, resource allocation, data management, and data communication. Job (program) management controls different jobs performed by the CPU. It tells the CPU in which order jobs should be processed. The

Figure 2–6
Different Functions of an
Operating System

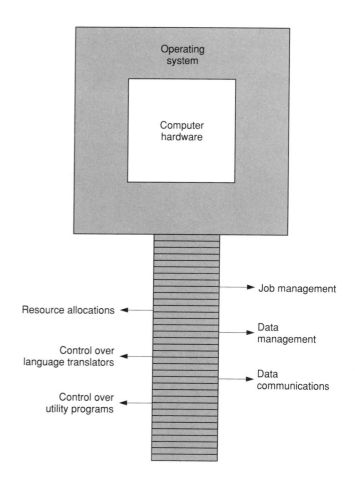

resource allocation function exercises a tight control over the existing computer resources. It tells the CPU, for example, which printer should be assigned to which job. The data management function controls the accuracy of the data. The communication function controls the transfer of data among different sections of the computer system.

The supervisor program, also known as the kernel, is responsible for controlling all the other programs within the operating system. These other programs include compilers, interpreters, assemblers, and utility programs for performing special tasks.

There are many types of operating systems available. In addition to single-tasking and multi-tasking systems, some operating systems are time-shared, meaning they allow several users to use the computer resources at the same time.

The majority of operating systems for microcomputers, such as MS-DOS, Apple PRODOS, and Apple Macintosh, are single-tasking operating systems. However, OS/2, the new operating system by IBM, and different versions of the UNIX operating system are designed to perform multi-tasking operations. Figure 2–6 summarizes the functions of an operating system.

Computer languages have developed through four generations and soon the fifth generation will appear in the marketplace.

The first generation of computer language is called **machine language**. Machine language consists of a series of 0s and 1s that represent data or instructions. Machine language, as the name indicates, is machine dependent —a code written for one computer will not work on another computer. It is a time-consuming process to write a machine language program.

The second generation of computer language is called **assembly language.** Assembly language is a higher level language than machine language. Assembly language also is machine dependent. It uses a series of short codes, or mnemonics, to present data or instructions. Compared with machine language, it is easier to code in assembly language. Some of the commands used by a typical assembly language may include ADD, SUBTRACT, and LDA (load register A, meaning store a value in a location called A).

The third generation of computer languages are machine-independent and are called **high-level languages**. Many high-level languages are available, and each is designed with a unique objective. For example, COBOL is used mostly for business data processing, and FORTRAN is used for scientific applications. High-level languages are more English-like, are mostly self-documenting, and are easier to learn and code than earlier generations. Self-documenting means that codes written in these languages are pretty much understandable as you read them and usually do not need additional documentation to explain them. However, a strict format must be followed to successfully implement a program written in these languages.

The **fourth generation languages,** or 4GLs as they are known, are the easiest computer languages on the marketplace from a user's point of view. These languages are user-friendly, and the commands are powerful and easy to learn, particularly for people with minimal computer training. 4GLs are sometimes called non-procedural languages. This means the user does not need to follow a rigorous format while using these languages.

4GLs use macro codes—codes that can take the place of several programming lines. For example, in a 4GL you might issue the PLOT command, which is a macro code. This command may take the place of 100 or more lines of a program in a high-level language. If you want to draw a fancy graph in a high-level language, you might have to write hundreds of lines of code. In a 4GL, one simple command will do the job for you.

Many 4GLs are available. IFPS (interactive financial planning system), NOMAD, and FOCUS are some examples.

The fifth generation languages, also called **natural language** processing (NLP), are the ideal computer languages for people with minimal computer training. These languages are designed to make possible a free-form conversation between you and the computer. Just imagine if you could say to your computer, "What product generated the highest sales last year?" and your computer, equipped with a voice synthesizer, could respond, "product X." This would be wonderful! CLOUT, INTELLECT, and Q&A are some examples of this type of language. Research has been steady in this area and it sounds promising.

2–9

HIGH-LEVEL LANGUAGES

There are several hundred computer languages available. The reason for such diversity is the specific application of each language in a given discipline. Some are for business, some for science, and some for other specific uses.

2–9–1

FORTRAN

FORTRAN (FORmula TRANslator) was invented in 1954. It is the oldest procedural language. FORTRAN is generally used for scientific applications. However, recent versions have been used successfully for business applications as well. Because of its long history, many applications have been written in this language.

A FORTRAN program consists of a series of statements. A FORTRAN statement contains a key word, variable names, and a symbol.

A key word is a command that tells the computer to do a certain task. READ, WRITE, and DO are examples of FORTRAN key words.

Variable names are addresses or locations that store data. For example, in the statement

```
A=20
```

A is a variable that contains the value 20.

Symbols, such as + (addition), − (subtraction), * (multiplication), and / (division) are used for mathematical operations. A FORTRAN program usually consists of executable and nonexecutable statements. Executable statements are either assignment, control, or input/output statements.

Assignment statements, as the name indicates, are used to assign a value to a variable. For example, the statement

```
A=55
```

assigns the value 55 to variable A.

Control, branch, or loop statements are used to either change the normal operation of a program, such as to transfer the control from one location to another (the command GOTO), or they are used to execute a certain portion of a program for a specific number of times (the DO and IF-THEN-ELSE commands).

Input/output statements control the input and output of data in the program. For example, READ is used to send information to the computer, and WRITE is used to send information out of the computer.

Nonexecutable statements are used for declaration purposes. For example, at the beginning of a FORTRAN program, you must declare your data types as integer, real, or character. Integer data are whole numbers, such as 59, 62, and 35. Real data uses decimal points, such as 299.65 and 1.57. Character data are a combination of digits and characters, such as Bob and 16ABC. The FORMAT command is another example of a nonexecutable statement. This command tells the computer how to print a line or how to read from an input medium such as a punch card.

FORTRAN is available for both micro and mainframe computers.

COBOL

2–9–2

COBOL (COmmon Business Oriented Language) has been in use since the early 1960s. It has gone through several variations, but now it is fairly standard and portable. Portability means that a program written for one computer will work on another computer with either no changes or with minimal modifications. COBOL is English-like and self-documenting. Programs written in COBOL are much easier to read than programs written in FORTRAN. COBOL is more suitable for business data processing because of its character-handling and report-generation facilities.

A COBOL program is divided into four major parts called divisions. The identification division includes the name of the program, name of the programmer, and the date. This section is useful for future reference and changes to the program. The environment division includes input/output support. This division identifies the type of computer and I/O devices that were used to read and compile the program. The data division identifies record layouts for both input and output records. The exact formats of data are identified in this division. The procedure division tells the computer what operations must be performed.

Similar to FORTRAN, COBOL includes commands for assignment, control, and I/O operation. For example, the statement

```
MOVE 30 TO HOURLY-PAY
```

is an example of an assignment statement in COBOL. This statement assigns the value 30 to a variable called HOURLY-PAY. Commands such as IF and PERFORM are used for control operations. READ and WRITE are used for I/O operations. In COBOL, a statement consists of three parts: words, symbols, and phrases beginning with a COBOL word. There are three types of COBOL words:

- Reserved words, such as ADD, SUBTRACT, PERFORM, and MOVE, have special meaning to the COBOL compiler and cannot be used by the program as variable names.
- User-defined words are different variables and addresses created by a programmer. For example, STATE-TAX, HOURLY-PAY, and COMMIS-SION-RATE.
- System names are supplied by the manufacturer of a particular computer. For example, a code name for a particular card-reader, tape drive, or a printer.

COBOL, aside from being wordy, is an ideal language for business data processing. It is not suitable for scientific applications. COBOL compilers are available for both micro and mainframe computers.

BASIC

2–9–3

BASIC was invented in 1964 at Dartmouth College. It has gone through many revisions. The BASIC language is available for most computers regardless of their size or sophistication. BASIC has not targeted a specific application area. BASIC was designed to be used in an interactive conversational mode, and it is useful for both scientific and business applications.

BASIC includes statements for assignment, control, and input/output operations. The assignment operation is done by the LET statement. For example, the statement

```
LET A=55
```

assigns the value 55 to an address called A. The LET statement is not needed in the majority of BASIC versions; just A = 55 will do the job.

Control operations are performed by commands such as GOTO, IF-THEN, and FOR-NEXT. The GOTO statement is used to transfer control from one location to another. The IF-THEN statement is used for conditional transfer. In the statement

```
IF HOURS>40 THEN 100
```

if the number of hours worked is greater than 40, the computer performs line 100. The FOR-NEXT statement is used for performing a task a certain number of times. For example, the code

```
FOR X=1 TO 100
     .
     .
     .
NEXT X
```

performs the tasks between the FOR and NEXT statements 100 times.

Input/output operations are done by the READ and PRINT commands. The READ statement either reads data from a data line or from a data file. The PRINT statement is used to display the output either to a CRT, printer, or to another file.

BASIC comes with many built-in functions. You also can define your own functions to perform a specific task.

The most attractive feature of BASIC is its simplicity and ease of use. Its most serious drawbacks are lack of portability and structure. This means there are many different versions of BASIC and only limited types of data can be handled by this language. Numbers and characters are the only types of data handled by BASIC.

2–9–4   PASCAL

PASCAL was named for Blaise Pascal, a French mathematician who was a pioneer in computer development history. PASCAL was first implemented in 1970. Ever since, it has been a widely used language, especially in the academic environment.

The major objective of PASCAL is to promote well-structured and readable programs. This language tries to eliminate or at least minimize the number of GOTO statements in a program. Programs with too many GOTO statements are difficult to debug.

PASCAL is a block-structured language. A block starts with BEGIN and ends with END. Data definition is accomplished with a VAR statement. In PASCAL, the programmer can define any type of data such as integer, real, and character.

Assignments are accomplished with the := sign combination. For example,

```
A:=23;
```

assigns the value 23 to variable A. The assignment statement must end with a semicolon (;).

Control statements in PASCAL use IF-THEN-ELSE, DO-WHILE, PERFORM-UNTIL, and CASE commands. The CASE statement is equivalent to a series of IF-THEN-ELSE statements.

The I/O operations are done by the READ, READLN, WRITE, and WRITELN commands.

By using rigorous data type declaration and the block structure features, PASCAL delivers readable and easy to understand programs. PASCAL is particularly suitable for microcomputer implementation because of its processing speeds and its reasonable memory requirements. However, relatively poor character handling is its major drawback.

C   2-9-5

The **C** programming language was developed at Bell Laboratories by Dennis Ritchie in 1972. It enables a programmer to exercise substantial control over the computer hardware. It is English-like and includes an excellent data structure, which is the capability of defining any type of data such as integer, real, and character.

C was first used for developing system software such as the UNIX operating system. Recently it has been used for application development. 1-2-3 Release 3.0 (the most popular spreadsheet program) has been rewritten in C.

C includes diverse data types including integer, character, and real similar to other languages discussed earlier. It has its own format for assignment statements, for example, Total = 10;. Each statement must end with a semicolon (;).

C includes several commands for branching and looping. Among these are WHILE, DO WHILE, FOR, and SWITCH-CASE.

Input/output operations are done by using PRINTF (print format) for displaying the output and GETS for reading input data to the computer.

C is extremely portable, concise, and flexible. It is gaining popularity daily.

SUMMARY

In this chapter, we reviewed the hardware and software components used in a typical computerized information system. A variety of input and output devices including CRTs, printers, and plotters were introduced. Different memory devices for both main and secondary storage were explained. We explored the criteria for computer classification and briefly discussed operating systems. The chapter concluded with a discussion of computer software including a survey of five of the most popular high-level languages.

REVIEW QUESTIONS

*These questions are answered in Appendix A.

  *1. What is the most popular input device? Why?

  2. What is the difference between a keyboard and a typewriter?

3. What are some of the applications of a touch screen? Mouse?

*4. What are some of the obstacles in using a voice-recognition system as an input device?

5. What are the differences between main and secondary memory?

*6. What is a main memory made of?

7. Which main memory device is volatile? Which one is non-volatile?

8. What is a secondary memory made of?

9. What are some of the common examples of secondary storage devices?

10. What are some of the commonly used output devices?

*11. In choosing a printer, what criteria should be considered?

12. How are computers classified?

13. What are the differences between a microcomputer and a mainframe?

14. Why is it difficult to draw a clear line between these computers?

15. What is a computer program? What are some of the ingredients of a computer program?

*16. What are some of the classes of computer languages? Which class is closest to the computer? To human language?

17. What is an operating system? What are its functions?

18. What are some of the unique features of FORTRAN?

*19. Why is COBOL most suitable for business data processing?

20. Why is BASIC so popular? What are some of the limitations of BASIC?

21. What are some of the unique features of PASCAL? C?

22. Visit your computer lab. What kinds of input devices are available? What are some of the output devices?

23. Can the printers in your lab generate graphs? Do you have a color graphics printer or plotter?

24. Visit a local bank. Ask about the applications of the MICR device.

25. Ask your instructor to tell you how multiple choice and true/false questions are graded. Besides speed, what are some other advantages of using computers to grade tests?

26. What is the fastest printer on your campus or in an organization that you are familiar with? What are some of the applications of high speed printers?

27. What input device is used in a computerized grocery store? In a fancy department store?

28. What types of secondary storage devices are available on your campus? What device is used mostly by mainframe computers? By micros?

29. Using the classifications of computers presented in this chapter, what types of computers are available on your campus? Hint: micros, minis, mainframes, or super computers?

30. What operating system is used by the mainframe computer(s) on your campus? What are the functions of an operating system?

31. What computer languages are taught on your campus? What language is the most popular language for business majors? For engineering majors?

32. Ask your instructor to compare and contrast the computer languages introduced in this chapter.

Assembly language	High-level languages	Operating system
Bar code	Input devices	Optical character reader
BASIC	Keyboard	Optical disk
Bubble memory	Light pen	Output devices
C	Machine language	PASCAL
COBOL	Magnetic disk	Printer
CRT	Magnetic tape	Semiconductor memory
Data tablet	Mouse	Touch screen
FORTRAN	Natural language	Voice-recognition system
Fourth generation language		

Multiple Choice

1. The most widely used input device is the

   a. mouse

   b. keyboard

   c. touch screen

   d. light pen

   e. plotter

2. Which of the following is best for rapid cursor movement?

   a. mouse

   b. keyboard

   c. touch screen

   d. light pen

   e. plotter

3. Main memory consists of

   a. magnetic tape

   b. semiconductor memory

   c. bubble memory

   d. both b and c

   e. none of the above

4. For storing vast amounts of data, it is best to use

   a. magnetic disks

   b. magnetic tape

   c. optical disks

   d. main memory

   e. secondary memory

5. Computers are classified based on

   a. cost

   b. memory size

   c. speed

   d. sophistication

   e. all of the above

6. A typical operating system consists of
   a. supervisor programs
   b. exercise programs
   c. control programs
   d. a and b
   e. a and c

7. Which of the following is not an operating system?
   a. DEC
   b. UNIX
   c. OS/2
   d. MS-DOS
   e. all of the above

8. High-level languages are best described as
   a. more difficult to learn than low-level languages
   b. less powerful than low-level languages
   c. self-documenting
   d. unavailable at this time
   e. machine dependent

9. An example of a high-level language is
   a. machine language
   b. ASCII
   c. DOS
   d. BASIC
   e. assembly language

10. The kernel is another name for the
   a. main memory
   b. supervisor program
   c. storage device
   d. operating system
   e. secondary memory

True/False

1. Touch screens rely on light detection or pressure-sensitive devices to determine which item is selected from a menu.

2. Secondary memory is volatile.

3. The current trends show that small computers will never be able to perform the tasks of large computers.

4. Regardless of the language being used, the computer will always understand the source code without further translation.

5. A typical computer language includes commands for assignment and branching statements.

6. An operating system is a set of programs that controls and supervises computer hardware and software.

7. Machine language and assembly language are machine independent.

8. Fourth generation languages (4GLs) are sometimes called non-procedural languages because the user does not need to follow a rigorous format.

9. A computer program is basically a series of instructions.

10. Of the main memory devices, only bubble memory is volatile.

Multiple Choice	True/False	ANSWERS
1. b	1. T	
2. a	2. F	
3. d	3. F	
4. c	4. F	
5. e	5. T	
6. e	6. T	
7. a	7. F	
8. c	8. T	
9. d	9. T	
10. b	10. F	

The World of Microcomputers

3

3–1

INTRODUCTION

In this chapter we discuss microcomputer fundamentals. Hardware and software for micros are explained, and different classes of application software are introduced. We present guidelines for successful selection and maintenance of microcomputers and we discuss the advantages of micros compared to mainframes. The chapter concludes with a hands-on session with a microcomputer.

3–2

DEFINING A MICROCOMPUTER

The terms personal computer, PC, micro, and **microcomputer** refer to the smallest type of computer when measured by such attributes as memory, cost, size, speed, and sophistication. Although small, the ever-increasing power and capability of personal computers sometimes blur the difference between PCs and larger computers.

Since the beginning of the microcomputer era in about 1975, the capability of these computers has improved beyond imagination. Still, some experts believe this is only the beginning and there is much more to be done by these computers.

A typical microcomputer consists of input, output, and memory devices. Figure 3–1 illustrates a typical microcomputer system. The **input device** is usually a keyboard. A PC keyboard is similar to a typewriter keyboard, with some additional keys. Figure 3–2 displays an IBM enhanced keyboard. Other input devices include the mouse, touch technology, light pens, graphics tablets, optical character readers (OCR), magnetic ink character recognition (MICR), cameras, sensors, and bar codes. In the future, there may be voice input devices as well.

The most common **output devices** for microcomputers are a monitor—sometimes called a CRT (cathode-ray tube) or VDT (video display terminal)—and a printer. The output generated on the monitor is called soft copy, and the printed output is referred to as hard copy. Other kinds of output devices include cameras and plotters.

There are two types of monitors. The majority of microcomputers use a monochrome screen. As the name indicates, this type of screen generates one

Figure 3–1
A Typical Microcomputer System. (Cobalt Productions/ Macmillan).

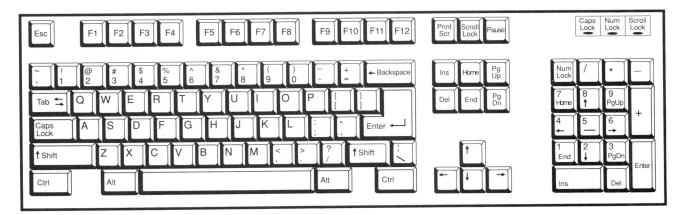

Figure 3-2
An IBM Enhanced Keyboard

color, such as green or amber. Monochrome monitors can generate graphics output if your computer is equipped with a graphics card or graphics adapter.

The other type of monitor is a color monitor—sometimes referred to as an RGB (red-green-blue) monitor. Color monitors come in several types: CGA, EGA, and VGA.

The sharpness of images on the display monitor is referred to as the resolution. The intersection of a row and a column is called a pixel; the greater the number of pixels, the higher the resolution. CGA, EGA, and VGA monitors present different resolutions. A CGA (Color Graphics Adapter) monitor displays 320 by 200 pixels in four colors.

An EGA (Enhanced Graphics Adapter) monitor displays 640 by 350 pixels in 16 colors. More advanced versions of EGA monitors can display 640 by 480 pixels in 16 colors and 320 by 200 pixels in 256 colors.

A VGA (Video Graphics Array) monitor can display 640 by 480 pixels in 16 colors and 320 by 200 pixels in 256 colors. The most recent graphics add-on board, this card was introduced in 1987 by the IBM PS/2 series computers.

Boards or cards are used to upgrade or expand the computer's capacities. These boards or cards perform many tasks. Some are used to expand memory, others are used as peripheral devices.

The processing part of a microcomputer is the CPU (central processing unit). Also called the microprocessor, the CPU includes three components. The main memory stores data, information, and instructions. The arithmetic logic unit (ALU) performs arithmetic and logical operations. Arithmetic operations include addition, subtraction, division, and multiplication. Logical operations include any types of comparisons, such as sorting (putting data into a particular order) or searching (choosing a particular data item). The control unit serves as the commander of the system. It tells the microcomputer what to do and how to do it. Figure 3-3 shows two different microprocessor chips or microchips.

3-3

MORE ON THE KEYBOARD

As you can see in figure 3-2, an enhanced keyboard is divided into three sections. Across the top are 12 function keys. Some keyboards have the function keys on the left. With most application software, these keys perform special functions, or they can be programmed to perform a particular task. For

A.

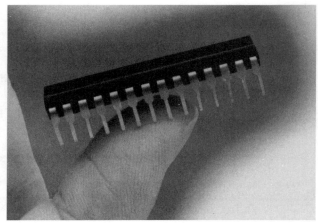

B.

Figure 3–3

A. The Motorola MC 68020 Microprocessor in the Protective Ceramic Package (Courtesy of Motorola, Inc.). B. A Microprocessor. (Courtesy of Radio Shack, A Division of Tandy Corporation).

example, Lotus 1-2-3, dBASE, and WordPerfect use function keys F1 through F10 for performing different tasks.

The middle part of the keyboard is similar to a typewriter keyboard. However, there are some special keys that a typewriter does not have—the Alt key and Ctrl keys, for example.

On the right side of the keyboard is a numeric keypad similar to that of an adding machine, used for cursor movement or, when the Num Lock key is pressed, to facilitate numeric data entry.

The purpose of function keys and some of the special keys varies in different application programs. For example, in WordPerfect, the F1 key performs undelete operations. In 1-2-3 or dBASE, it accesses on-line help.

3–4

OTHER NECESSARY DEVICES

Besides typical input/output devices, some additional devices are required for effective use of a microcomputer. These devices include disk drives and adapter cards.

3–4–1

Disk Drives

Disk drives are used to read and store data or information from and to a disk into the memory. Disk drives come in various capacities. You may have one or more floppy disk drives, and you also may have a **hard disk** drive. As you will read later, hard disks are capable of storing large quantities of information. The capacity of a hard disk is many times greater than a **floppy disk**. A floppy disk can hold from 360K (kilobytes) to 1.44M (megabytes) of information. The capacity of a hard disk varies from 5M to 300M or more.

The capacity of a storage device is measured in terms of bits or bytes. A bit (BInary digiT) is the smallest piece of information understood by a computer. A bit is either a 1 or a 0, indicating either an on or an off condition. A byte is a string of eight bits acting as a single piece of information. A byte is roughly equivalent to one character. For example, if you type "Susan" on your

Table 3–1

0 or 1 is equal to one bit
8 bits is equal to one byte
1,024 (2^{10}) bytes is equal to one kilobyte (K)
1,048,576 (2^{20}) bytes is equal to one megabyte (M)
1,073,741,824 (2^{30}) bytes is equal to one gigabyte
1,099,511,627,776 (2^{40}) bytes is equal to one terabyte

computer, it will occupy approximately five bytes of memory. Table 3–1 shows various memory equivalents.

Adapter Cards   3–4–2

Adapter cards are used to attach a particular option to the system unit. They are installed in expansion slots (channels) inside the system unit. Typical adapter cards may include the following:

- Disk drive card for connecting disk drives to the system unit
- Display card for connecting CRT to the system unit
- Memory card for connecting additional RAM to the existing memory
- Clock card for connecting a clock to the system unit
- Modem card for connecting a modem to your PC
- Printer interface card for connecting a printer to your computer

The original IBM PC has five expansion slots, the IBM XT and AT have eight slots. The adapter cards usually have outlet ports that are accessed at the back of the system unit. It is important to remember that the newer PCs do not require as many adapter cards. Ports are either parallel or serial and are used to connect devices to the system. You must connect a serial device to a serial port and a parallel device to a parallel port. Serial devices transfer one bit of data at a time, parallel devices transfer groups of bits at a time.

3–5
TYPES OF PRIMARY MEMORIES

There are two kinds of memory: main, or **primary memory,** and auxiliary, or secondary memory. Main memory is the heart of the microcomputer, usually referred to as **RAM** (Random-Access Memory). This is volatile memory—data stored in RAM are lost when you turn off your computer. To avoid this type of loss, you should always save your work on a storage device, such as a disk.

Three other types of memory also are referred to as main memory, but the user does not have direct control over them. These include:

- **ROM** (Read-Only Memory): A prefabricated chip supplied by vendors. This memory stores some general-purpose instructions or programs—DOS commands, for example.
- **PROM** (Programmable Read-Only Memory): By using a special device, the user can program this memory. However, once programmed, the user cannot erase this type of memory.

■ **EPROM** (Erasable Programmable Read-Only Memory): This type of read-only memory can be programmed by the user and, as the name indicates, erased and programmed again.

3-6
TYPES OF SECONDARY MEMORIES

Because the main memory of a microcomputer is limited, expensive, and volatile, secondary storage devices are used for mass data storage. **Secondary memory** is nonvolatile, and can be broadly classified into magnetic and optical.

3-6-1
Magnetic Storage Devices

Magnetic storage devices include floppy disks, mini-floppy disks, hard disks, and the Bernoulli Box. The capacity of a floppy or hard disk depends on its technical features. There are three types of standard disks: 3-½ inches, 5-¼ inches, and 8 inches. The most recent floppy just entering into the market is a 2-inch floppy.

Disks can be single-density, double density, or high-density. Density refers to the amount of information that can be stored on a disk. They can also be single-sided or double-sided. A 5-¼ inch, single-sided, single-density floppy can hold roughly 125K; a 5-¼ inch, single-sided, double-density floppy can hold about 250K; a 5-¼ inch, double-sided, double-density floppy can hold approximately 360K; and a high-density disk (sometimes called quad-density) can hold up to 1.2M. A 3-½ inch floppy disk can store 720K per side, or 1.44M on a double-sided disk.

A hard disk (sometimes called a Winchester disk) can be either 14, 8, 5-¼, or less than 4 inches in diameter. The capacity of these devices varies from 5 megabytes to 1 gigabyte.

A Bernoulli Box is a removable medium. This means after finishing your computer work you can pull this device out and store it in a safe location. This is not possible with a hard disk. A Bernoulli Box uses high-capacity floppy disks to store 10M or more of information. Generally speaking, it is less damage-prone than a hard disk, because the Bernoulli Box drive head, which records the data, does not move as a hard disk drive head does. In a Bernoulli Box the floppy disk moves toward the stationary read/write head. Figure 3-4 shows a Bernoulli Box.

Figure 3-4
A Bernoulli Box (Cobalt Productions/Macmillan)

Currently, the most commonly used secondary storage device is the 3-½ inch floppy disk. However, at the beginning of the PC era 5-¼ inch floppy disks were the most commonly used secondary storage devices. A 5-¼ inch disk is enclosed in a permanent vinyl jacket to protect the disk. A floppy disk is made of plastic material coated with magnetic material. After using a floppy disk you should put it back in its paper cover to protect it against dirt and dust. Don't put your fingers on exposed portions of the disk or data loss may result. Figure 3–5 highlights important areas of a 5-¼ inch disk.

Optical Technologies   3–6–2

Three types of optical storage have attracted much attention in recent years: CD ROM, WORM, and erasable optical disk. The advantages of optical technology devices are their durability and storage capacity. The major drawback of optical technology is its slow speed. However, the speed problem is being resolved gradually.

As the name indicates, **CD ROM** (compact disk read-only memory) is a permanent device. Information is recorded by disk-mastering machines. A CD ROM is similar to an audio compact disk. It can be duplicated and distributed throughout the organization. Its major application is for large permanent databases; for example, public-domain databases such as libraries, real estate information, and corporate financial information.

WORM (Write Once, Read Many) also is a permanent device. Information can be recorded once and cannot be altered. Its major drawback compared

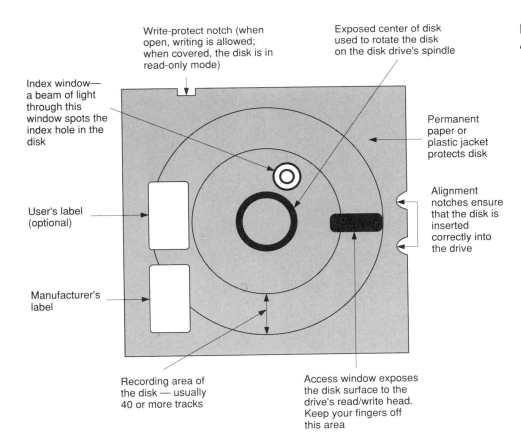

Figure 3–5
A 5-¼ Inch Floppy Disk

Write-protect notch (when open, writing is allowed; when covered, the disk is in read-only mode)

Exposed center of disk used to rotate the disk on the disk drive's spindle

Index window—a beam of light through this window spots the index hole in the disk

Permanent paper or plastic jacket protects disk

User's label (optional)

Alignment notches ensure that the disk is inserted correctly into the drive

Manufacturer's label

Recording area of the disk — usually 40 or more tracks

Access window exposes the disk surface to the drive's read/write head. Keep your fingers off this area

Figure 3-6
Optical Storage Devices for
Microcomputers

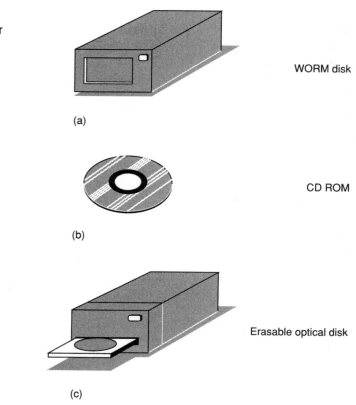

WORM disk

(a)

CD ROM

(b)

Erasable optical disk

(c)

to CD ROM is that you cannot duplicate the disk. You use a WORM for storing information that must be kept permanently; for example, information related to annual reports, nuclear power plants, airports, and railroads.

An **erasable optical disk** is used when high-volume storage and updating are essential. The information can be recorded and erased repeatedly. Figure 3-6 shows these different technologies.

3-7

MEMORY CAPACITY AND PROCESSOR SPEED

Microcomputer RAM capacity usually starts at 256K, but most vendors now offer 512K or 640K PCs. PCs with capacities of 1 to 4 megabytes are becoming more common and, in the future, will approach minicomputer capacity.

When you purchase a computer, you should calculate the memory requirements for your computing needs. Although you may have a PC with 640K of RAM, all of it is not accessible to you. A large portion of this memory is used by the application software. As an example, Lotus 1-2-3 Release 2.01 uses almost 200K of RAM. So in a 640K PC, you are left with only 440K of user memory.

Another consideration regarding your computer is speed. The speed of the processor is measured in megahertz (MHz) and usually varies from 4 MHz to 33 MHz. Soon, speeds of 50 MHz or more may be available. The higher the processor speed, the faster the computer.

A factor that has direct effect on speed is the word size of the processor. Word size indicates the number of characters that can be processed simultaneously. Word size varies from 8 to 32 bits for microcomputers. The bigger the word size, the faster the computer. The speed of your microcomputer may have a direct effect on your business operation. With a faster computer you can process more information in a shorter period of time. However, you should consider the additional cost incurred by buying the more powerful PCs and the marginal benefit to be gained.

3–8 GENERAL CAPABILITIES OF MICROCOMPUTER SOFTWARE

A microcomputer can perform a variety of tasks by using either commercial software or software developed in-house. In-house developed software is usually more expensive than commercial software. However, this software is customized and should better fit your needs. Thousands of software programs are available for PCs. The following are typical commercial programs and applications available for microcomputers.

Word Processing Software

3–8–1

A microcomputer used as a **word processor** is similar to a typewriter with a memory. With a word processor, you can generate documents, make deletions and insertions, and cut and paste. Word processing programs are becoming more sophisticated, and some of these programs provide limited graphics and data management features.

There are many word processing programs on the market. Some of the most popular ones are Multimate from Ashton-Tate, Officewriter from Office Solutions, WordPerfect from WordPerfect Corp., Wordstar from WordStar International, PC-Write from Quicksoft, Word from Microsoft, and Volkswriter from Lifetree Software, Inc.

Spreadsheet Software

3–8–2

A spreadsheet is simply a table of rows and columns. **Spreadsheet software** can be broadly classified into two types.

The first type is a dedicated spreadsheet. This means that the program performs only spreadsheet analysis. VisiCalc (by Visicorp) is a good example. The other type of spreadsheet package is integrated software, which means it can perform more than one type of analysis. You can use 1-2-3, for example, to perform spreadsheet analysis as well as maintaining a database and doing graphics. Some experts believe 1-2-3 is not a truly integrated package because it does not offer word processing and communication. However, although this is true, 1-2-3 can easily use these features from other software.

Other popular integrated packages include Electronic Desk from the Software Group, Inc., Framework from Ashton-Tate, Smart Software System from Innovative Software, Inc., Symphony from Lotus Development Corporation, UniCalc from Lattice, Inc., Excel from Microsoft, SuperCalc 5.0 from Computer Associates International, Inc., and Quattro from Borland International.

The number of jobs that can be performed by a spreadsheet program is unlimited. Generally speaking, any application suitable for a row and column analysis is a candidate for a typical spreadsheet. For example, you can use a spreadsheet to prepare a budget, and then, manipulating variables, the spreadsheet can perform some impressive "what-if" analysis. You could reduce your predicted income by 2 percent and ask the spreadsheet to calculate the effect of this change on other items in the spreadsheet.

3–8–3   ## Database Software

Database software is designed to perform database operations such as file creation, deletion, modification, search, sort, merge, and join (combining two files based on a common key). A **file** is a collection of records, a record is a collection of fields, and a field is a collection of characters.

Popular database programs include Business Filevision from Telos Software Products, dBASE III PLUS and IV from Ashton-Tate, PC-File III from Buttonware, Inc., Q&A from Symantec, Paradox from Ansa Software, Omnis Quartz from Blyth Software, DataEase from DataEase International, FoxBase and FoxPro from Fox Software, and R-Base from Microrim Corporation.

A database also can be compared to a table of rows and columns. The rows correspond to a record, and the columns correspond to the fields within the record. Two common applications of a database are sorting and searching records. In sort operations, the operator enters a series of records in any order then asks the database management program to sort the records in ascending or descending order, based on the data in the fields. Search operations are even more interesting. You can search for data items that meet certain criteria. You can, for example, search for all the MIS students who have GPAs greater than 3.6 and who are under 20 years of age. Some databases (such as Q&A) allow you to search for key words within a text file.

3–8–4   ## Graphics Software

Graphics software is designed to present data in graphic format. With this software, data can be converted into a line graph to show a trend, to a pie chart to highlight the components of a data item, and to other types of graphs for various analyses. Masses of data can be converted to a graph and, in a glance, you can discover the general pattern of the data. Graphs can highlight patterns and correlation of data items. They also make data presentation a more manageable job. Integrated packages such as 1-2-3 or Symphony have graphics capabilities, or you can use a dedicated graphics package.

Three popular graphics packages are Energraphics from Enertronics Research, Inc., Harvard Graphics from Software Publishing Corporation, and Freelance from Lotus Development Corporation.

3–8–5   ## Communications Software

Using a modem and **communications software,** your microcomputer can connect you to a wealth of information available in public and private databases. Several executives can simultaneously work on the same report in several different states or countries by using communications software. The report is sent back and forth to each location until it is completed. With communications software and a modem, remote job entry becomes an easy task. A modem converts computer signals (digital signals) to signals that can be transferred on a telephone line (analog signals).

Some programs, such as Symphony, include a communications program within the package itself. However, there are many other communications software products on the market, among them Crosstalk from Microstuf, Inc., On-Line from Micro-Systems Software, Inc., PFS: Access from Software Publishing Corp., and Smartcom II from Hayes Microcomputer Products, Inc.

Desktop Publishing Software

3–8–6

Desktop publishing software is used to produce professional-quality documents (with or without graphics) using relatively inexpensive hardware and software. All that is needed is a PC, a desktop publishing software package, and a letter-quality or laser printer. Desktop publishing has evolved as a result of three major factors: inexpensive PCs, inexpensive laser printers, and sophisticated and easy-to-use software.

Desktop publishing enables you to produce high quality screen output, and then transfer it to the printer in a "what you see is what you get" (WYSIWYG) environment. You can use desktop publishing for creating newsletters, brochures, training manuals, transparencies, posters, and books (see fig. 3–7).

A.

B.

Figure 3–7
A. Desktop Publishing Combines Text, Graphics, and Illustrations (Courtesy of Hewlett-Packard).
B. With Desktop Publishing, Business Professionals Can Prepare High Quality Documents (Courtesy of Hewlett-Packard)

There are several desktop publishing software packages available. Pagemaker from Aldus and Ventura Publisher from Xerox Corporation are two of the most popular ones.

3–8–7   Financial Planning Software

Financial planning software works with large amounts of data and performs diverse financial analyses. These analyses include present value, future value, rate of return, cash flow, depreciation, and budgeting.

Some popular programs for financial planning are DTFPS from Desk Top Financial Solutions, Inc., Excel from Microsoft Corp., Finar from Finar Research Systems, Ltd., Javelin from Javelin Software Corp., Micro-DSS/Finance from Addison-Wesley Publishing Co., 1-2-3 from Lotus Development Corporation, IFPS from Execucom Systems, and Micro Plan from Chase Laboratories, Inc.

With these programs, you can plan and analyze your financial situation. For example, you can calculate how much your $2,000 IRA will be at 10 percent interest in 30 years, or you can discount all future cash flows into today's dollar. You can figure out how much you have to deposit in the bank in order to save $60,000 in 10 years for your child's education.

3–8–8   Accounting Software

Aside from spreadsheet software, which has widespread applications in the accounting field, there are many dedicated **accounting programs** that are able to perform accounting tasks. The tasks performed by these programs include general ledgers, account receivables, account payables, payrolls, balance sheets, and income statements. Depending on the price, these programs vary in sophistication.

Some of the more popular accounting programs are One Write Plus from Gerat American Software, Business Works PC from Manzanita Software Systems, 4-in-1 Basic Accounting from Real World Corp., Peachtree from Peachtree Software, Inc., and DacEasy Accounting from Dac Software, Inc.

3–8–9   Project-Management Software

A project consists of a series of related activities. Building a house, designing an order-entry system, or writing a thesis are examples of projects. The goal of **project-management software** is to help decision-makers keep the time and budget under control by resolving scheduling problems. Project-management software helps managers to plan and set achievable goals. It also highlights the bottlenecks and the relationships among different activities. These programs enable you to study the cost, time, and resource effect of any change in the schedule.

Popular project-management programs include Harvard Total Project Manager from Software Publishing Corp., Micro Planner 6 from Micro Planning International, Microsoft Project from Microsoft Corp., Superproject Expert from Computer Associates, and Time Line from Symantec.

3–8–10   Computer-Aided Design (CAD) Software

Computer-aided design (CAD) software is used for drafting and design. CAD has replaced the traditional tools of drafting and design such as T-square, triangle, paper, and pencil, and it is being used extensively in the architectural and engineering industries. CAD software does not belong only to the large corporations any more. With the new 286-, 386-, and 486-based PCs and significant price reduction, small companies and individuals can afford this software. Because the new PCs have larger memory and are significantly faster than earlier PCs, they are able to take advantage of the majority of features offered by CAD programs.

There are several CAD programs on the market including AutoCAD from Autodesk, Cadkey from Cadkey, and VersaCAD from VersaCAD (see fig. 3–8).

3–9
GUIDELINES FOR SELECTING A MICROCOMPUTER

There are many kinds of microcomputers on the market, making the selection task a difficult one. In this section and the next, we provide you with some general guidelines regarding the purchase and maintenance of a microcomputer. These guidelines will help you choose a suitable computer and maintain it more easily.

A.

B.

Figure 3–8
A. A CAD System for Detailed Architectural Design (Larry Hamill/Macmillan). B. A CAD System for Design of a Multi-component Product (Larry Hamill/Macmillan). C. A CAD System of an Indy Car Rear Wing (Larry Hamill/Macmillan)

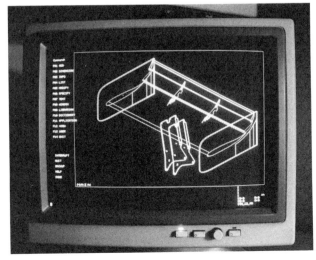

C.

Before you start looking, you should define your requirements. Sometimes this is called the "wish list" approach. When you are ready to buy, you should have a clear idea of the microcomputer you need and the specific applications you want it to handle. Remember, if you need a particular kind of software, you must have the hardware to run it.

After defining your software and hardware needs, you should look at technical support and vendor reputation. Important factors regarding selection and maintenance of a microcomputer follow.

Good software should:

- be easy to use
- be able to handle your business volume
- have good documentation
- have training available
- have updates available (free of charge or for a minimum charge)
- have local support
- come from a reputable vendor
- have a low cost

Good hardware should:

- have a comfortable keyboard
- have function keys
- have a general operating system (OS/2, MS-DOS, PC-DOS, or UNIX)
- have 16-bit or bigger processor (word) size
- be expandable (memory and peripheral)
- have adequate channel capacity or expansion slots
- have a low cost

A good monitor should:

- be separated from the system unit (not be built-in)
- be easy to read
- have a standard number of characters per row and column (80 columns by 25 rows)

A good disk drive should:

- have a built-in, not separate, disk drive
- have adequate storage capacity
- have a hard disk option

A good printer should:

- have a standard printer interface (without additional devices)
- produce quality output
- have high speed

- have a reasonable amount of noise suppression
- let you change tape, ribbons, or toner cartridge easily
- have a low cost

A good vendor should:

- have a good reputation
- have a knowledgeable staff
- have training available for hardware and software
- have a hot line available
- support newsletters and user groups
- provide a "loaner" in case of break down
- provide updates (trade-in options)

A good contract should:

- have a warranty period
- state a flexible time for repair
- limit down time and inconvenience by providing flexible repair visits and timely repair of the computer
- have reasonable terms for contract renewal
- allow relocation or reassignment of the present contract
- observe confidentiality issues

3-10
TAKING CARE OF YOUR MICROCOMPUTER

To maintain the health of your microcomputer you should follow these guidelines:

- Protect your microcomputer against dirt, dust, and smoke.
- Make backups and keep your backups in different locations.
- Avoid any kind of liquid spills.
- Maintain steady power. Use surge protectors and lightning arresters.
- Protect the machine from static by using humidifiers or antistatic spray devices.
- Do not use a disk that you are not familiar with (to avoid computer viruses—the deadly programs that can corrupt data).
- Don't download information to your computer from unknown bulletin boards. (Downloading means importing information from other computers by using a telephone line.)
- Acquire insurance for your computer equipment.

3-11
ADVANTAGES OF MICROCOMPUTERS

Generally speaking, a microcomputer offers several advantages compared to a mainframe computer. With extended memory and increased speed, microcomputers can perform on a smaller scale many of the tasks performed by a mainframe. We can summarize the advantages of microcomputers compared with mainframes as follows:

- They are easier to use.
- They are less threatening to non-computer experts.
- The user has more control.
- They are relatively inexpensive.
- They can be portable.

3–12

YOU AND YOUR PC: A HANDS-ON SESSION

If the disk operating system (DOS) is in drive A (the top disk drive, or the left disk drive, in a two-drive system), when you turn the computer on, your microcomputer will ask for the date. Most IBM or IBM-compatible computers come with a DOS disk. Either type the date in the desired format or press Enter to skip this prompt. The computer then asks you for the time. Either type the time in the desired format or press Enter. Now you are at the A> prompt. Figure 3–9 shows how your screen looks during the getting-started procedure.

If your computer has a hard disk this procedure is slightly different. You will start the system from the hard disk, and your prompt will be C> instead of A>. From the prompt, or disk operating system mode, you can go to any application software. For example, pull the DOS disk out of the drive, insert the Lotus System disk, type 123, and press Enter to load 1-2-3 into RAM.

When you are at the A> prompt, you are in RAM. We call this area a working or temporary area. This means any work in this area will disappear if you turn the computer off. To make your work permanent, you must transfer it to a **permanent area**. Any application program provides you with some type of save or copy command for transferring your work from RAM to disk. The permanent area can be either floppy disk, hard disk, or cassette. Your work stays in the permanent area until you erase it.

Beginning computer users are always worried about making mistakes. What happens if you make a mistake? Don't panic. Your mistakes easily can be corrected. Some computers and application programs have an UNDO command. In the worst case, you can correct your mistake by typing over your previous material. Remember, any address or cell in the computer memory can hold only one value at a time. As soon as you type a new value, the old one disappears.

Figure 3–9

Starting the System

```
Current date is Tue 1-01-80
Enter new date (mm-dd-yy): 1-1-91
Current time is 0:00:52.89
Enter new time: 15:25


Microsoft(R) MS-DOS(R)  Version 3.30
          (C)Copyright Microsoft Corp 1981-1987



A>
```

3–13
DEFINING A COMPUTER FILE

A computer file is basically an electronic document. One way to create a document is to enter it using the keyboard. As soon as you save the document, you have generated a computer file.

To differentiate one file from another, you must save each file under a unique name—a file name. A file name is any combination of up to eight valid characters (MYFILE, for example). Valid characters include letters of the alphabet (upper- or lowercase), digits 0 through 9, the underscore, and some special characters. If you provide a name longer than eight characters, some application programs give you an error message, others truncate the name and accept only the first eight characters. In addition to a file name, a file is usually saved with a file extension (MYFILE.TXT, for example). Some application programs automatically provide a file extension when you save the file. In other application programs, providing a file extension is the user's responsibility.

There are several characters that have special meanings in different application software. The asterisk (*) can represent up to eight characters. The question mark (?) can represent any single character. These two characters are called **wild card** characters. These wild cards can significantly improve your efficiency while working with application programs. For example, all your 1-2-3 graphics files are identified by *.PIC. The * represents any file name, and the PIC indicates that your file is a 1-2-3 graphics file.

As an illustration of the usefulness of these wild card characters, suppose that you want to copy all your 1-2-3 graphics files from the disk in drive A to the disk in drive B. You would simply type the DOS command COPY *.PIC B:. If the * wild card feature was not available, you would have to type the COPY command as many times as the number of graphics files.

3–14
TYPES OF DATA

Any application program or computer language accepts different types of data. The most commonly used data types are numeric and alphanumeric.

Numeric data include any combination of digits 0 through 9 and decimal points. Numeric data can be integer or real. Integer data include only whole numbers without any decimal points, for example, 656 or 986. Real data include digits and decimal points, 696.25 or 729.793, for example. Real data are sometimes called floating point data, which means the decimal point can move—222.2, 22.22, or 2.222, for example. Another type of real data is fixed point data, which means that the decimal point is always fixed.

Nonnumeric, or alphanumeric, **data** (sometimes called labels or strings) include any types of valid characters. For example, Jackson or 123 Broadway Street. Remember, you cannot perform any arithmetic operations with nonnumeric data or labels.

3–15
TYPES OF VALUES

Computers usually handle two types of values: variables and constants.

Variables are valid computer addresses (locations) that hold different values at different times. For example, when you specify A=65, A is the variable and 65 is the constant. When you specify B="Brown", B is the variable and Brown is the constant. As soon as you enter a new value into this variable, the old value disappears. The **constant** is always fixed. Figure 3–10 illustrates this concept.

Figure 3–10
An Example of a Variable and a
Constant

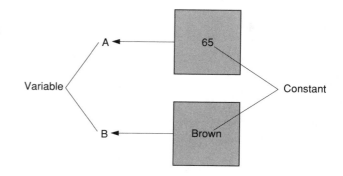

3–16
TYPES OF FORMULAS

There are two types of formulas or functions handled by computers: user-defined and built-in.

User-defined formulas or functions are a combination of computer addresses designed to perform a certain task. For example, the area of a triangle can be presented as A=B*H/2 meaning base multiplied by height divided by 2. In this case, A is a formula or a function. You can enter different values for B and H and a different value for A (the area of the triangle) will be calculated.

Built-in formulas or functions are already available within the application program or the computer language. As soon as the user provides values for a given variable or variables, the application program or the computer language calculates these formulas. For example, SQRT(X) is a function that calculates the square root of a variable, X. The X or any other information needed by these functions is called an argument. As soon as you provide a value for X, the square root is immediately calculated. For example, SQRT(25) is equal to 5. The function FV(payment,interest rate,term) calculates the future value of a series of equal payments with a given interest rate over a period of time (term).

3–17
PRIORITY (PRECEDENCE) OF OPERATIONS

When application programs perform arithmetic operations, they follow a series of rules. These **priority rules** are as follows:

1. Expressions inside parentheses have the highest priority.
2. Exponentiation (raising to power) is performed next.
3. Multiplication and division have the third highest priority.
4. Addition and subtraction have the lowest priority.
5. When there are two or more operations with the same priority, operations proceed from left to right.

The following examples should make this clear. A program uses * for multiplication, ^ for exponentiation, and / for division. If A=5, B=10, and C=2, a computer will calculate the following answers:

```
A+B/C=10
(A+B)/C=7.5
A*B/C=25
(A*B)/C=25
A^C/2=12.50
```

In this chapter we discussed microcomputers in general. Input and output, and primary and secondary memory devices were explained. General capabilities of microcomputers were introduced, and we presented a series of guidelines for successful selection and maintenance of a microcomputer. We discussed the advantages of microcomputers compared to mainframe computers. The chapter concluded with a hands-on session. We explained computer files, data, values, formulas, and the priority of operations.

SUMMARY

REVIEW QUESTIONS

*These questions are answered in Appendix A.

1. What is a microcomputer? What components does a typical minicomputer have?

*2. What are some typical input devices for a PC ?

3. What are some typical output devices for a PC?

4. What is the difference between a primary memory device and a secondary memory device?

5. What is RAM? ROM? PROM? EPROM?

*6. What is the most commonly used secondary memory device for a PC?

7. What are optical technologies? What are their advantages?

8. How do you measure the memory capacity of a PC?

9. Besides memory, what other attributes are important when you buy a computer?

10. What is the difference between a floppy and a hard disk?

11. What is the speed range for a typical microcomputer?

*12. What is the memory size of a typical personal computer?

13. What constitutes good software?

14. What constitutes good hardware?

15. What factors constitute a good contract?

*16. List important things to do when caring for your computer.

17. What are some application programs for a PC?

18. What are some of the advantages of a personal computer compared to a mainframe computer?

19. What is permanent memory in a PC? What is temporary memory?

20. How do you send information from RAM to a disk?

*21. How do you correct your mistakes?

22. What is a computer file?

23. What is a wild card character?

24. Name some different types of data.

25. What is a variable? A constant?

*26. What is priority of operations?

27. What symbols are used for arithmetic operations?

28. Turn on a PC. What do you see? Turn it off. Insert the DOS disk in drive A and turn the computer back on. What do you see this time?

29. Enter the correct date and time into your computer. What happens if you make a mistake?

30. Type DIR and press Enter. What is displayed?

31. How many generations of micros have we seen? What are the most powerful PCs on the market?

32. What types of PCs do you have on your campus? Describe different input/output devices used by the PCs in your school micro lab. Do you have a Bernoulli Box in the lab? What are some of the advantages of a Bernoulli Box over a hard disk?

33. What are the most commonly used disks on your campus? 3-½ or 5-¼? Compare and contrast these two types of storage devices.

34. Consult computer magazines to find out which computer at the present time is using optical disks.

35. Out of 10 application software packages introduced in this chapter, which ones are available on your campus? What are the applications of each?

36. If you want to buy a PC for your personal use, how do you start shopping? What attributes make a PC attractive?

KEY TERMS

Accounting software	Graphics software	PROM
Built-in formulas	Hard disk	RAM
CD ROM	Input device	ROM
Communications software	Microcomputer	Secondary memory
Computer-aided design	Nonnumeric data	Spreadsheet software
Constants	Numeric data	User-defined formulas
Database software	Output device	Variables
EPROM	Permanent area	Wild card
Erasable optical disk	Primary memory	Word processor
File	Priority rules	WORM
Financial planning software	Project-management software	
Floppy disk		

ARE YOU READY TO MOVE ON?

Multiple Choice

1. Choose the correct ranking of monitor display resolutions from lowest to highest:
   a. VGA, CGA, EGA
   b. EGA, VGA, CGA
   c. EGA, CGA, VGA
   d. CGA, EGA, VGA
   e. none of the above

2. Which of the following is not a typical adapter card?
   a. printer interface card
   b. clock card
   c. disk drive card
   d. display card
   e. punch card

3. Of the various types of main memory, the user has direct control over
   a. ROM
   b. REM
   c. RAM
   d. PROM
   e. all of the above

4. At the present time, the most commonly used secondary storage device is the

  a. 5-¼ inch floppy disk

  b. 3-½ inch floppy disk

  c. Bernoulli Box

  d. hard disk

  e. none of the above

5. The major advantage(s) of optical storage technology is (are)

  a. storage capacity

  b. cost

  c. durability

  d. both a and c

  e. all of the above

6. When we refer to memory and storage capacity sizes, we use the term K (as in 360K). 1K equals approximately

  a. 1 byte

  b. 1,000 bytes

  c. 1,000,000 bytes

  d. 1,048,576 bytes

  e. none of the above

7. Word size directly affects

  a. the speed of the computer

  b. the ability of the user to understand what is being said

  c. the maximum amount of data that can be displayed on the CRT

  d. the choice of which type of disk drive to use

  e. the meaning of the function keys on the keyboard

8. Which of the following are disadvantages of mainframes when compared to microcomputers?

  a. they are more difficult to use

  b. they are more threatening to non-computer users

  c. the user has less control

  d. they are relatively more expensive

  e. all of the above

9. After "booting" the computer with the DOS disk (loading DOS and entering the date and time), you are at

  a. the Lotus Access Menu

  b. the DOS prompt (A>)

  c. the parallel/serial interface

  d. the BASIC prompt

  e. none of the above

10. An example of alphanumeric data would be

  a. 123

  b. 123.

  c. LOTUS-123

  d. A=(123−2)/4

  e. none of the above

True/False

1. The terms personal computer, PC, and microcomputer refer to different types of computers.
2. A typical microcomputer consists of input, output, and memory devices.
3. Monochrome (or amber) CRTs cannot generate graphic output.
4. The purpose of function keys and special keys on a computer keyboard do not vary in different application programs.
5. The capacity of a hard disk is greater than the capacity of a floppy disk.
6. A WORM drive can be recorded and erased repeatedly when high volume storage and updating are essential.
7. Typical microcomputer software packages and applications include spreadsheet, database, graphics, communications, and word processing.
8. The first step in selecting a microcomputer is to define your needs, then think about software.
9. The commands DIR *.* and DIR ????????.??? produce the same results.
10. Expressions inside parentheses have the lowest priority when it comes to performing arithmetic operations.

ANSWERS

Multiple Choice	True/False
1. d	1. F
2. e	2. T
3. c	3. F
4. b	4. F
5. d	5. T
6. b	6. F
7. a	7. T
8. e	8. T
9. b	9. T
10. c	10. F

Computer-Based Information Systems

4

4–1

INTRODUCTION

In this chapter we review the basics of a computer-based information system (CBIS) and look at the components and objectives of these systems. We introduce different classes of CBIS, including electronic data processing (EDP), management information systems (MIS), decision support systems (DSS), and executive information systems (EIS). Included is a brief discussion of artificial intelligence and its related technologies, including expert systems, natural language processing, and robotics. The chapter concludes with a discussion regarding the importance and versatility of CBIS.

4–2

COMPUTER-BASED INFORMATION SYSTEMS

Generally speaking, a **computer-based information system** (CBIS) is an organized integration of hardware and software technologies and human elements designed to produce timely, integrated, accurate, and useful information for decision-making purposes.

The hardware elements discussed so far include input, output, and memory devices. The type of device used varies from one application to the next and from one organization to the next.

The software used includes commercial programs or software developed in-house or both. The particular application or organization determines the type of software employed in a CBIS.

The human element includes system users, programmers, systems analysts, and so forth. We discuss system professionals in detail in Chapter 9.

To design a CBIS, you first must clearly define the objective of the system. Then you must collect and analyze the data. Finally, information must be provided in a useful format for decision-making purposes.

There are many CBIS applications in both private and public organizations; for example, a CBIS for inventory control. This system provides information about inventory so that the inventory manager can know how much of each product is on hand, what items have been ordered, what items are back ordered, and so on.

Another example of a CBIS is for forecasting sales for the next period. This CBIS, using the most recent past data and some types of mathematical or statistical models, provides the best possible forecast. The sales manager then can use this information for planning.

A CBIS for cash flow analysis provides information to the financial manager regarding all the cash inflows and outflows. Using this information, the manager can establish a balance between the incoming and outgoing cash.

A final example of a CBIS is for a police department. This CBIS could provide information such as crime statistics, crime forecasts, and police protection allocation.

4–3

A CBIS MODEL

Any CBIS includes seven components: data, database, process, information, information systems life cycle (ISLC), environment, and design specifications.[1] Figure 4–1 shows this model.

---

[1] Hossein Bidgoli and James Vigen, *Introduction to Management Information Systems: A User's Perspective* (Dubuque, Iowa: Kendall/Hunt Publishing Company, 1986).

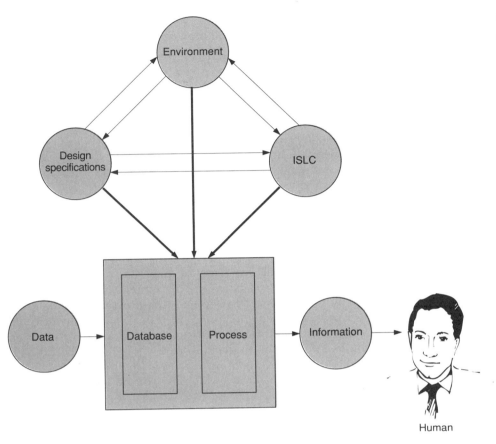

Figure 4–1
A Conceptual Model for a CBIS

Data   4–3–1

When developing a CBIS, the information needed by the user directly affects the type of data used.

If an organization has defined its strategic goals, objectives, and critical success factors to ensure a viable and growing organization, the data component can be structured rather easily and the CBIS has potential for success. On the other hand, if there are conflicting goals and objectives, or if the company is not aware of which factors are critical to its success, many problems can occur to destroy the confidence in a CBIS or minimize its effectiveness. If the CBIS is not designed to evolve as changes take place, then the system may do more damage than good.

Of course, the objectives of the organization ultimately resolve the questions of the sources of data—external or internal sources—and whether the data are past- (performance), present- (operational), or future- (budget or cash flow) oriented. The urgency of need and the availability of data in many forms, including aggregated (lump sum) or disaggregated (itemized), can then be addressed.

Disaggregated data allow for a greater focus on specific business problems. This, in turn, reduces the tendency to bias decisions based on intangible qualities. Disaggregated data are needed when, for instance, sales are analyzed by product, territory, or salesperson, and costs are analyzed by cost center or product. Aggregated data limit the decision-maker's ability to focus on specific factors.

CBIS users have a need not only to receive specific output but receive it in an understandable and appropriate format for ease of use in decision-making.

4-3-2   Database

The type of database is not important to the user, only the existence and availability of the database is the issue. We discuss different types of database models in Chapter 6. If the CBIS does not provide what the user wants, the success of such a system is questionable.

In addition, managers at higher levels are less willing to expend valuable personal or staff time to manually gather, process, and interpret available data. Thus, data need to be treated as a common resource so that they can be used readily.

4-3-3   Process

Development of a CBIS generally includes a wide range of transaction processing reports and some models for decision analysis. In many cases the models are built into the system or can be accessed from external sources.

Formal information is generated by a CBIS, and informal information is received through informal channels, which may include rumors, unconfirmed reports, and stories. Because the user has both formal and informal information available and will use this information in decision-making, a good CBIS should enable the user to work with both kinds of information when problem solving.

A CBIS should, therefore, include a wide range of models to support all levels of decision-making. Users should be able to do inquiry and report generation and interface with a large number of subroutines that can be linked. The capability to grow with the system requires that the initial CBIS enable the user to redefine, generate, restructure, and incorporate new information into the modeling analysis. Eventually, the purpose of the process component of the CBIS is generation of the most useful type of information for decision-making purposes.

4-3-4   Information

The nature of information is determined by its usefulness to the end user. It is the usefulness of this information that determines the success of a CBIS. The system must be responsive to the end user in four main areas. It must be timely, integrated with other data and information, consistent and accurate, and relevant. If the information lacks any of these basic features, incorrect decisions, misallocation of resources, and overlooked windows of opportunity will result. If the system cannot provide a minimum level of confidence, then the CBIS will not be used or the system will be severely discounted.

Perhaps the greatest requirement for information is that it provide a fundamental base from which the end user can explore different options, or better yet, gain an insight into the particular task at hand.

In addition to the nature of information, the user/system interface must be flexible and easy to use. Menu-driven systems have attracted much attention in recent years. These systems provide flexibility and ease of use, particularly to users with minimum computer background. The CBIS should provide information in diverse formats, including graphics, tabular, exception type, and so forth. Graphic reports highlight the business situation in an easy to understand pictorial fashion. Exception reports highlight those situations that are outside of the specified range. A CBIS that has many options for receiving or gaining access to information has a better chance for success because it uses methods of information transfer that are better understood by the user.

Information Systems Life Cycle   4–3–5

As with all systems, the CBIS has a well-defined life cycle—the information systems life cycle (ISLC). Unless the system has a radical transformation, each information system has exploration (introduction), establishment (growth), maintenance (maturity), and decline (death) periods.

A CBIS has a life cycle because of technological changes and varying information needs of the key decision-makers. Within the system itself, each subsystem has its own life cycle. The exploration stage is crucial to the acceptance of the CBIS (but not necessarily its success). The growth period may be slowed by delays in the expansion of the CBIS, technical problems, the availability of the CBIS to the end-users, and the reluctance by the end users to accept the CBIS. If the delays can be overcome, the growth period of the CBIS offers a greater opportunity for it to be accepted. Finally, if the CBIS improves the quality of the work accomplished, searches out new areas and new ways to service end users, and lowers the cost of providing information, it will also be more readily accepted.

Next, the information systems life cycle should increase the usage and reputation of the CBIS through quality and improvement of features, such as graphics and external databases, which give greater flexibility and greater user enthusiasm.

The final stage in the information systems life cycle is the decline period. This can be crucial to the organization's success. If there is not a planned death or review of the CBIS, the organization may be saddled with a CBIS that takes a disproportionate amount of the organization's resources relative to its contributions. A periodic review may force the current CBIS to be drastically overhauled or eliminated in favor of a new system. Figure 4–2 shows the four CBIS states of life.

Environment   4–3–6

Users of computer-based information systems occupy three organizational levels: top management (strategic), middle management (tactical), and lower

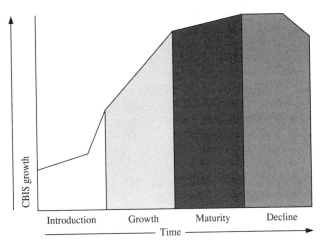

Figure 4–2
Four States of a CBIS Life Cycle

management (operational). Each organizational level assumes a different role in the development and use of CBIS.

Support in the form of policies and encouragement from top management is necessary for a CBIS to be successful. General resistance to CBIS at all levels of the organization can be seen in habit patterns, lack of familiarity with the system, and feelings of insecurity regarding the system. Usually, people are accustomed to hard copy data regarding company policies, financial reports, progress reports, and so on. So visualization of data on a CRT is new and unfamiliar to many people.

Learning how to access the computer is also an activity that shakes the user's security. Resistance is further compounded by the boring nature of data input, extraction, and all the mechanical elements associated with operating the computer.

Security and confidentiality are other factors in resistance. Who has access to a user's data? Who has access to the data formerly stored in the minds of decision-makers? Is pirating a possibility? Users are concerned that creative ideas and secured data may become sources of power for unauthorized individuals. Even if data are not pirated through internal or external sources it is possible that data may disappear because of software or hardware malfunctions. Have security measures been properly implemented into the system to prevent the accidental erasure of important documents? Are backups adequate and timely? Has the user been adequately trained? Have policies been established for the displaced employees? These are all important questions that must be addressed if the system is going to be successful.

4-3-7   Design Specifications

After a careful review of the information system's life cycle and a precise definition of the environment of a particular CBIS, the design specifications should be decided on. Comprehensive design specifications play a crucial role in the CBIS by creating consistency in computer use, increasing the adaptability of the existing CBIS to growing technology, increasing the chances of acceptance by the users, and, finally, by serving as a guideline for CBIS use. The most important design specification variables are types of design (task force vs. individual), provision for change (modularity in design), functional specifications and performance criteria, and system documentation.

Traditionally, a CBIS has been designed largely by data processing personnel. As a result, the designs have not always gained the full support of the users. The emerging issue of task force design emphasizes the participation of all affected personnel in the design of the CBIS. This particular method could increase the commitment of users and give them a chance to express their views regarding the use of the CBIS.

Acquisition and utilization of computer technology should not be a one-shot operation. Rather, it should be a continuous and evolutionary process. Design specifications of the CBIS model should consider the ways and methods by which a particular organization might adapt to the growing technology. Modularity in design could provide such an opportunity. Modularity should be considered in relation to hardware acquisition, software acquisition, systems design principles, and, most importantly, software development. To achieve this goal, an organization should set a master plan for its CBIS applications. The plan should include all the related activities for the next three to five years and should be continuously reviewed and revised. The plan should clearly specify where the organization is with regard to its CBIS projects and where it is planning to be. All the affected personnel should have input to the CBIS master plan.

To stay within the range of the predefined objectives for the CBIS, the designer should keep in mind the functional specifications of the system. Functional specifications include the following:

- Time, cost, and other resource estimations (how much time and money is needed to design and implement a particular CBIS)
- Specific objectives of the CBIS
- Input and output specifications
- A description of system functions and characteristics
- Accuracy of reports
- Reliability of reports
- Degree of acceptance and use of the CBIS

A comprehensive written document that describes the details and step-by-step operation of the CBIS can be very helpful. This document also may aid in improving the performance of existing systems.

4–4
CLASSES OF CBIS

Different types of CBIS have been designed to provide specific information. Based on their objectives, the intended audiences, and the technology used, CBIS systems have been classified as EDP, MIS, DSS, and EIS. Each system addresses a specific type of decision. Organizational decisions can be classified into three groups as follows:

Structured decisions, or programmable tasks, do not need a decision-maker for implementation because a well-defined standard operating procedure exists for the execution of these types of decisions. Record-keeping operations, payrolls, and simple inventory problems are examples of this type of task. Electronic data processing is mostly associated with this level.

Semistructured decisions are those that are not quite as well-defined by standard operating procedures as are structured decisions. However, these decisions include structured aspects that greatly benefit from information retrieval, mathematical and statistical models, and information-system technology in general. Sales forecasting, cash flow, and capital acquisition analyses are some decisions within this group.

Unstructured decisions are unique in nature, are mostly nonrecurring, and have no standard operating procedure that pertains to their implementation. In these circumstances, the decision-maker's intuition plays the most significant role and computer technology offers the least support. There are many instances of these types of decisions, including research and development, hiring and firing, and introduction of a new product. Future developments in artificial intelligence may be of great assistance to organizations confronted with these types of qualitative decisions.

Figure 4–3 shows various organizational levels and the types of decisions made at each level. This figure highlights the potential and applications of information technology in all levels of an organization.

Figure 4–3
Organizational Levels and Types
of Decisions

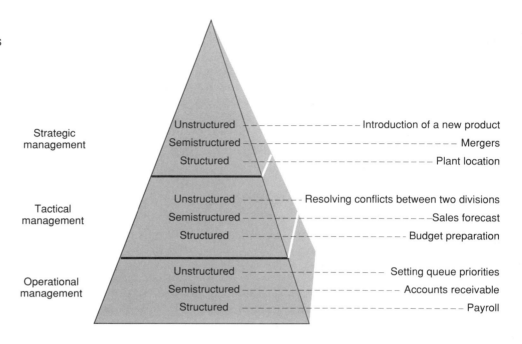

Strategic management	Unstructured — — — — — — — — — — — Introduction of a new product
	Semistructured — — — — — — — — — — — — — — — — — Mergers
	Structured — — — — — — — — — — — — — — Plant location
Tactical management	Unstructured — — — — — Resolving conflicts between two divisions
	Semistructured — — — — — — — — — — — — Sales forecast
	Structured — — — — — — — — — — — Budget preparation
Operational management	Unstructured — — — — — — — — Setting queue priorities
	Semistructured — — — — — — — Accounts receivable
	Structured — — — — — — — — — — — — — — Payroll

4–4–1 Electronic Data Processing

For the past 50 years, **electronic data processing,** or transaction processing, has been applied to such structured tasks as record keeping, simple clerical operations, and inventory control. Payroll, for example, was one of the first applications to be automated. The emphasis of these systems has been on data collection and data processing. Cost reduction is the major objective for the implementation of these systems.

A closer investigation of structured tasks reveals that computers are the most beneficial in this group of data processing operations. These tasks are either repetitive, such as printing 4,000 checks, or they involve enormous volumes of data, such as inventory control of a multinational textile company. When these systems are automated the human interface becomes minimal. For example, when a payroll system is automated, many checks are printed and sent to the recipients—there is no need for managerial judgment here.

4–4–2 Management Information Systems

Since their inception in the mid-1960s, **management information systems** (MIS) have been used to process information. The objective of these systems has been the production of timely, accurate, and useful information for middle management on a scheduled basis, such as weekly, bi-weekly, or monthly. Though an MIS supplies more information, it lacks flexibility and is not suitable for ad hoc applications. This is due to the sophistication in hardware and software technologies and the sophistication of users' requirements.

There are many applications of MIS in both private and public organizations. An automated budgeting system, cash flow model, and sources and uses of funds statements are some examples of MIS. Although cost reduction is an important factor for designing these systems, other factors, such as employee satisfaction and customer service, play an important role.

Decision Support Systems   4–4–3

There is no commonly accepted definition for **decision support systems** (DSS).[2] For our purpose we define a DSS as a computer-based information system consisting of hardware, software, and the human element designed to assist any decision-maker at any organizational level with emphasis on semistructured and unstructured tasks.

This simple definition underscores several requirements for a DSS:

- A DSS requires hardware, software, and human elements (designers and users)
- A DSS is designed to support decision-making
- A DSS should help decision-makers at all organizational levels
- A DSS emphasizes semistructured and unstructured tasks

DSS differs from EDP and MIS in several aspects: DSS uses both internal and external data; emphasizes the present and future; uses mathematical and statistical models, and because a DSS is easier to use, the user is more heavily involved in design, implementation, and utilization. A DSS is designed to serve as a decision companion. These systems and decision-makers work together to implement a decision. Where decisions are being made in the organization, there is a need for a DSS.

Executive Information Systems   4–4–4

In recent years, some new buzzwords have been introduced to the field of information systems. These are executive information systems (EIS), executive support systems (ESS), and executive management systems (EMS). Although their definitions and place among EDP, MIS, and DSS are still evolving, we consider these systems to be a branch of DSS. At the center of the systems, there is always a microcomputer that serves as an intelligent terminal. The microcomputer can serve as a stand-alone system or be used as a workstation to connect the executive decision-maker to a wealth of information from both internal and external databases.

Executive information systems attempt to deliver only information critical to a decision-maker and are user- or business-problem-driven. There is a heavy emphasis on providing an easily understood format in which executives use the information. One of the primary objectives of these systems is to eliminate the vast amounts of information bombarding executives. This objective is accomplished with exception reports and by reporting only the critical information. An EIS combines the decision-maker's imagination and judgment with the computer's ability to store, retrieve, manipulate, compute, and report internal and external information.

Executive information systems use integrated office technologies for planning, forecasting, and controlling managerial tasks. This kind of system may use the following:

- Touch screen
- Mouse

---

[2]Hossein Bidgoli, *Decision Support Systems: Principles & Practice* (St. Paul, Minnesota: West Publishing Company, 1989).

- Menu-driven interfaces
- Color screen
- Key commands (such as SOLVE, DISPLAY, DRAW, and PLOT)
- Local area network (LAN)
- Wide area network (WAN)
- Electronic mail
- Facsimile equipment
- Voice mail
- Electronic message distribution
- Teleconferencing (both audio and video)
- Graphics
- Spreadsheets
- Lap-top computers
- Scanners
- Integration of voice, data, and images through ISDN (Integrated Services Digital Network, which is discussed in Chapter 7)
- Image-transmission systems through facsimile

Comparing EIS with DSS, some specific advantages can be highlighted. An EIS provides:

- Easier user-system interface
- More timely delivery of information
- More understandable format for the information provided
- Increased executive productivity by reporting on key items
- A better understanding of the information and its interrelationships

We discuss distributed data processing in Chapter 7. For now, remember that through communications systems, an organization can share the same information among many decision-makers in an efficient way. By using a communications system, an executive can be connected to the wealth of information in public and private databases.

4–5

COMPARATIVE ANALYSIS OF EDP, MIS, DSS, AND EIS

EDP, MIS, DSS, and EIS are not unique technologies. Each technology addresses a particular user group. Table 4–1 provides a comparative summary of these four technologies.

EDP, MIS, DSS, and EIS can be developed from a series of design tools. Design tools are software technologies used to design and construct a CBIS. They can be either high-level programming languages (such as BASIC or FORTRAN) or computer packages, fourth-generation languages (4 GLs), or DSS generators. The 4 GLs and DSS generators (such as FOCUS, ORACLE, IFPS, and NOMAD) are more user friendly and powerful than traditional programming languages.

A CBIS uses internal or external data—different systems use different proportions for designing a CBIS.

Key Factor	EDP	MIS	DSS	EIS
Problem addressed	Structured	Structured	Structured/ semistructured	Structured/ semistructured
User	Lower management	Middle management	All management	Top management
Design team	Mostly DP professional	DP professional and the user	The user and DP professional	Top management and DP professional
Design tools	Mostly high-level language	High-level language and packages	Mostly packages	Mostly packages
Data used	Internal	Internal	Internal and external	Internal and mostly external
Interface mode	Mostly batch	Batch and interactive	Mostly interactive	Interactive

Table 4–1
EDP, MIS, DSS, and EIS Comparison

The interface mode is either batch or interactive. In the batch mode, periodic reports are generated. In an interactive mode, the user receives instant response from the system.

4–6
THE ARTIFICIAL INTELLIGENCE ERA

There is no commonly accepted definition for **artificial intelligence** (AI). Generally speaking, AI refers to a series of related technologies that try to simulate and reproduce human-thought behavior, including thinking, speaking, feeling, and reasoning.

AI technology applies computers to areas that require knowledge, perception, reasoning, understanding, and cognitive abilities. To achieve this, computers must:

- Understand "common sense"
- Understand facts and manipulate qualitative data
- Deal with exceptions
- Understand relationships among the facts
- Interface with humans in a free-format fashion (natural language)
- Be able to deal with new situations based on previous learning
- Be able to learn from experience

As an example of how AI works, suppose that you are searching your file cabinet for a document. Suddenly you find an old notebook that you used during junior high school. This notebook brings many different memories to your mind immediately—memories of your classmates, your close friends, possibly the teacher who taught you biology, the course in which you used this notebook. This can go on and on. Can computers perform in such a way? At this time, computers are not capable of doing these tasks and will probably not be capable of them in the near future.

Whereas traditional computer-based information systems (CBIS) are concerned with storage, retrieval, manipulation, and display of data, AI systems are concerned with the reproduction and display of knowledge and facts.

In traditional CBIS, programmers and systems analysts design and implement systems that help decision-makers by providing timely, relevant, accurate, and integrated information. In the AI field, "knowledge engineers" are trying to discover "rules of thumb," or **heuristics,** that will enable computers to perform tasks usually performed by humans or enable computers to duplicate human mental tasks, such as association and reasoning. Rules employed in AI technology come from a diverse group of experts in such areas as mathematics, computer science, psychology, economics, anthropology, medicine, engineering, and physics.

Some AI experts believe that AI is more of a concept than a solid field. AI encompasses a group of related technologies, among which are expert systems (ES), natural language processing (NLP), speech recognition, vision recognition, and robotics.

4–7

AI-RELATED TECHNOLOGIES

Of all the AI-related technologies, expert systems, natural language processing, and robotics have attracted the most attention.

4–7–1

Expert Systems

Generally speaking, **expert systems** mimic human expertise in a particular discipline to solve a specific problem in a well-defined area. If a problem is not specific and it has not been solved previously by an expert or a series of experts, that problem is not suitable for expert system implementation.

Although traditional computer-based information systems generate information by using data and models and a well-defined algorithm, expert systems work with heuristics. Heuristics are sometimes referred to as the general knowledge available in a discipline. Heuristic reasoning does not imply formal knowledge, but rather considers binding a solution to a problem without following a rigorous algorithm. For example, if we tell you that a canary is a bird, you know that a canary knows how to fly because it is a bird, or if we tell you John owns a horse, you quickly include this animal with other horses and separate them from millions of other animals.

Expert systems have been around since the 1960s and have been continually improved during the past 20 years. There are a variety of ES systems on the market.

News about expert systems is kept somewhat secret. Developers of these systems do not reveal the detailed information regarding technical capabilities of these systems until their final release. Practitioners and companies who are using these systems are also reluctant to reveal all the successes achieved by these systems because of the competitive advantages that may be gained by other users of these systems.

R1/XCON, developed by Digital Equipment Corporation in a joint effort with Carnegie-Mellon University, has been used by Digital Equipment Corporation for configuring VAX computers. This system uses more than 3,500 rules and more than 6,000 product descriptions to configure the specific components of VAX systems based on a particular customer order. When the specifications are defined, the system generates a series of diagrams highlighting the electrical connections and the layout for the 50 to 150 components in a typical VAX order. The system has been continuously improved by modifying the quality and quantity of the rules employed by the system. Until 1983, one out of a thousand orders configured by XCON were misconfigured due to missing or incorrect rules. All these correction incidences involved cases where a seldom-used component was part of the system.

Dipmeter Advisor, developed by Schlumberger Corporation, is another successful operational expert system. This system uses oil well log data and the geological characteristics of a well to provide recommendations concerning the possible location of oil in that region.

In the microcomputer environment, Expert Ease, developed by Human Edge Software Corporation for IBM PCs and PC compatibles, has demonstrated significant success. With this system, Westinghouse has achieved increased productivity in one factory by more than $10 million per year.

SRI International, working with the U.S. Geological Survey, has designed the Prospector System. This system provides advice and consultation to field teams during mineral exploration. This system predicted a deposit of molybdenum in the Cascade Mountains in northern California. This mineral deposit is expected to yield over $100 million. Figure 4–4 illustrates three commercial expert systems.

A.

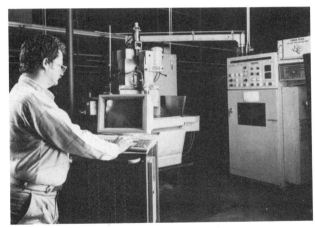

B.

Figure 4–4
A. An Expert System that Diagnoses the Cause of Cracks in Steel Weldments (Larry Hamill/Macmillan). B. Expert System for Troubleshooting and Repairing Complex Machine or Production Process Failures. Expert System Design to Help Technicians Diagnose and Repair Faulty Assemblies in Such Areas as Manufacturing and Service (Courtesy of Texas Instruments). C. Computer Battle Simulator at National Training Center, Ft. Irwin (Courtesy of RAMTEK Corp.)

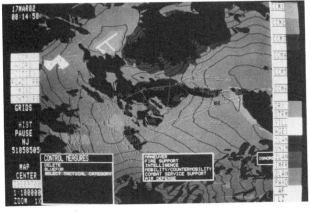

C.

4–7–2

Natural Language Processing

Computer-based information systems have been designed to be used by those who are somewhat computer literate. No matter how flexible and user-friendly these systems are, a specific method must be followed to operate these systems or perform queries.

As discussed in Chapter 2, four classes of computer languages have evolved. The first class, a machine language, is a binary system consisting of 1s and 0s. It is the closest to the computer and the farthest from human language. The second class, assembly language, consists of a series of short codes (mnemonics) that represent instructions to the computer. The third class is high-level languages. They are more application- and user-oriented and more English-like than previous languages. The fourth class, fourth-generation languages (4 GLs), are more forgiving than high-level languages and, most importantly, nonprocedural. The nonprocedural quality means that the user does not need to follow a rigid structure to communicate with a computer. The fifth class, natural languages, are the ideal languages from a user's point of view. These languages are supposed to enable a computer user to communicate with the computer in his or her native language.

The goal of **natural language processing** (NLP) is to provide a method for interface that is very similar to our native language. An NLP provides a free-format question-and-answer situation for a typical user.

There are several NLPs available. These natural or artificial languages include CLOUT for database management systems, LADDER for ship identification and location, and TDUS for electromechanical repair. Currently, none of these products are capable of providing a dialog comparable to a conversation between humans.

There are several serious obstacles that have to be overcome before a natural-language interface can be developed. Among these problems are ambiguity in our native language (one word may have several meanings), problems with ellipses (incomplete sentences), problems with metaphors (you say something and you mean something else), idioms, and similar sounding words.

At this time, NLP systems have been successful only when they are used within a well-defined context; however, research continues.

4–7–3

Robotics

Robots and **robotics** are some of the most successful applications of AI. Today's robots are the ones seen mostly in movies and factories. They are far from intelligent, but progress has been steady. At the present time, most are slow, clumsy, blind, and mostly stupid! Their major applications have been on assembly lines in factories where they are used as a part of computer-integrated manufacturing (CIM).

Industrial robots cost between $100,000 to $250,000. Their mobility is limited. A serious challenge that still exists is teaching robots how to walk. How does a robot learn to walk on a soft surface? Which foot has to go first? Even with all these problems, robots have been used successfully by the Japanese and in some American factories. At the present time, the majority of the robots in the world are operating on Japanese assembly lines. A typical robot has a fixed arm that moves objects from point A to B. Some robots have limited vision, in which case they can locate objects and pick them up as long as the desired objects are isolated from other objects.

The operation of a robot is controlled by a computer and a program. A computer program written for a robot includes such commands as when and how far to reach, which direction to go or turn, when to grasp an object, and how much pressure to apply. There are many computer languages for robot programming. T3, RCL, AL, AML, and PAL are just a few. Naturally, these languages are associated with a particular manufacturer of robots.

Personal robots have attracted a lot of attention in recent years. These robots have limited mobility, limited vision, and some speech capability. At the present time, they are used mostly as toys. Improvement in speech and vision should improve the usefulness of these robots.

In general, robots have some unique advantages compared to humans in the workplace:

- They don't fall in love
- They never ask for a raise
- They don't ask for a room with a window
- They aren't moody
- They are consistent
- They don't take coffee or meal breaks
- They don't argue with the boss
- They don't join unions
- They don't get emotionally hurt
- They don't get insulted
- They can be used in environments that are hazardous to humans, such as the spray painting of autos or radioactive work

Developments in AI-related fields such as ES, NLP, vision, and hearing will have a definite effect on future developments in the robotics industry. Figure 4–5 shows three commercial robots.

4–8
DO COMPUTERS THINK?

The issue of computer "intelligence" has been around since the early 1950s. This is a controversial issue, and different experts have different opinions. Computers play chess and, sometimes, even can win a game against a chess player. The question remains the same: When a computer plays a chess game, is this thinking?

Generally speaking, when a computer prints a paycheck and plays a chess game, there is more intelligence involved in the latter case, but is this really thinking? In our opinion, no. The algorithm, or road map, for thinking has been given to the computer. Because computers possess extensive memory and are extremely fast, they can play a chess game and win when facing a human player.

To make a computer a thinking machine, it must behave and simulate the human brain. To date we have not been able to understand how the brain functions, let alone how to design a computer that operates similarly to the human brain.

AI research in both the United States and Japan has been steady. Billions of dollars are being spent on it throughout the world. The result of this research undoubtedly will assist us to design more intelligent computers. The outcome of this research will improve the quality and effectiveness of robots, natural language processors, and expert systems.

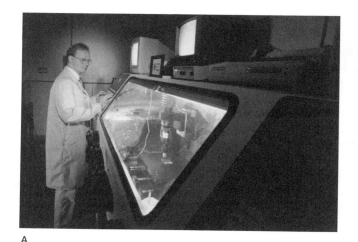

A.

B.

Figure 4-5
A. Robot. Computer Controlled
Positioner for the ND YAG Laser
(Larry Hamill/Macmillan). B.
GMF Model A-600 is a Four-Axis
Horizontally Articulated Arm,
Electric Servo Driven Robot.
Solution for High Speed Assem-
bly Requiring Gray Scale Vision
with GMF INSIGHT Integral Vi-
sion System (Larry Hamill/Mac-
millan). C. Robot/Vision (Cour-
tesy of GMF Robotics Corp.)

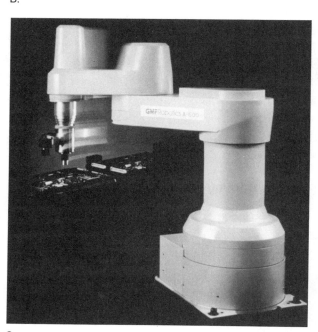

C.

4-9

WILL COMPUTERS REPLACE US?

This question is also difficult to answer. Certainly, computers have replaced many workers during the past fifty years. However, these were mostly clerical workers. Robots have and will replace many workers on the assembly lines. More and more giant corporations, such as AT&T, Ford, General Motors, and Chrysler, are using computer technologies in various stages of their operations to improve efficiency and effectiveness.

Word processing programs have almost made typewriter technology obsolete. Facsimile, voice mail, and electronic mail may soon take over a large portion of mail services. Teleshopping may replace many of the traditional shopping arrangements. Automatic point of sale (POS) and universal product codes (UPC) have eliminated certain clerical jobs by providing faster service with fewer employees.

However, many jobs will stay intact. Computers need humans as designers, programmers, and users. In addition, computers have created many jobs. We discuss the effect of computers in the work place in more detail in Chapter 9.

4–10
THE IMPORTANCE OF CBIS

Information is the second most important resource (after the human element) owned by any organization. Timely and accurate information is a weapon used by key decision-makers to enhance their competitive position in the market place. This important resource enables a decision-maker to manage the other crucial resources in the organization. Information is used to manage the four M's of resources in the organization: manpower, machinery, materials, and money.

To manage each of these resources, a specific information system has evolved. A **personnel information system** (PIS) is designed to provide information to assist decision-makers in the personnel department in carrying out their tasks in a more effective way.

A **logistic information system** (LIS) is designed to manage all the machinery and equipment in the organization. The logistic information system is a sophisticated automated database that provides the decision-maker with timely and accurate information regarding all the machinery: the date of purchase, when they were last serviced, when they need the next service, their price, when they should be replaced, and so on. Such a system can save money by providing a decision-maker with timely information regarding the repair or replacement of a piece of equipment.

A **manufacturing information system** (MFIS) is primarily useful for managers responsible for inventory control. Its objective is to reduce the total inventory costs to the lowest level consistent with the company's desired level of service.

The goal of a **financial information system** (FIS) is to provide diverse financial information to finance executives in a timely manner. A FIS uses internal and external data, mathematical and statistical models, and a user-friendly interface to achieve this goal.

In the next chapter we talk about the versatility of CBIS in more detail.

SUMMARY

In this chapter we reviewed the fundamentals of computer-based information systems. Different classes of CBIS including EDP, MIS, DSS, and EIS were discussed. The chapter introduced artificial intelligence as the new trend in the information systems field. Expert systems, natural language processing and robotics are three promising applications of AI technology. The chapter concluded with a discussion regarding the importance of CBIS in the business world.

REVIEW QUESTIONS

*These questions are answered in Appendix A.

1. What is a CBIS? What are seven major components of a CBIS?

2. What are some examples of a CBIS?

*3. What are four classes of CBIS?

4. How is EDP different from MIS?

5. How is MIS different from DSS?

*6. If we introduce the three focal points—data, information, and decision—which system (EDP, MIS, DSS) emphasizes which focal point? Explain.

7. What is an EIS?

8. How is EIS different from DSS?

*9. What are some of the technologies used by an EIS?

10. What are two unique characteristics of each of the four technologies: EDP, MIS, DSS, and EIS?

11. What is AI? Is AI a solid discipline or is it a concept? Discuss.

12. What are some of the successful applications within the AI discipline?

13. What should an AI computer do? How are these computers different from the traditional computers?

14. How do you define an expert system? Why are they called expert systems?

*15. What are some of the applications of expert systems? What are some successful examples?

16. What is NLP? How are NLPs different from traditional computer languages?

17. What are robots? Where would a robot be a good substitute for humans?

18. Will computers really think? Discuss.

19. Will computers replace us? Discuss.

20. Why is a CBIS important?

*21. What are the four M's?

22. How will a CBIS manage the four M's?

23. What are some CBIS applications in a university? In a bank? In a law firm? In a CPA firm?

24. Let us say you have been asked to establish a CBIS for the president of your school. The main objective of this system is to monitor students' enrollment. What are the seven components of this system as discussed in this chapter? What specific information will be generated by this system?

25. Why will a CBIS experience a life cycle similar to a product life cycle? What factors cause such a cycle?

26. Boeing Corporation markets a system under the EIS name. Conduct some research on this system. What are some of the specific tasks performed by this system? Who should be using this system?

27. By consulting MIS journals, research two of the commercial expert systems on the market. What are some of the unique applications of these systems? Why are they called expert systems?

28. There are several commercial natural languages on the market. Research two of these products. What are some of the unique advantages of these products compared to traditional high-level languages? What is performed by a natural language? Why are they called natural languages?

29. Research a commercial robot. What can a robot do that a human cannot? Why are the Japanese using so many robots in their assembly lines?

30. Computers play chess. Is this an AI application? Can they beat a master chess player? Discuss.

Artificial intelligence	Heuristics	Personnel information system	**KEY TERMS**
Computer-based information systems	Logistic information system	Robotics	
Decision support systems	Management information system	Semistructured decisions	
Electronic data processing		Structured decisions	
Executive information system	Manufacturing information system	Unstructured decisions	
Expert systems	Natural language processing		
Financial information system			

Multiple Choice

1. The highest priority in designing a CBIS is
   a. providing information in a useful format
   b. collecting and analyzing internal and external data
   c. defining the objective of the system
   d. choosing the hardware and software to be used
   e. none of the above

2. The most important aspect of the database component of the CBIS to the user or manager is
   a. the existence and availability of the database
   b. the type of database models
   c. the hardware and software being used for the database
   d. the programming language used to write the database
   e. the number of people needed to install the database

3. The CBIS must be responsive to the user by providing information that is
   a. integrated with other data and information
   b. relevant
   c. timely
   d. consistent and accurate
   e. all of the above

4. Generally, a CBIS has a well-defined life cycle consisting of the following ordered stages:
   a. introduction, decline, maturity, growth
   b. introduction, growth, maturity, decline
   c. growth, maturity, introduction, decline
   d. growth, introduction, maturity, decline
   e. maturity, growth, decline, introduction

5. Comprehensive design specifications play a crucial role in the CBIS by
   a. creating inconsistency in computer utilization
   b. decreasing the chances of acceptance by the users
   c. increasing the uncertainty of the system
   d. increasing the adaptability of the existing CBIS to growing technology
   e. decreasing the usefulness of the system

6. A DSS differs from EDP and MIS in the following aspects except that
    a. a DSS uses both internal and external data
    b. a DSS emphasizes the past
    c. a DSS uses mathematical or statistical models
    d. a DSS is adaptable to ad hoc problems
    e. the user is more heavily involved in design, implementation, and utilization of DSS

7. Which of the following is not an AI technology:
    a. EDP
    b. NLP
    c. ES
    d. robotics
    e. speech recognition

8. The goal of NLP is
    a. to replace people with machines
    b. to allow computers to deal with semistructured and unstructured problems
    c. to provide ad hoc analyses
    d. to provide a more natural interface between user and computer
    e. to use heuristics to solve problems

9. When we say that information is used to manage the 4 M's, we are referring to
    a. marketing, management, manufacturing, methods
    b. minimization, maximization, mathematics, modules
    c. material, manpower, money, machinery
    d. miniaturization, models, modernization, manuals
    e. none of the above

10. Programmable tasks that do not require a decision maker for implementation are best suited for
    a. AI technologies
    b. EIS
    c. DSS
    d. MIS
    e. EDP

True/False

1. A computer-based information system contains hardware elements, software elements, and human elements.

2. The data component of the CBIS can be structured easily if the organization has not defined its strategic goals, organizational objectives, and critical success factors.

3. An effective and efficient CBIS should incorporate the ability to use only formal information in problem solving analyses.

4. A CBIS goes through the information systems life cycle because of technological changes and varying information needs of the users.

5. Users of CBIS occupy three organizational levels: strategic, tactical, and operational.

6. Different types of CBIS have been designed and, based on their objectives, the intended audiences, and the technology used, have been classified as EDP, MIS, DSS, or EIS.

7. A DSS is designed to make a decision and implement it.

8. EIS is considered to be separate and distinct from DSS.

9. Artificial intelligence (AI) refers to a series of related technologies that try to simulate and reproduce human thought behavior.

10. Expert systems work with models and well-defined algorithms.

Multiple Choice	**True/False**	**ANSWERS**
1. c	1. T	
2. a	2. F	
3. e	3. F	
4. b	4. T	
5. d	5. T	
6. b	6. T	
7. a	7. F	
8. d	8. F	
9. c	9. T	
10. e	10. F	

Computer-Based Information Systems In Action

5

5–1

INTRODUCTION

This chapter reviews the application of CBIS in the five major areas of business, including finance, manufacturing, marketing, personnel, and strategic planning. The input and output of these systems and the software support for the implementation of these systems are highlighted.

5–2

CBIS IN SUPPORT OF FINANCE

A **financial CBIS** collects accounting, budgeting, auditing, and other internal and external financial data from various sources to generate information related to financial management and financial control. Figure 5–1 illustrates a conceptual model for a financial CBIS.

Financial management deals with cash flow analysis by trying to balance the cash inflows and cash outflows. Cash inflows are all the income from various sources. Cash outflows are all the expenditures.

The goal of a financial CBIS is to provide diverse financial information in a timely manner to finance executives. A financial CBIS uses internal and external data, mathematical and statistical models, and a user-friendly interface to achieve this goal. By using what-if, goal-seeking, and sensitivity analyses, a financial CBIS should be able to highlight and analyze different financial scenarios.

In what-if analysis, the system may assist the decision-maker to investigate the effect of a change in interest rate on several financial portfolios. For example, if the interest rate drops by 2 percent, what is the effect on a particular investment? In goal-seeking analysis, the system may assist a decision-maker to manipulate different variables for achieving a financial goal. For example, if the goal is a 14 percent return on investment, then what type of investment projects should be considered or how much cash is needed to achieve this financial goal? In sensitivity analysis, the system can assist the user to study

Figure 5–1

A Conceptual Model for a Financial CBIS

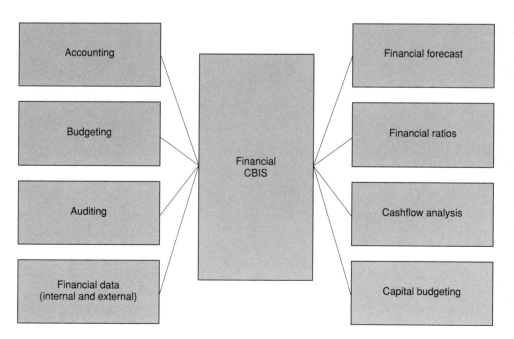

the range of change of different variables, such as the various changes in the stock market, the interest rate, and so on.

One of the most common outputs from a financial CBIS is a **financial ratio** analysis. To measure the financial strength of a company, many analysts use financial ratio analysis. To perform this task, a series of financial ratios are computed and are compared with those of other companies in the same industry or with the past years' ratios of the company itself. However, ratio analysis for determining a company's financial strength can be misleading. These ratios can be manipulated to distort a company's actual financial situation. If these ratios are calculated periodically in a straightforward manner, they can be a good basis for further financial investigation. Some of the most commonly used ratios are as follows:

Return on investment ($R = I/E$)
where: R = return on investment
      I = net income
      E = owners' equity
Earnings per share ($G = I/S$)
where: G = earnings per share
      I = net income
      S = number of shares outstanding
Price to earnings ratio ($C = P/G$)
where: C = price to earnings ratio
      P = market price per share
      G = earnings per share
Quick ratio ($Q = A/L1$)
where: Q = quick ratio
      A = quick assets (all assets—goods)
      L1 = current liabilities
Debt to equity ratio ($D = L2/E$)
where: D = debt to equity ratio
      L2 = total liabilities
      E = owners' equity

A financial CBIS easily can generate these and many other ratios. The input data for these ratios come from the balance sheet and the income statement. A decision-maker can perform financial analysis by using these ratios as the starting point. The financial CBIS provides tremendous flexibility by providing on-line access to the internal and external financial data and by performing diverse financial analyses.

Capital budgeting analysis is another common output from a financial CBIS. Many financial analyses are classified under the capital budgeting domain. **Present value, future value,** and **internal rate of return** are some of the most important techniques used in capital budgeting analysis. **Net present value** (NPV) discounts a future cash outflow to today's value considering different interest rates. For example, if you are promised $20,000 ten years from today, how much is today's value of this note at a given interest rate?

The **internal rate of return** (IRR) calculates an interest rate generated by a project. To use this model, the financial CBIS requires the data on cash inflows and cash outflows of a project. These data can be collected from the database of the financial CBIS or can be collected from external sources. By using these cash flows, the system calculates the IRR of a project. For example, if the IRR of a project is 12 percent, you should implement this project if a bank lends you

Table 5–1
Applications of CBIS in the Financial Environment

What-if analysis with budget preparation
What-if analysis with budget allocation
Goal-seeking analysis with budget

Creation of an integrated budget that includes:
    Sales
    Production
    Raw material
    Cost of goods sold
    Direct labor
    Overhead
    Operating expenses

Auditing applications:
    For staff scheduling to create a compatible audit team
    To provide more cost-effective service to clients

Monitoring cost trends
Monitoring profit trends
Capital budgeting analysis
Funds allocation
Timing of borrowing decisions
Cash flow analysis
Financial projection
Setting financial objectives
Investment structure analysis: Determining what should be included in the investment structure and how much

money under 12 percent. Beyond this rate you are advised not to implement the project because you will lose money. At a 12 percent interest rate, the net present value of the project is zero. In other words, you neither lose nor gain by this investment. Table 5–1 summarizes the applications of a CBIS in the financial environment.

5–3

SOFTWARE SUPPORT FOR FINANCIAL CBIS

There are many software packages available for financial analysis. Spreadsheet packages have been used in the financial environment since their introduction. Database packages are used for data management and search and sort operations in financial databases. Forecasting packages are used to provide financial forecasts. Other packages, such as IFPS (Interactive Financial Planning System) by Execucom, Forecast Plus by Walonick Associates, and Smart Forecasts by Smart Software, Inc., are some examples of software packages frequently used in the financial environment.

5–4

CBIS IN SUPPORT OF MANUFACTURING

A **manufacturing CBIS** collects invoices and order-scheduling data from the accounting department. Shipping and storage data are collected from the warehousing department. Information relating to loading, trip logs, and costs is collected from the transportation department. Information relating to current

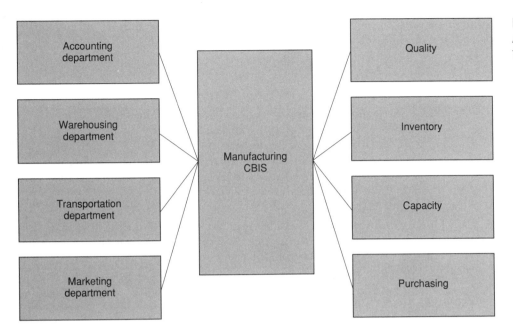

Figure 5–2
A Conceptual Model for a Manufacturing CBIS

and potential customers and competitors is collected from the marketing department. A manufacturing CBIS processes these data and generates information related to product quality, inventory, capacity, and purchasing.

Information related to quality ensures proper handling of defective items and the setting of optimal control limits. A tight monitoring system guarantees the production of desirable products that are acceptable to the customers. Information related to the inventory subsystem deals with the amount and timing of orders. The correct amount and proper timing of the orders can save an organization money. Information related to the capacity subsystem is concerned with short- and long-term capacity planning. How much should be produced and what is the optimum plant size are important issues addressed by this subsystem. Information related to the purchasing subsystem is concerned with suppliers and vendors. Where should the company purchase its raw materials? Who are the best vendors? Figure 5–2 illustrates a conceptual model for a manufacturing CBIS.

A manufacturing CBIS is useful primarily for managers responsible for inventory control.[1] Their objective is to reduce the total inventory costs to the lowest possible level consistent with the level of desired service. The total inventory costs consist of carrying or holding costs, which vary directly with inventory level, and purchasing or ordering costs, which vary inversely with the number of units ordered. Therefore, the two key decisions in inventory management are when to order and how much to order. If the demand for finished goods inventory is constant and known in advance, the **economic order quantity** (EOQ) model balances these two inventory costs and identifies the optimum order quantity.

The EOQ model has been used by many businesses for minimizing inventory costs. The outcome of this model is the optimum order quantity or the

---

[1]Mohsen Attaran and Hossein Bidgoli, "Developing an Effective Manufacturing Decision Support System," *Business Magazine*, October–December 1986.

number of units to be ordered that will minimize the business's total inventory costs. This model uses the following formula and variables:

$$EOQ = \sqrt{\frac{2*A*B}{C*P}}$$

where: A = annual inventory requirements (annual sales)
B = cost of placing an order (ordering cost)
C = single unit cost (sales price)
P = percentage of inventory value allotted for carrying costs
EOQ = number of units to order that will minimize the business's total inventory cost

This formula makes it possible for the user to compute the EOQ for many products with different selling prices and different annual sales. Using this model, the inventory manager can perform various on-line what-if analyses until a desirable solution is reached.

Decisions about how much and when to order can be made with little management intervention, using the manufacturing CBIS. The system uses the accounting and purchasing/inventory files in the database to determine the total holding and ordering costs. The EOQ model will determine the optimum quantity to order. The specific vendor is then selected from information provided by the procurement/purchasing file.

Another area in which a manufacturing CBIS can be helpful is in inventory control decisions by using a **material requirement planning** (MRP) system. The MRP schedules what is needed in each time period and plans the acquisition of the items. To derive maximum benefit from an MRP system, a large integrated database is needed.

The MRP requires input regarding what should be produced, when it is needed, a record of the actual inventory level, a record of the lead times needed to replenish inventory levels, product structure, raw materials, and components and subassemblies. These data can be obtained from various files in the manufacturing CBIS database. For example, data regarding lead times and actual inventories are obtained from inventory files. The number of finished goods needed during each time period and the part numbers of components required to make each product are gained from production files, and so forth.

Management then uses the MRP model to determine what quantity to order. The MRP model also will generate some optional management reports. This output usually includes what should be ordered, what orders should be canceled, exception reports (items that need management attention), and how well the system is operating. If properly designed and integrated, the manufacturing CBIS is a powerful support tool that enhances the effectiveness and capabilities of decision-makers in a manufacturing environment. With the use of a manufacturing CBIS, it becomes easier to collect more data, make forecasts, schedule operations, remove bottlenecks, perform sensitivity and what-if analyses, and optimize, monitor, and control the system. These features offer today's production manager—pressed more than ever to maximize efficiency, quality, and flexibility—unprecedented benefits in the management of resources.

Table 5–2 summarizes applications of CBIS in the manufacturing environment.

Demand forecasting

Master scheduling

Order processing

Capacity planning

Shop-floor planning

Computer-aided design (CAD)

Computer-aided manufacturing (CAM)

Computer-integrated manufacturing (CIM)

Product design

Forecasting expected delivery dates

New-product planning

Material requirement planning (MRP)

Inventory management

Dispatching work to workstations

Capacity control

Robot selection

Production/sales/inventory (PSI) planning

Manufacturing/distribution coordination

Facility location analysis

Table 5–2
Applications of CBIS in the Manufacturing Environment

5–5
SOFTWARE SUPPORT FOR MANUFACTURING CBIS

Spreadsheet software is used for various what-if analyses. Database software is used for search and sort operations. Statistical packages are used for quality control as statistical sampling. Project management software is used to control the time and budget of production operations. Other specific software packages include AutoCAD for drawing and drafting and MRP software for production planning and control. Several specific software packages for CAD/CAM and project management were highlighted in Chapter 3.

5–6
CBIS IN SUPPORT OF MARKETING

A **marketing CBIS** collects information related to consumers, competition, market, and cost and provides timely, accurate, and integrated information regarding the **marketing mix** including price, promotion, place, and product.

The price component of the marketing mix helps decision-makers to establish a competitive price for their product. Because either over- or under-pricing is costly, use of a marketing CBIS can be beneficial.

The promotion component of the marketing mix helps decision-makers to establish the most efficient and effective promotional campaign. For example, it helps them decide how to advertise. Which advertising media should be selected? How much budget should be allocated to each medium?

The place component helps decision-makers establish the most effective and efficient channel between the wholesalers, retailers, and the consumers. It helps manufacturers establish effective dealership and distribution centers.

The product component helps decision-makers produce the most desirable product acceptable to consumers, considering all the important dimensions such as price, style, customer's taste, and service.

Figure 5-3
A Conceptual Model for a Marketing CBIS

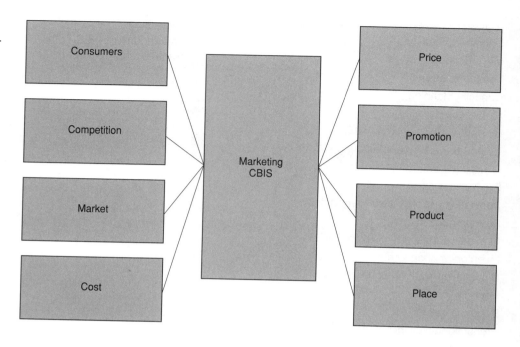

The growing use of CBIS as a management tool is having a significant effect on marketing practice.[2] The intensified need for a wide variety of marketing information that supports strategic and tactical decision-making strongly suggests that organizations should consider implementing a marketing CBIS.

In many instances, these systems are designed, developed, and implemented in a mainframe environment and supported by a centralized EDP department. In other cases, elements of the marketing CBIS have been developed with microcomputer support. Such decentralized systems enable greater flexibility and timeliness; the tradeoff is the extreme challenge these decentralized systems represent to system security and control. In either case, it is necessary for the marketing line managers to be directly involved in the design, implementation, and control of the marketing CBIS.

The marketing CBIS is a necessary element in the organizational infrastructure that provides the foundation for a successful marketing program. Marketing managers have long recognized the acute need for accurate and timely information that supports marketing decision-making in a cost-effective way. The increasingly competitive and dynamic marketing environment has made marketing information the key element in marketing plans. Fortunately, the dramatic decline in the cost of the hardware and software necessary for a marketing CBIS will enable more marketers to take advantage of its benefits.

Figure 5-3 illustrates a conceptual model for a marketing CBIS. Table 5-3 summarizes applications of CBIS in a marketing environment.

---

[2]Hossein Bidgoli and Robert Harmon, "Marketing Decision Support System," *Business Insights,* p. 3, no. 1, Spring, 1987.

Product evaluation

Pricing

Sales territory assignment

Advertising analysis

Media selection

Salesperson routing

Marketing research

Demographic analysis

Profitability analysis

Market share analysis

Product distribution analysis

Monitoring sales objectives analysis

Sales forecasting for new products

Distribution-center analysis

Table 5–3
Applications of CBIS in a
Marketing Environment

5–7
SOFTWARE SUPPORT FOR MARKETING CBIS

Spreadsheet software can be used in the marketing environment for diverse what-if analyses. Database software is used for various search and sort operations. For example, salesperson analysis, territory analysis, and statistical analysis software are used for market research and data analysis. There are other software and on-line databases available to marketing managers. The Nielson Retail Index and Teenage Market Study databases are examples of such databases.

5–8
CBIS IN SUPPORT OF PERSONNEL

A **personnel CBIS** is designed to provide information to assist decision-makers in the personnel department in carrying out their tasks more effectively. A personnel CBIS deals with the human element, the most valuable resource in the organization. Due to the complexity and diversity of skills used by a typical large organization, retention and promotion of a skilled labor force is a challenging task. Affirmative action decisions, minority employees, and work force planning all have made management of human resources more complex. When designed properly, an effective personnel CBIS can be a valuable tool for human resource directors. A personnel CBIS collects employees' personal data, such as types of skills, job market data, and government requirements. The output of this system includes recruitment analysis, scheduling assignment, work force planning, and affirmative action statistics. Figure 5–4 shows a conceptual model for this system, and Table 5–4 summarizes the applications of a CBIS in the personnel environment.

5–9
SOFTWARE SUPPORT FOR PERSONNEL CBIS

Database software probably is the most versatile type of software used in the personnel environment. This software is used to establish on-line databases that use diverse personnel data. Spreadsheet software is used for what-if analysis. Project management software is used to control personnel projects. Statistical

Figure 5-4
A Conceptual Model for a Personnel CBIS

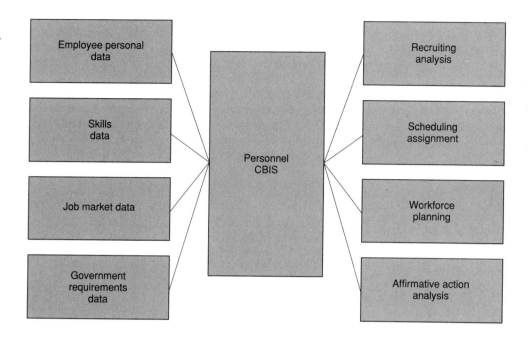

software is used for statistical analysis, statistical sampling, compensation analysis, and so forth.

5-10

CBIS IN SUPPORT OF STRATEGIC PLANNING

Strategic planning is a tool to aid management in strategic decision-making.[3] The purpose of strategic planning is to accomplish a sufficient process of innovation and change in the firm. As such, strategic planning involves the following general tasks:

- Formulation of long-term goals and objectives
- Selection of strategies to achieve goals and objectives
- Balancing of internal competencies and resources to take advantage of external opportunities and reduce the effect of external threats

Strategic planning within business organizations should, at the very least, include the functional areas of marketing, production, finance, and personnel. Within each functional area certain decisions must be made with a high degree of effectiveness and efficiency. Table 5-5 summarizes the major functional areas and strategic decisions within each area.

The essence of the ideal strategic decision-making process is timely and integrated information that is readily accessible to those who need it.

The goal of a **strategic CBIS** is to help chief executives make long-range strategic decisions even though the majority of these decisions are either semistructured or unstructured. A strategic planning CBIS can generate timely

---

[3]Hossein Bidgoli and Mohsen Attaran, "Improving the Effectiveness of Strategic Decision-Making Using an Integrated Decision Support," *Information and Software Technology*, p. 30, no. 5, June 1988.

Table 5–4
Applications of a CBIS in a
Personnel Environment

Recruitment analysis

Candidate-selection analysis

Skills inventories

Work force analysis

Employee-scheduling analysis

Job-appraisal analysis

Compensation analysis

Job-person assignment models to assign the best
person to the job

Labor force planning with what-if

Salary administration with what-if

Personnel policy and planning

Training and skill development analysis

Staff selection, assessment, and evaluation

Job evaluation

Attitude surveys

Resource allocation in personnel departments

Table 5–5
Strategic Decisions Within
Each Functional Area

Marketing	Production	Finance	Personnel
Product range	Plant size and share	Assets and their structural components	Labor force size and skill
Product quality	Equipment type and age	Cash flow	Industrial relations
Product profitability	Supply sources for equipment and materials	Profitability	Manpower training and development
Sales and service organization	Output design	Sources and uses of funds	Organization structure
Market size and share	Innovative capabilities		Management

information regarding long-range planning, corporate planning, forecasting, and decisions as to new products and new plants.

Figure 5–5 illustrates a conceptual model for a strategic planning CBIS, and Table 5–6 summarizes the applications of a CBIS in a strategic planning environment.

5–11
SOFTWARE SUPPORT FOR STRATEGIC PLANNING

Basically, all the software discussed under financial, manufacturing, marketing, and personnel CBIS are directly or indirectly related to strategic planning. Forecasting software, plant location software, resource allocation software, and on-line external databases are some examples.

Figure 5-5
A Conceptual Model for Strategic Planning CBIS

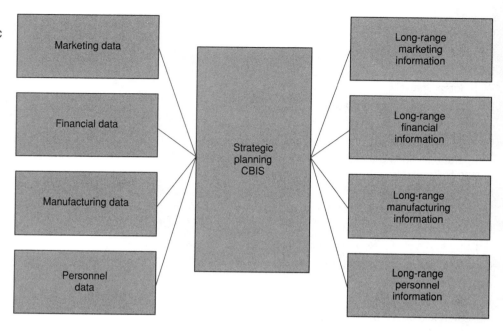

Table 5-6
Applications of a CBIS in a Strategic Planning Environment

Market research
Competition analysis
Identification of relevant environment
Long-range marketing planning
Long-range manufacturing planning
Long-range financial planning
Long-range personnel planning
Prioritizing corporate objectives
Plant-location analysis
New-product planning
Merger and acquisition analysis
Profitability analysis

SUMMARY

In this chapter we reviewed the applications of a CBIS in five major business areas: finance, manufacturing, marketing, personnel, and strategic planning. The input and output of a CBIS in these areas were explained. A brief discussion of software support in these functional areas was presented. Using these software packages, these CBISs can be implemented with reasonable cost and moderate developmental time.

REVIEW QUESTIONS

*These questions are answered in Appendix A.

1. What are the input and output of a financial CBIS?
2. What are financial ratios? Why are they used?
*3. What are some of the shortcomings of financial ratios? Why can they be misleading?
4. What are capital budgeting techniques?

5. List five applications of a CBIS in the financial environment.

6. What are some of the financial software packages available?

7. What are the input and output of a manufacturing CBIS?

8. What is the outcome of an EOQ model?

*9. What is needed to calculate an EOQ?

10. What is MRP?

11. What are the outcomes of an MRP system?

12. What are some of the applications of CBIS in the manufacturing environment?

13. What are the input and output of a marketing CBIS?

*14. What is the marketing mix? How can CBIS provide the information related to the marketing mix?

15. What are some of the applications of a CBIS in the marketing environment?

16. What are some examples of marketing software?

*17. What are the input and output of a personnel CBIS?

18. What are some of the applications of CBIS in the personnel environment?

19. What are some examples of software in the personnel environment?

*20. What is strategic planning?

21. What are the input and output of a strategic planning CBIS?

22. What are some of the applications of CBIS in the strategic planning environment?

23. By using the following balance sheet and income statement calculate the following financial ratios: return on investment, earnings per share, price-to-earnings ratio, quick ratio, and debt-to-equity ratio.

BALANCE SHEET
ASSETS   19xx

Current Assets:
  Cash. $4,309,000
  Accounts Receivable.   2,070,000
  Inventory   580,000
  Total Current Assets   6,959,000
  Long-Term Investment   500,400
  Plant and Equipment   400,500
  Less: Accumulated Depreciation   58,000
  Net Plant and Equipment   342,500
  Total Assets $7,859,900

CURRENT LIABILITIES AND OWNERS' EQUITY

Current Liabilities:
  Accounts Payable. $4,000,500
  Taxes Payable   2,000,500
  Total Current Liabilities.   6,001,000
Bonds Payable   550,000
Stockholders' Equity
  Common Stock, $15.00 par value.   150,000
  Retained Earnings   1,158,900
  Total Stockholders' Equity.   1,308,900
  Total Liabilities and Stockholders' Equity $7,859,900

INCOME STATEMENT

Sales	$7,800,000
Cost of Goods Sold	1,500,000
Gross Margin	6,300,000
Operating Expenses	
Selling Expenses	900,500
Administrative Expenses	1,250,000
Total Operating Expenses	2,150,500
Net Operating Income	4,149,500
Interest Expenses	15,000
Net Income Before Taxes	4,134,500
Income Taxes at 46%	2,232,630
Net Income	$1,901,870

24. If the annual sales of Alpha Tek is $2,000,000, cost of placing an order is $2, single unit cost is $15, and percentage of inventory value allotted for carrying cost is 10 percent, what is the EOQ?

25. Consult a manufacturing firm in your area and find out what type of CBIS support is available. Do they have an operational MRP system? Do they have any robots? If yes, what do the robots do?

26. Consult a service organization, such as an advertising agency or research and development company, and find out if they have any marketing CBIS in place. If the answer is yes, what are some specific applications of such a system? If they do not have such a system, how is their marketing function carried out?

27. Consult the city hall or county office in your area and find out how their personnel department runs. What types of computer support do they have? How do they generate affirmative action statistics? Do they have a computerized skills inventory?

28. Contact the office of a chief executive officer of one of the organizations in your area. What type of computer support is available to this executive? How does this executive conduct long-term planning? Does the executive receive daily reports from a CBIS? If yes, what is included in a particular report? Are graphics used extensively? Discuss.

KEY TERMS

Capital budgeting	Internal rate of return	Material requirement planning
Economic order quantity	Manufacturing CBIS	
Financial CBIS	Marketing CBIS	Net present value
Financial ratio	Marketing mix	Personnel CBIS
Future value		Strategic CBIS

ARE YOU READY TO MOVE ON?

Multiple Choice

1. Common outputs from a financial CBIS include
   a. ratio analyses
   b. order quantities
   c. capital budgeting
   d. both a and b
   e. both a and c

2. A manufacturing CBIS can incorporate
   a. EOQ models
   b. MRP schedules
   c. ratio analysis
   d. both a and b
   e. all of the above

3. The data collected and entered into a marketing CBIS are related to
   a. consumers, competition, market, and cost
   b. price, promotion, place, and product
   c. the marketing mix
   d. manpower, machinery, money, and material
   e. none of the above

4. The most versatile software used in a personnel CBIS is
   a. communications software
   b. database software
   c. word processing software
   d. programming languages
   e. none of the above

5. Cash flow analysis is a typical output of a
   a. manufacturing CBIS
   b. personnel CBIS
   c. financial CBIS
   d. marketing CBIS
   e. none of the above

6. Managers responsible for inventory control would use a
   a. manufacturing CBIS
   b. personnel CBIS
   c. financial CBIS
   d. marketing CBIS
   e. none of the above

7. A package available to marketing managers for use with a marketing CBIS is
   a. IFPS
   b. AutoCAD
   c. Nielson Retail Index database
   d. both a and b
   e. none of the above

8. Which of the following would a strategic planning CBIS use as input?
   a. marketing data
   b. financial data
   c. manufacturing data
   d. personnel data
   e. all of the above

9. Sales assignments and demographic analysis are primarily applications of a
   a. manufacturing CBIS
   b. personnel CBIS
   c. financial CBIS

    d. marketing CBIS

    e. none of the above

10. A financial CBIS makes use of

    a. EOQ models

    b. what-if and sensitivity analyses

    c. employee databases

    d. CAD/CAM techniques

    e. all of the above

True/False

1. A financial CBIS uses only internal data; it does not use external data.

2. A manufacturing CBIS collects data from various departments and generates information related to product quality, inventory, capacity, and purchasing.

3. Work force planning and scheduling assignments are examples of a personnel CBIS output.

4. Strategic planning within business organizations need not include the functional areas of marketing, production, finance, and personnel.

5. A strategic planning CBIS is best suited for long-range decisions that are either semistructured or unstructured.

6. IFPS is a manufacturing CBIS software package.

7. The EOQ model and the MRP system are often used in marketing CBISs.

8. Ratio analysis with a financial CBIS always gives a true picture of the company's financial strength.

9. Spreadsheet software is used for what-if analyses, and database software is used for search and sort operations.

10. Whether a marketing CBIS is developed on a mainframe or a microcomputer, it is necessary for the marketing managers to be directly involved in its design, implementation, and control.

ANSWERS

Multiple Choice	True/False
1. e	**1.** F
2. d	**2.** T
3. a	**3.** T
4. b	**4.** F
5. c	**5.** T
6. a	**6.** F
7. c	**7.** F
8. e	**8.** F
9. d	**9.** T
10. b	**10.** T

Database and Information Systems

6

6–1

INTRODUCTION

In this chapter we review database principles. The role of the database in design and implementation of a CBIS is emphasized. Types of data models (sometimes called data structures) are introduced, and functions performed by a typical **database management system** (DBMS) are highlighted. The chapter concludes with a discussion of new trends in database design, including distributed databases and database machines.

6–2

DEFINING A DATABASE

A **database** is simply a collection of relevant data stored in a central location. In this chapter, an overview of this important component of any computer-based information system (CBIS) is provided, as well as guidelines and instructions for the design and implementation of a database in the CBIS environment.

Databases are used even in manual systems. A file cabinet is a good example of a database. Various information and data are stored using a series of manila folders. However, in this type of database, speed and accuracy are not high. Figure 6–1 shows an example of a manual database. In this chapter, we are interested exclusively in computerized databases to satisfy the specific need of a CBIS.

In computer terminology, a database is defined as a series of integrated files. A file is a series of related records. A record is a series of related fields. Figure 6–2 illustrates data hierarchy.

To make these definitions more clear, consider a database as the information related to all the students, faculty, and staff of a state university. One file includes all the student records—their names, social security numbers, GPAs, and so forth. Another file includes all the faculty records. And the third file belongs to the staff of the university.

The database is closely associated with DBMS software. A DBMS is a series of computer programs used to create, store, maintain, and access a database. The features offered by a particular DBMS depend on its type and level of sophistication. For example, dBASE is a sophisticated DBMS for microcomputers. Several other DBMSs for microcomputers were highlighted in

Figure 6–1

An Example of a Manual Database

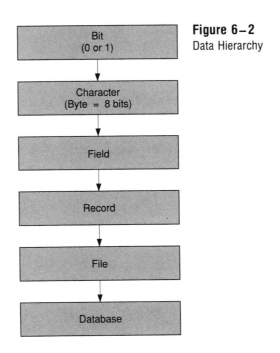

Figure 6–2
Data Hierarchy

Chapter 3. Figure 6–3 illustrates the relationship among DBMS, database, and application programs.

As this figure indicates, an application program written in a high-level language accesses the database through the DBMS software. In other words, DBMS software serves as the gatekeeper for the database.

In comparison with a flat file environment, the database environment offers unique advantages:

- Independence between data and application programs, meaning the same data can be used by several application programs.
- More information can be generated from the same amount of data. In other words, a given set of data can be manipulated in many ways.
- One-of-a-kind requests can be fulfilled easily.
- Data duplication is minimal. This is true because only one occurrence of each data item is maintained.
- Data management is enhanced and improved. This is possible because there is only one set of data for all the users.
- More sophisticated security measures (discussed in the next chapter) can be implemented.

Design and implementation of a database is done by **database administrators** (DBAs). The scope of the responsibility of DBAs depends on the complexity of the database. Some organizations devote an entire group to database design and maintenance. In smaller organizations one person may carry the entire responsibility of database design. The following are some of the responsibilities of a DBA:

- Designing and implementing a database
- Establishing security measures

Figure 6–3
The Relationship of DBMS, Database, and Application Programs

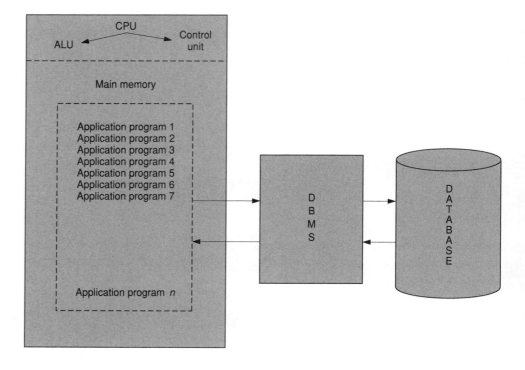

- Establishing recovery procedures
- Documenting the database
- Establishing database performance evaluations
- Adding new database functions
- Fine-tuning existing database functions

In a database environment, both a DBA and database administration are critical, and careful consideration is needed in order to establish an effective database administration office and DBA.

Generating a database increases cost and creates more complexity in CBIS operation. However, the implementation of an effective CBIS requires an on-line and comprehensive database regardless of its cost and complexity.

6–3

THE ROLE OF A DATABASE IN CBIS DESIGN AND USE

Any CBIS is designed to provide timely and relevant information either by performing data analysis or modeling analysis or both. Data analysis includes various query operations on a database. Modeling analysis applies some types of models to the data available in the database and provides some additional information that is not directly available within the data themselves. To make this discussion more clear, consider the following example. The data presented in table 6–1 have been extracted from the corporate database of On-Line Automated, a wholesaler of electronic devices.

By manipulating these data, we can discover who has the highest total sales, who has the lowest total sales, which city has the highest total sales, and which city has the lowest total sales.

Can anything be predicted about the future by examining these data? Can any statistical conclusion be drawn, either for the salespersons or the sales

Table 6–1
On-Line Automated Corporate Database

| Salespersons | Cities (figures in thousands) | | | | |
	L.A.	Denver	Portland	St. Paul	Detroit
Sue	100	600	680	600	625
Jack	150	510	750	500	980
Bob	180	580	900	480	640
Robin	200	610	830	900	720
Mary	600	920	650	600	690
Becky	250	630	490	400	950
Silvia	350	640	500	600	250
John	750	510	610	720	700
Melanie	550	650	450	950	900

regions? Using such simple data analysis, the answer to these questions is no. Using modeling analysis, however, we can provide answers to these questions and more. Using a simple forecasting model, we can generate a forecast for total sales for any city or salesperson. Statistical models can be used to compare the performances of cities or salespersons and to spot significant differences.

As you can see, for any type of analysis, a sophisticated database is needed. A DBMS maintains data as one of the most valuable resources in the organization and provides access to the authorized users.

6–4

A DATABASE AS A CORPORATE RESOURCE

A sophisticated database in a typical business organization may include relevant data related to four major functional areas: finance, marketing, manufacturing, and personnel. Figure 6–4 illustrates a corporate database, and table 6–2 highlights detail data items that should be maintained in these individual databases.

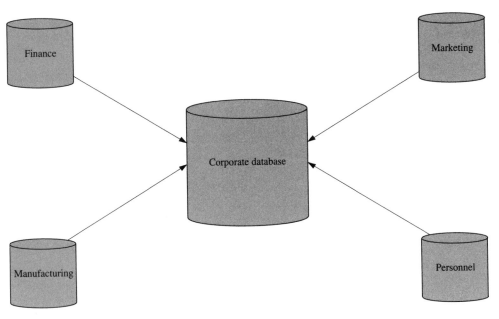

Figure 6–4
A Corporate Database

Table 6–2
Corporate Database: A
Typical Example

Functional Area	Data to be Collected and Maintained
Finance	Payroll
	Costs
	Taxes
	Income/loss statements
	Balance sheets
	Cash flow
	Sources of funds
	Uses of funds
Manufacturing	Warehousing
	Transportation
	Purchasing
	Inventory
	Production
	Technology
	Legal environment
Marketing	Economy
	Consumer behavior
	Competitors
	Sales
	Promotional activities
	Advertising
Personnel	Wages and salaries
	Contracts
	Skills inventory
	Personal history
	Training

6–5

DESIGNING A DATABASE

To design a database, you first must identify a data model. A **data model** is a procedure for creating and maintaining a database. You also must define a data dictionary. A **data dictionary** includes definitions of all the data used in a database, their types, their sizes, and so forth. Figure 6–5 illustrates a data dictionary.

Figure 6–5
An Example of a Data Dictionary

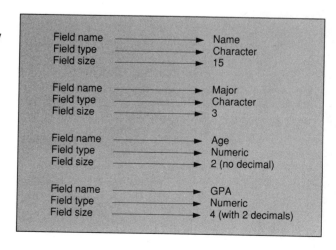

Finally, the type of organization should be identified. Types of organization include sequential, random, and indexed-sequential. In the sequential organization, all of the records are stored and accessed one after the other. This method is similar to a cassette tape and it is slow. If you want to access the seventh song on the tape, you either must listen to the first six songs or fast forward through them. This method usually is used for archiving files. Random organization enables you to access a record directly regardless of its storage location. In indexed-sequential organization, a file can be accessed either sequentially or randomly.

The Flat File Model   6-5-1

A file management system, or a **flat file model,** is simply a file or a series of files that contain records and fields. These files are called flat because there are no relationships between them, and because they have no repeating groups. The flat file system does not allow sophisticated database operations performed by other data models. Table 6-3 illustrates an example of a flat file system.

Basic data management operations such as file creation, deletion, updating, and simple data query can be performed using this model. However, as mentioned earlier, this type of data model is limited in its capacity to support complex CBIS requirements.

The Relational Model   6-5-2

A **relational model,** the most popular model, uses a mathematical construct called a relation (table), which is simply a table of rows and columns of data. Rows are records (tuples) and columns are fields (attributes). Different relations can be linked on the basis of a common field (key). To clarify this concept, look at the two relations in tables 6-4 and 6-5.

As you can see, the common field in these two relations is the customer number. A relational DBMS can use these two relations to generate a report like the one in table 6-6.

The relational model is straightforward. Creation and maintenance of this type of database are easy, as are additions and deletions of records. Overall,

Table 6-3
An Example of a Flat File

Name	Major	Age	GPA
Mary	MIS	25	3.00
Sue	CS	21	3.60
Debra	MGT	26	3.50
Bob	MKT	22	3.40
George	MIS	28	3.70

Table 6-4
A Customer Relation

Customer No.	Name	Address
2000	Adams	2020 Broadway
3000	Baker	119 Jefferson
9000	Clark	7521 Madison

Table 6–5
An Invoice Relation

Invoice No.	Customer No.	Amount	Method of Payment
111	2000	$2000	Cash
222	3000	$4000	Credit
333	3000	$1500	Cash
444	9000	$6400	Cash
555	9000	$7000	Credit

Table 6–6
Invoice and Customer
Relations Are Joined Using
Customer Number

Invoice No.	Customer Number	Amount	Method of Payment	Name	Address
111	2000	$2000	Cash	Adams	2020 Broadway
222	3000	$4000	Credit	Baker	119 Jefferson
333	3000	$1500	Cash	Baker	119 Jefferson
444	9000	$6400	Cash	Clark	7521 Madison
555	9000	$7000	Credit	Clark	7521 Madison

relational models offer a great degree of flexibility. General operations handled by a relational model include the following:

- Creation of relation
- Updating (insertion, deletion, and modification)
- Selection of a relation or a sub-relation
- **Join operation** (putting two relations side by side)
- **Projection** (selection of a subset of a field or a subset of a series of fields)
- General query operation

A major shortcoming of this model is in dealing with complex database operations. Establishing many relations, with the key included in each one, may use a great deal of disk space, and modification may be time-consuming. This model may limit insertion of new records. Advance planning may resolve some of these problems.

Overall, the relational model is more suitable for applications when a shorter developmental time is needed.

6–5–3   The Hierarchical Model

Like the relational model, a **hierarchical data model** is made up of records (called nodes), each of which can have several fields. The presentation is similar to a one-dimensional array (a table with only one column or one row) or tree structure. The relationships between the records are called branches. The node at the top of the hierarchy is called the root, and every node of the tree except the root node has a parent. The nodes with the same parent are called twins or siblings. For example, P1 and P2 in figure 6–6 are twins.

In the hierarchical model the connections between files do not depend on the data contained within the files. The connections are defined initially when the database is designed and are maintained for the entire life of the database. For example, file X is linked to file Y regardless of their contents. The connection between records is hierarchical.

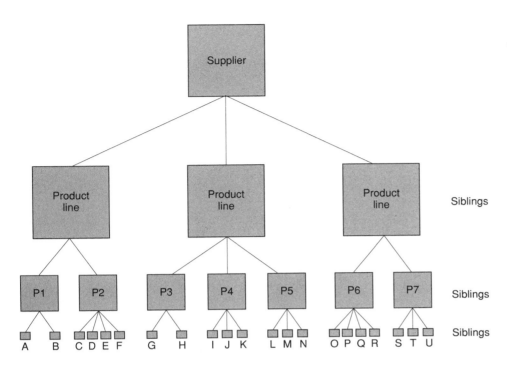

Figure 6-6
An Example of the Hierarchical Model

The hierarchical model is sometimes called an upside-down tree (a tree with its roots up). Figure 6-6 illustrates an example of a hierarchical model; it indicates that a supplier may supply three different families of products. In each family, there may be several different product categories. As an example, supplier X may supply soap, shampoo, and toothpaste. Within each product category there may be many brands of the same product— for example, nine different shampoos or five different toothpastes. Such a relationship is called a one-to-many data structure, which means a parent can have many children; however, each child has only one parent. In the hierarchical model, a search in the parent node can lead you to children nodes and vice versa. Any updating in a parent node should automatically update the children nodes.

The operations associated with the hierarchical model include file creation, file updating (insertion, deletion, addition, and modification), queries, retrieval of the next descendent record, and retrieval of the parent record.

When compared to the relational data model, the hierarchical model is less flexible, primarily because the designer should know the data relationships of a particular system ahead of time.

The Network Model   6-5-4

The **network model** is very similar to the hierarchical model. However, the records and fields of a network model are organized differently. Figure 6-7 illustrates the customer/invoice relations in a network model.

As can be seen in this figure, in place of related key fields, there is a connection between the invoice number, the customer number, and the method of payment. In this case, the customer number no longer needs to remain in the invoice record. As figure 6-7 illustrates, invoice numbers are connected to the customer number in the same order in which they were entered (see table 6-4).

The network model is not as flexible as the relational model. Also, the data relationships must be defined ahead of time to see if the network model will be suitable for a particular CBIS operation. Operations associated with a

Figure 6–7

An Example of a Simple Network
Model

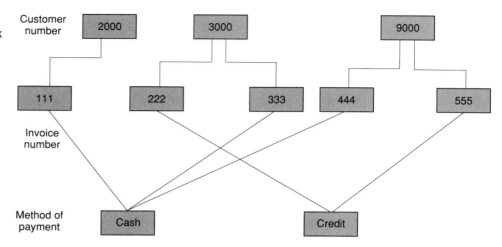

network model include file creation, file updating (insertion, deletion, addition, and modification), and queries.

The network model can be considered to be an enhanced version of the hierarchical model. In this data structure the relationship can be one-to-many (simple network) as well as many-to-many (complex network). Figure 6–7 illustrates a one-to-many relationship. Each child (invoice) has two parents (method of payment and customer number). Figure 6–8 illustrates a many-to-many relationship. In a real estate agency, each agent is selling several properties. For example, agent A-1 sells properties P-1, P-2, and P-6 while property P-1 has been listed under agents A-1 and A-2. In a many-to-many relationship, the parent-child relationship breaks down, because any record can be the parent and any record can be the child.

6–6

DATABASE MANAGEMENT SYSTEMS FUNCTIONS

A database management system (DBMS), regardless of its data structure (data model), must be able to perform the following operations for effective use in a CBIS environment. In these examples, we use the relational model for simplicity. However, these operations are available in other types of data models.

■ **Basic data-management operations.** The basic data-management operations include database creation, modification, deletion, addition, insertion, and maintenance. These operations are supported even in a file (flat file) management system.

Figure 6–8

An Example of a Complex Network Model

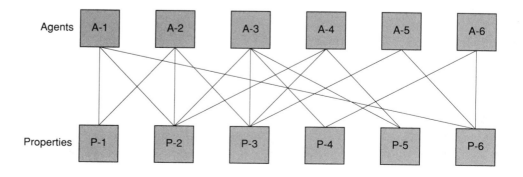

- **Basic arithmetic operations.** These include simple arithmetic operations performed on different records and fields in a database, including addition, subtraction, multiplication, and division. These basic operations may be quite useful for simple query operations, such as calculating the average salary for both male and female employees or finding the maximum and minimum salary for each sex.

- **Projection operation.** This function may be a special case of a general query operation that generates a subset of the fields. For example, in a student database that includes each student's name, GPA, age, sex, address, and nationality, a projection operation could generate a listing of the names and GPAs of all these students or a mailing list for mailing the students' transcripts.

- **Search (Query).** This function may include different searches on a database for specific conditions. As an example, a triple-criteria search on our example student database is as follows:

```
DISPLAY ALL STUDENTS FOR GPA >= 3 AND MAJOR = "CS" AND AGE <= 22
```

  Query operations can include as many criteria as the number of fields in the database. The search can include an AND search (all criteria specified must be met), an OR search (only one of the specified criteria must be met), and a NOT search (opposite criteria must be met or supply an alternative). AND, OR, and NOT are referred to as Boolean operations.

- **Sort. Sort operations** put the database in a specific order. Data can be sorted with one key or multiple keys in ascending or descending order.

- **Summary.** The summary operation may be a special case of basic arithmetic operations and basic query operations. For example, you could generate a subtotal of all MIS students and all accounting students in the student database.

- **Union (merge) operation.** This operation enables a user to combine two files, tables, or relations, thereby generating a third file, table, or relation that includes all the information from the first two files, tables, or relations. In other words, the union operation does concatenation (joining) over the existing data. Table 6–7 presents this operation on a student database. File 3 is the union of files 1 and 2. Remember, to perform the union operation, the two databases must be **union compatible**. This means they must include the same number of fields and data type.

Table 6–7
An Example of a Union Operation

File 1		File 2		File 3 (union of files 1 and 2)	
Student	**Major**	**Student**	**Major**	**Student**	**Major**
Bob	MIS	Mary	Marketing	Bob	MIS
Barry	CS	Sherry	MIS	Barry	CS
James	MIS	Sandy	Math	James	MIS
Sue	Accounting			Sue	Accounting
				Mary	Marketing
				Sherry	MIS
				Sandy	Math

Table 6–8
An Example of a Join Operation

	Relation 1		Relation 2		Relation 3 (joining of relations 1 and 2)	
Customer	Purchase No.	Customer	Purchase Amount	Customer	Purchase No.	Purchase Amount
Barry	112	Barry	$2000	Barry	112	$2000
James	118	James	$5000	James	118	$5000
Susan	129	Susan	$1000	Susan	129	$1000
Bob	135	Bob	$1500	Bob	135	$1500

Table 6–9
An Example of an Intersection Operation

	Relation 1			Relation 2			Relation 3 (intersection of relations 1 and 2)		
Student	Major	GPA	Student	Major	GPA	Student	Major	GPA
Bob	CS	3.60	Tom	ACC	2.90	Tom	ACC	2.90
Bobby	MIS	3.80	Jerry	CIS	3.70			
Tom	ACC	2.90	Don	MGT	3.90			

- **Join operation.** This operation combines two or more files, tables, or relations within a database on a common field in order to generate the third file, table, or relation. Table 6–8 illustrates one example of this operation in which the common key is the customer name.
- **Intersection operation.** This operation generates the intersection of two relations in a third relation containing a common tuple(s) (common rows). The relations must be union compatible. Table 6–9 illustrates this operation. The result of the intersection of relations 1 and 2 is relation 3, which contains only one row (tuple), the one belonging to the first two relations.

6–7

NEW TRENDS IN DATABASE DESIGN AND USE

Several new trends, including natural language processing, distributed databases, and database machines, have recently developed in database design and use.

The advancement in natural language processing will have a definite effect on the design and use of databases. Natural language processing should give the CBIS user easier access by providing an interface more similar to the user's native language. How nice it would be to pick up a microphone and ask your database to print a listing of overdue accounts! We discussed natural language processing as a branch of AI in Chapter 4. At the present time, no full-featured natural language is available because of the ambiguities in our native languages.

Currently, these issues may be of limited practical importance; however, they may be quite significant in the near future, and this may have a direct effect on the design and use of CBISs.

Distributed Databases 6–7–1

So far in our discussion, we have assumed a central database for all the users of a CBIS. However, several factors indicate a database that is a **distributed database** (distributed throughout an organization) is better than a centralized database:

■ Economic constraints. For remote users of a CBIS (those users who are not located in the same place where the CBIS is located), it may not be economically feasible to access the central database all the time. It may be more economical to store some of the data at the remote site(s).

■ Lack of responsiveness. A centralized database may not be responsive to the immediate needs of a CBIS user. A distributed database provides an immediate response to a user's request.

■ Enhanced sophistication in microcomputers. The increasing sophistication and decreasing cost of microcomputers has made distributed processing more feasible and the use of these computers a more viable option in a distributed environment. This is even more promising with the introduction of multi-user PCs.

■ Change in data processing organizational structure. Since the mid-1970s, there has been a trend toward distributed processing. This trend certainly includes database design and implementation. When considering user needs, the responsiveness of this type of system is evidently higher than that of a centralized system.

■ Security issues. Although the security of a distributed system versus a centralized system is a debatable issue, in a distributed system the damage and failure may be localized.

These issues support a distributed DBMS. In distributed databases, the data are not located at the same site as the user or the computer. There are some specific advantages of a distributed DBMS: local storage of data decreases response times and communication costs; data distribution involving multiple sites minimizes the effects of a computer breakdown, restricting it to its point of occurrence; the size and number of users are not limited by one computer's size or processing power; multiple, integrated small systems might cost less than one large computer; most important of all, a distributed database need not be constrained by the physical organization of data. The corporate data can be stored in any location and can be accessed from any other location.

This type of database may follow the data model discussed earlier; however, more than one user can access the same database at the same time. DBAs must design specific features and access codes in order to allow only one user to update the database at any time, otherwise data discrepancies may occur.

Security issues are more important in a multi-user environment, since the system can be accessed from both inside and outside the organization. Security policies must be clearly defined and the authorized users must be identified. The scope of users' access and their times of access also must be clearly defined. Generally speaking, the designer of a database and CBIS must bear in mind that not all applications are suitable for distributed processing.

A distributed database may be designed in several configurations. Figure 6–9 illustrates one example of this type of database.

In the next chapter, we discuss distributed processing and security issues in detail.

Figure 6–9
An Example of a Distributed Database

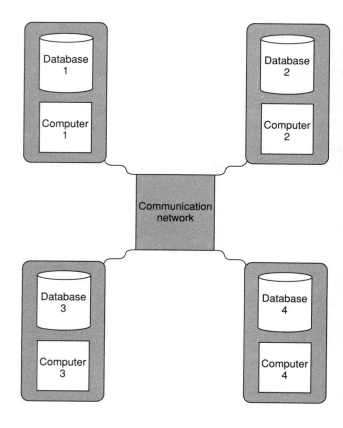

6–7–2   Database Machines

Database machines have attracted some attention in recent years because they enhance efficiency. Database machines simply serve as back-end processors to the main computer system. Because a second processor handles the entire operation related to the DBMS, the first processor (the main computer system) can be dedicated to the application programs. In other words, database machines provide an environment for parallel processing and multi-tasking (performing more than one task at the same time). This technology has not existed long, so it is difficult to judge its effectiveness, but it seems to have merit in complex business environments. However, its real effectiveness is yet to be seen.

SUMMARY

In this chapter we reviewed database and database management systems. The role of a database in the design and use of a CBIS was discussed. We defined database models, including flat file, relational, hierarchical, and network. DBMS functions were explained and we presented several examples. The chapter concluded with a discussion of distributed databases and database machines. In the next chapter, we discuss distributed processing in detail.

REVIEW QUESTIONS

*These questions are answered in Appendix A.

1. What is a database?

2. What are some of the advantages of a database environment compared to flat files?

*3. What are some of the responsibilities of a DBA?

   4. Why is a database so crucial in CBIS design?

   5. What is data analysis?

   6. What is modeling analysis?

  ***7.** What is a data model?

   8. What are three types of access methods?

   9. Why is the sequential access method slow?

  10. Compare and contrast the flat file, relational, hierarchical, and network data models. What are the unique advantages of each type of model?

  11. List seven DBMS functions.

  12. What is a join operation? Projection? Merge?

 ***13.** What does union compatible mean?

  14. For what types of DBMS functions is union compatibility needed?

  15. What is a distributed database?

 ***16.** Why and how may a distributed database increase the responsiveness of a CBIS?

  17. Is security higher or lower in a distributed environment? Discuss.

  18. What is the role of natural language processing in database design and use?

  19. What is a database machine?

 ***20.** What are some of the advantages of a database machine?

  21. Design a database of the students in your class and perform the seven basic DBMS functions. Hint: You may have to set up several small databases or relations.

  22. What is the most logical way to organize a file cabinet? How do you transfer the same principle to a computerized database?

  23. Contact a real estate agency in your area and find out how are they managing information related to different properties. What type of report is generated by a computerized database in such a setting? How does the city hall in your area manage its real estate properties?

  24. Set up a database similar to table 6–1. This table should include 10 student names and 5 test scores. What type of information will be generated by such a table (database)? Who can benefit the most from this table?

  25. Assume that you have been asked to set up a database for all the students in your school. What will you include in this database? What type of information will be generated by this database? Who will be the prime user of this database?

  26. Computerized search in the library of your school is a good example of an automated database. Consult your librarian and find out how this computerized database works. What type of information is included in this database? Compare and contrast this database with a manual database. What are some of the obvious advantages of this computerized database over the manual database? What type of data model is used by such a database (flat file, hierarchical, relational, or network)?

  27. What type of database management system is available in your school? What are some of the functions of this DBMS? Is there any distributed database available? Discuss.

  28. Consult computer magazines and find out the strengths and weaknesses of a database machine. Who are some of the vendors of these machines? Who are some of the prime users of database machines?

  29. Discuss the role of a natural language processing system in the design and use of a database. Will it become easier to use a database? Discuss.

KEY TERMS

Data dictionary	Distributed database	Projection
Data model	Flat file model	Query operations
Database	Hierarchical data model	Relational model
Database administrator	Intersection operation	Sort operations
Database machines	Join operation	Union (merge) operation
Database management system	Network model	Union compatible

ARE YOU READY TO MOVE ON?

Multiple Choice

1. Which of the following represents the data hierarchy in a computerized database system from smallest component to largest component?

   a. field, record, file, database

   b. record, file, field, database

   c. database, file, record, field

   d. file, record, field, database

   e. file, database, record, field

2. A DBMS is

   a. the database itself

   b. the person in charge of the database

   c. a series of computer programs

   d. a Master of Science degree in Databases

   e. none of the above

3. Responsibilities of the DBA include

   a. designing and implementing the database

   b. documenting the database

   c. adding new database functions

   d. both a and c

   e. all the above

Questions 4 and 5 refer to the following database:

Student	Exam 1	Exam 2	Exam 3	Final
Bill	95	92	95	
Mary	80	86	97	
John	90	95	93	
Alice	65	75	85	
Bob	85	87	86	

4. The results of an analysis are as follows:

   Bill had the highest score on exam 1
   John had the highest score on exam 2
   Mary had the highest score on exam 3

   What kind of analysis was performed?

   a. statistical analysis

   b. modeling analysis

   c. simple data query

    d. sensitivity analysis

    e. none of the above

5. The result of an analysis is as follows:

> Alice has shown constant improvement and will score a 95 on the final exam

   What kind of analysis was performed?

    a. statistical analysis

    b. modeling analysis

    c. simple data analysis (query)

    d. sensitivity analysis

    e. none of the above

6. In a relational database, different relations can be linked by the

    a. table

    b. tuple

    c. attribute

    d. key

    e. none of the above

7. To be effective, a DBMS must be able to perform the following operation(s):

    a. basic arithmetic operations

    b. search

    c. sort

    d. all of the above

    e. b and c only

8. Boolean operations include

    a. add, subtract, multiply, divide

    b. +, −, *, /

    c. sort, summary, join

    d. flat file, relational, hierarchical

    e. AND, OR, NOT

9. Which of the following is (are) not an advantage(s) of distributed databases?

    a. increases response times and communication costs

    b. minimizes the effects of computer breakdown

    c. not constrained by the physical organization of data

    d. size and number of users is not limited by one computer's size or processing power

    e. all the above are advantages

10. The hierarchical database model is sometimes called

    a. a flat file

    b. an upside-down tree

    c. a network model

    d. a many-to-one relationship model

    e. none of the above

True/False

1. A database is a collection of relevant data stored in a central location.

2. With a flat file system, data duplication is minimal and data management is enhanced and improved.

3. The database administrator (DBA) designs and implements the database.

4. When designing a database, a data model must be identified, a data dictionary must be defined, and the type of access must be identified.

5. Sequential access is generally faster than random access.

6. Flat files allow highly sophisticated database operations because there are no relationships between them.

7. The hierarchical database model is less flexible than the relational database model.

8. The relationships in the network model are always one-to-many.

9. In distributed databases, the data are always located at the same site as the user or the computer.

10. Database machines serve as back-end processors, providing an environment for parallel processing and multi-tasking.

ANSWERS	**Multiple Choice**	**True/False**
	1. a	1. T
	2. c	2. F
	3. e	3. T
	4. c	4. T
	5. b	5. F
	6. d	6. F
	7. d	7. T
	8. e	8. F
	9. a	9. F
	10. b	10. T

Distributed Processing and Information Systems

7

7–1

INTRODUCTION

In this chapter we discuss principles of distributed processing and networking. We look at the components, topologies, and different types of networking systems and discuss the role of distributed processing in a CBIS environment. Office automation and teleconferencing as two of the important applications of networking also are discussed. The chapter concludes with a brief discussion of computer security threats.

7–2

DEFINING DATA COMMUNICATIONS

The electronic transfer of data from one location to another is called data communication. The efficiency and effectiveness of any CBIS is measured in terms of the timely delivery of relevant information. Data communications enable a CBIS to deliver information where and when it is needed.

In previous chapters, we assumed that the data were gathered and processed in one location. However, many times data are not collected in the same location. They may be collected in different cities, states, and even countries. By using a data communication system, the organizational limits do not impose any boundaries. Data can be collected anywhere, processed, and delivered to any location throughout the world. An effective data communication system can significantly improve the effectiveness of a CBIS by improving the flexibility of data collection and transmission. By using a portable computer and a communication system, an executive can communicate with the office at any time and from any location.

7–3

COMPONENTS OF A DATA COMMUNICATION SYSTEM

A typical data communication system may include the following components:

- Sender and receiver devices
- Modems
- Communication lines
- Communication software
- Communication control unit

Figure 7–1 illustrates a basic configuration of a data communication system.

7–3–1

Sender and Receiver Devices

The sender or receiver device may include one of the following devices:

- An input/output device, or a dumb terminal, which is used only for sending or receiving information and has no processing power.
- A smart terminal, which is an input/output device with a limited degree of processing capability. This device can perform certain processing tasks; however, it is not a full-featured computer. This type of device is used on factory floors and assembly lines for data collection and transmission to the main computer system.

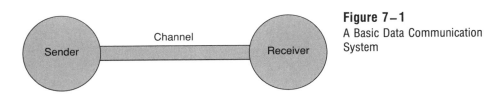

Figure 7–1
A Basic Data Communication System

- An intelligent terminal, a workstation, or a microcomputer, which serves as an input/output device and also as a stand-alone system. Using this type of device, the remote site is able to perform processing tasks without the support of the main computer system.
- Other types of computers (mini, mainframe, and so on).

Modems

7–3–2

A **modem** (modulator-demodulator) is used to convert digital signals into analog signals that can be transferred over a regular telephone line. Analog signals are continuous wave patterns, such as the human voice. Digital signals are distinct electrical signals. Figure 7–2 illustrates these two different signals.

Once the analog signals arrive at their destination, another modem converts them back to digital signals. Figure 7–3 illustrates a direct-connect modem. Direct-connect modems are plugged directly into the phone line so that you do not need a phone to use them.

To use a regular telephone for data communications, you need to use a device called an acoustic coupler (see fig. 7–4). To establish communications after you dial the receiving computer, you must place the telephone handset into the cups of the acoustic coupler. Acoustic couplers have switches to turn the modem on and off and to switch between data and voice communications.

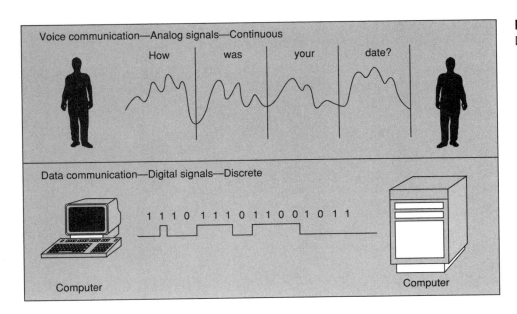

Figure 7–2
Digital and Analog Signals

Figure 7–3
A Direct-Connect Modem (Cobalt Productions/Macmillan)

Modems generally are classified as dumb and smart modems. With a dumb modem, you must dial the number yourself from the telephone. With a smart modem, you can dial the number from the keyboard. Some modems include an auto-dial feature that directly dials a number for you. With some modems, you can store several phone numbers in memory and have the modem automatically dial the number for you. Some smart modems include an auto-answering feature that enables them to receive the incoming call and direct it to your computer. They automatically disconnect as soon as the communication is over.

To establish a communication link, the two devices must be synchronized. This means both devices must start and stop at the same point. Synchronization is achieved through **protocols**—rules that govern a communication system. Protocols provide compatibility among different manufacturers' devices. Figure 7–5 illustrates a micro-to-micro network system.

Figure 7–4
An Acoustic Coupler (Courtesy of Radio Shack, A Division of Tandy Corp.)

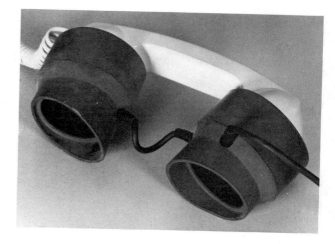

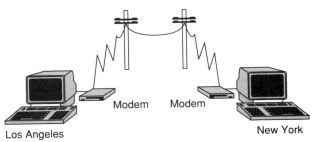

Figure 7–5
A Micro-to-Micro Network
System

Communication Lines   7–3–3

Communication lines, or channels, are used to connect the sender and receiver. Communication lines can be any one or a combination of regular telephone line, coaxial cable, microwaves, satellites, and fiber optics.

Each type of communication line has its advantages and disadvantages. When choosing a communication line, you usually consider the quality of transmission, security of the line, throughput of the line (how much information can be transferred at a time, which is measured in bits per second, or bps), and the range of the line.

Telephone lines have been the major method of communication to date because the system is already well established. However, speed and security issues make these lines less attractive than other options, particularly since the lines are not suitable for continent-to-continent transmission.

The ordinary telephone line is sometimes called a dial-up system, meaning you dial a number to establish a communication link. Telephone services are offered through common carriers, such as AT&T, Sprint, and MCI. Telephone lines are reasonably inexpensive, but they can be slow and often are busy during prime time.

An alternative to an ordinary telephone line is a leased line, which is a dedicated line. A leased line is more reliable, faster, and always available. However, it is more expensive than the common carriers.

Coaxial cables are thick cables that can be used for both data and voice transmissions. They also can be used as underwater cables for continent-to-continent communications. Figure 7–6 illustrates a coaxial cable.

Satellite systems cover a broad geographical range, but these devices are not completely secure either. The messages are sent through an earth station to the satellite (uplink) and the satellite sends the messages to a dish antenna (downlink). Satellite channels are fast and have very high capacities—one satellite is equivalent to over 100,000 voice telephone lines.

Microwave systems have a shorter range, similar to radio signals, but they suffer from the same problems as the satellite.

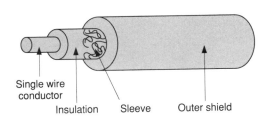

Single wire
conductor

Insulation   Sleeve   Outer shield

Figure 7–6
A Coaxial Cable

Fiber optics communication appears to be the wave of the future. Fiber optics use tubes of glass half the diameter of a human hair to form a light path through wire cables. This method is capable of high-quality transmission, high throughput, and very high security.

A communication channel can be either a point-to-point or a multi-point channel. In a point-to-point system, only one device uses the line. In a multi-point system, several devices share the same line. All these communication methods may be used at the same time in a complex network system. The system designer or engineer must implement a series of measures to ensure a comprehensive security system that protects the entire input/process/output cycle.

7–3–4   Communication Software

Communication software is a dedicated program that enables a user to send messages from one site to another one. Several of these types of software were highlighted in Chapter 3.

7–3–5   Communication Control Unit

The communication control unit (CCU) is usually a minicomputer or a microcomputer that serves as a front-end processor in a network. The CCU performs some processing tasks, such as data condensation, error checking, and simple processing, for the host computer. In the network, this unit improves the effectiveness of the host computer by enabling the host to concentrate on the important networking tasks.

7–4

DATA-PROCESSING ARCHITECTURES

During the past 50 years, with advancements in the computer field, three types of data-processing architectures have emerged: centralized, decentralized, and distributed data processing.

7–4–1   Centralized

A **centralized processing** system uses one central location for performing all data-processing tasks. In the early days of computer technology this type of processing was justified because data-processing personnel were in short supply; economies of scale, both in hardware and software, could be realized; and only large organizations could afford computers.

In some cases, however, a centralized processing system has a major shortcoming—it may not be responsive to user needs, because the data collection and processing functions may not take place in the same location. Nowadays, the economy-of-scale issue is no longer valid because of the decreasing cost and increasing sophistication of microcomputers.

7–4–2   Decentralized

With a **decentralized data-processing** system, each office, department, or division has its own computer. All data-processing tasks can be implemented within each separate organizational unit.

A decentralized data-processing system is certainly much more responsive to the user than centralized processing. However, there are some problems with decentralized systems, including lack of coordination between organizational units, excessive costs of having many systems, and duplication of efforts.

Distributed Data Processing   7–4–3

Distributed data processing (DDP) solves two of the major problems associated with the first two types of data-processing architectures: lack of responsiveness in centralized processing, and lack of coordination in decentralized processing. Distributed data processing has overcome these problems by maintaining centralized control and decentralized operations.

In DDP, the processing power is distributed among several locations. Databases, processing units, or input/output devices may be distributed. A good example is in the newspaper publishing business, where reporters and editors are scattered throughout the world. Reporters gather news stories throughout the world, enter them into their terminals, edit them using a communication channel, and forward them to the editor in charge. The reporter and the editor can be thousands of miles apart. Since the mid-1970s, with advancements in networking and mini- and microcomputers, this type of data-processing architecture has gained popularity.

Some of the unique advantages of a DDP system include:

■ Design modularity—computer power can be added or deleted based on the needs

■ System reliability—failure of a system can be limited to only one site

■ User orientation—the system is more responsive to user needs

■ Redundant resources as a security measure—if one resource fails, a redundant component will take over

■ Unused processing power can be accessed by an overused location

Figure 7–7 illustrates these three different architectures.

7–5

Mode of transmission, line configuration, and line efficiency are important concepts in a distributed environment.

Transmission modes include synchronous and asynchronous. In **synchronous** transmission, several characters are blocked together for transmission. At the beginning and end of each block there are empty bits, but these bits make up a small percentage of the total number of messages. Synchronous transmission is used to reduce overall communication costs.

In **asynchronous** transmission, each character is sent through a channel as an independent message. Each message is one character long, and the character is preceded by a start bit and ended with a stop bit. This type of transmission is more expensive than a synchronous transmission; however, it may be more accurate. Figure 7–8 illustrates an asynchronous configuration.

IMPORTANT CONCEPTS IN A DISTRIBUTED ENVIRONMENT

Figure 7–7
Three Data-Processing
Architectures

Centralized data processing

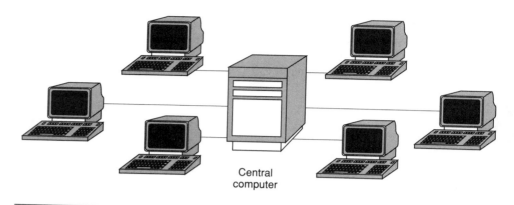

Central
computer

Decentralized data processing

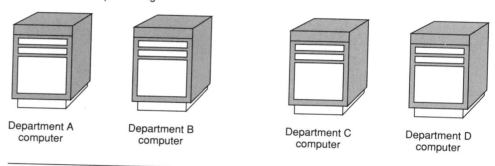

Department A
computer

Department B
computer

Department C
computer

Department D
computer

Distributed data processing

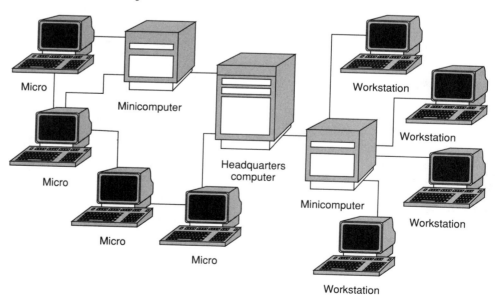

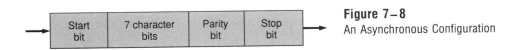

Figure 7-8
An Asynchronous Configuration

The types of line configurations include simplex, duplex, and half-duplex. In a **simplex** configuration, the communication can take place in only one direction—a warehouse sending its daily transactions to the main office, for example. In **half-duplex,** communication takes place in both directions, but not at the same time—a warehouse sending its daily transactions to the main office, and then receiving the main office inventory status. In a **full-duplex** configuration, communication can take place in both directions at the same time. Figure 7-9 illustrates these three configurations.

Improving the line efficiency is done either by multiplexing or concentration. **Multiplexing** takes place when a high-speed line is shared by multiple devices or users through a device called a multiplexer. When multiple devices can share one line, then you may need only one line. For example, two lines at 3,200 bits per second can be combined by a multiplexer on a single 6,400-bps line.

Concentration is a more advanced feature than multiplexing. It enables a greater number of input channels to be combined in one output channel through a device called a concentrator. For example, four 3,200-bps lines could share a 6,400-bps line using a concentrator. A concentrator may store and format some of the traffic. This storage function is not possible with a multiplexer.

7-6

NETWORK TYPES

There are two major types of network systems: LAN (local area network) and WAN (wide area network). LANs have received a great deal of attention in recent years. A **LAN** system connects peripheral equipment in close proximity. Usually this kind of system is limited to a certain geographical area, such as a building, and it is usually owned by one company. However, some systems cover a broad geographical range and are still referred to as LANs. A LAN is usually a prerequisite for an automated office. In an automated office, word processing, electronic mail, and electronic message distribution are integrated by using a LAN system. We discuss office automation later in this chapter. To establish a LAN system, careful planning and a thorough assessment of the information needs of a particular organization are required.

A **WAN** system does not limit itself to a certain geographical area. It may be in several cities, states, or even countries. It usually is owned by several different parties. As an example of a WAN system, consider a company that has its headquarters in Washington, D.C., and 30 offices in 30 states. With a WAN system, all these offices can be in continuous contact with the headquarters and can send and receive information. Remote data entry becomes a real possibility in a WAN system. An airline reservation system is another example of a WAN system. You can reserve an airline ticket in the United States, and then pick it up in Asia or Africa. A WAN system may use all the technologies discussed earlier. For example, it may use all the different communication channels, terminals of different sizes and sophistication, a multiplexer, and so on. Figure 7-10 illustrates a WAN system.

Figure 7–9
Line Configurations

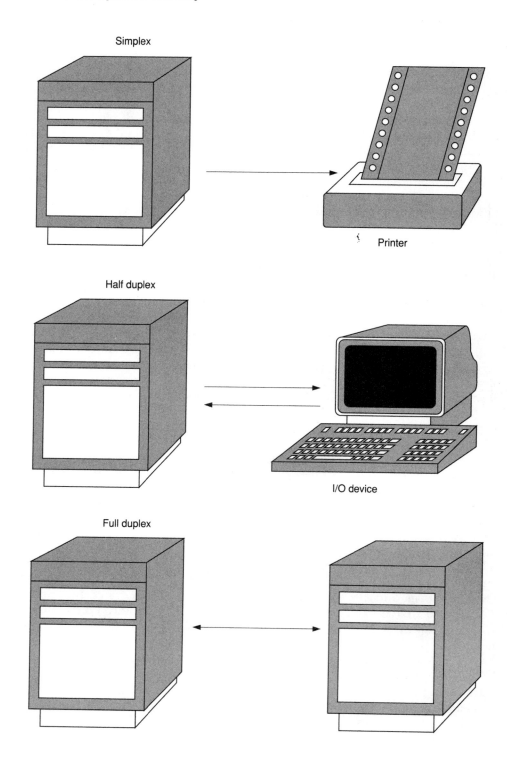

Simplex

Printer

Half duplex

I/O device

Full duplex

7–7

NETWORK TOPOLOGIES

There are several architectures (**topologies**) for a network system, each with its own advantages and disadvantages. Depending on the organizational structure, functions, and needs, one or several of these architectures may be implemented. The commonly used topologies are star, ring, bus, tree, and web networks.

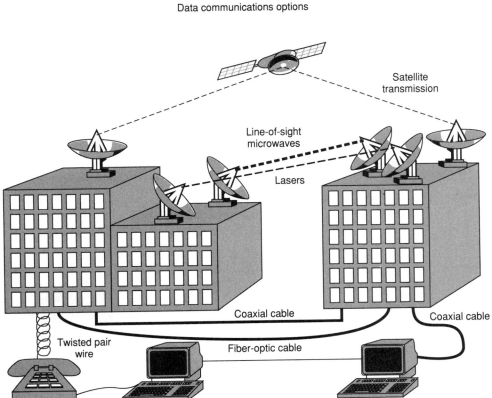

Data communications options

Figure 7–10
An Example of a WAN System

Star Network   7–7–1

The star network usually consists of a central computer (host computer) and a series of nodes (terminals). The main processing power is supplied by the host computer. The breakdown of any of the nodes will not affect the operation of the entire network; however, if the host computer goes down, the entire network is no longer operable. Figure 7–11 illustrates a star network.

Ring Network   7–7–2

A ring network does not have a central host computer. There may be a variety of computers and input/output devices used in this architecture. If any one of the nodes or computers goes down, the effect over the entire network would be minimal. Figure 7–12 illustrates this type of network.

Bus Network   7–7–3

The bus network, which is commonly used in a LAN system, connects a series of different nodes (see fig. 7–13). The failure of any of the nodes does not have an effect on any other node. This type of network is usually used for resource sharing in an organization. For example, a bus network can enable 20 PCs to use one high-speed laser printer or a hard disk with 300M of memory.

Figure 7–11
A Star Network

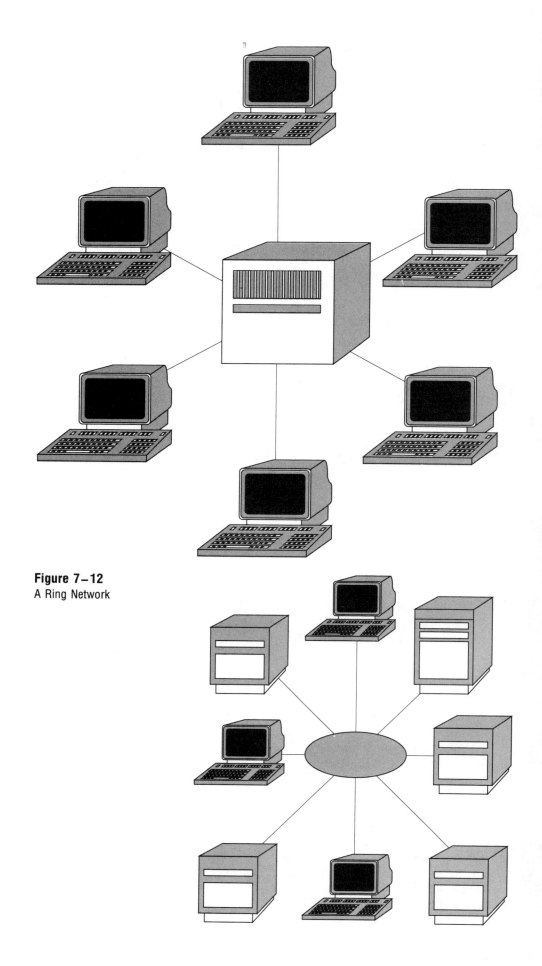

Figure 7–12
A Ring Network

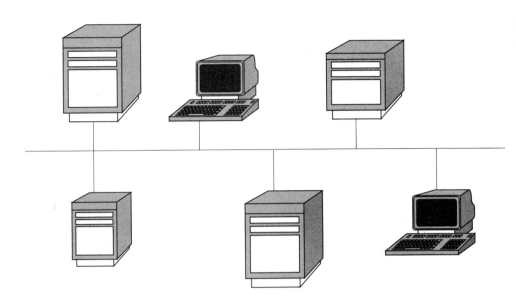

Figure 7–13
A Bus Network

Tree Network   7–7–4

A tree network combines computers with different powers in different organizational levels (see fig. 7–14). This network may use microcomputers at the bottom, minicomputers at the middle, and a mainframe computer at the top. Companies that are organized in a tree (hierarchical) fashion are the main candidates for this type of network.

Failure of nodes at the bottom may not have a significant effect on the performance of the entire network; however, the middle nodes and, especially, the top node—which has control over the entire operation of the network—are extremely important for the operation of the network.

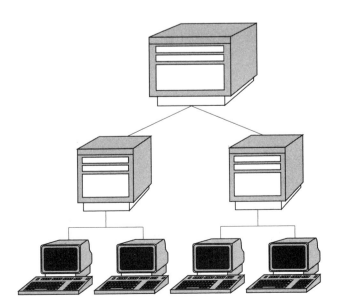

Figure 7–14
A Tree Network

Figure 7–15
A Web Network

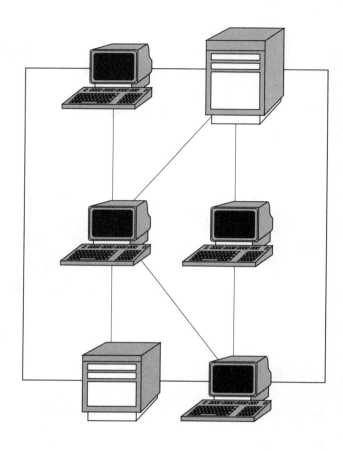

7–7–5	## Web Network

In a web network, every node (which may differ in size and configuration from the others) is connected to every other node (see fig. 7–15). This type of architecture is the most reliable. Failure of one or a few of the nodes may not cause a major problem to the entire network operation. However, this type of architecture is costly and difficult to maintain.

7–8

APPLICATIONS OF TELE-COMMUNICATIONS

There are many applications of telecommunications and networking. Office automation and teleconferencing are two of the most popular applications.

7–8–1	## Office Automation

Increasing sophistication and decreasing costs have made microcomputers affordable for even medium and small organizations. This new development has changed the traditional office environment.

Office automation or office automated systems consist of a series of related technologies, such as electronic mail, electronic message distribution, text processing and reprographics, voice mail, micrographics, and facsimile.

An electronic mail (E-mail) system delivers messages electronically. An E-mail system reduces the amount of paper flow throughout the organization and expedites information delivery by disseminating the information to all authorized users immediately. With an E-mail system, a decision-maker can send and receive messages, copy messages, save them on computer files, and set up private and public mailing lists. An E-mail system enables the user to deliver a message to the recipient without a third-party intervention, which enhances the privacy of communication. This type of system also improves the effectiveness of communication by delivering a message to the right person. At the present time, E-mail systems have some limitations. For example, you cannot send blind carbon copies, and you cannot send graphics. However, it is expected that these problems will be resolved in the near future.

Electronic message distribution is very similar to an E-mail system. You can send a message to several employees through your computer terminal. You also can request a reply from the recipients.

Text processing and reprographics include creation and dissemination of forms and documents electronically. All the features of word processing, such as document creation, modification, cut, and paste, are available.

Voice mail is an enhanced version of a telephone answering machine. You can send and receive your voice messages through a telephone system within or outside your office. You can forward a message as it was received or add to it, and then forward it to one or several recipients.

Micrographics is the process of reducing texts and graphs on hard copy documents to a fraction of their size and storing these documents on film. The micrographics process helps an organization save space, resulting in significant cost savings.

Facsimile, or fax, machines send a hard copy document from one location to another through an ordinary telephone line. Fax machines can be integrated with PCs and laser printers in an automated office. This means the output from a PC can be directly faxed to another location or to another computer without producing hard copy.

The goal of the automated office is to use all these ingredients to make the office operation more effective. In a sophisticated office, voice, data, and images are transmitted on a single line. This capability improves the quality of the information processing. The automated office should improve the effectiveness of decision makers by providing timely access to the information needed for decision-making purposes. The technology is available in the form of integrated services digital networks (ISDNs). ISDNs are discussed later in this chapter. When costs are reduced and telecommunication systems are improved, we should see more applications of office automation.

Teleconferencing   7-8-2

A **teleconferencing** system is an interactive electronic communication system that connects several people in several locations. A teleconferencing system can include different types of technologies. In its simplest form, it may include a meeting room and a basic telecommunication system, which may be a telephone connected to a microphone. A teleconferencing system can enable face-to-face interaction, interaction between local groups, or interaction with remote groups.

It also can include computer conferencing: the user contacts a central computer and sends or receives information to or from a central database.

Many organizations have reported significant savings by using a teleconferencing system, which enables executives to conduct meetings from their own offices. The advancement in telecommunication systems should make teleconferencing more affordable to even smaller organizations. The major drawbacks of teleconferencing systems are security and the lack of human touch.

7–9
PBX NETWORK

A **private branch exchange** (PBX) is a computer system that switches telephone signals in an organization. A PBX system replaces the same equipment available from the local telephone companies. There are several advantages to establishing a PBX system privately. The cost may be cheaper, and a PBX provides services that may not be available through the local telephone company. These services may include voice mail, networking microcomputers, and combining voice and data messages.

7–10
ISDN NETWORK

Until the advent of the **Integrated Services Digital Network** (ISDN), the computer user had to have separate lines for voice, data, and images. An ISDN allows the networking of telephones, PCs, mainframes, printers, and fax machines. The ISDN is the most recent communication system. It uses an ordinary twisted-pair telephone line and digital transmission technology to send voice, data, and image information over the same line. The ISDN will make the analog modems obsolete.

Today's fastest modems transmit data at 19,200 bits per second. An ISDN, on the other hand, can transmit data at 64,000 bps, which will be improved with the advancement of the technology. Figure 7–16 illustrates an example of an ISDN network.

Figure 7–16
An Example of an ISDN Network

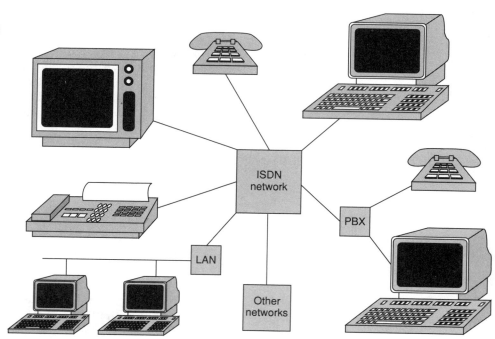

SECURITY IN A NETWORK ENVIRONMENT

Computer security is an important managerial and technical issue, and organizations should be aware of underlying factors. Some factors are controllable, some are partially controllable, and some are completely uncontrollable. Some potential security threats are summarized in table 7–1.

The majority of computer threats are created by insiders. A comprehensive security system should allow only authorized employees to have access to the computer facilities. Table 7–2 summarizes the threats posed by insiders.

The damage from natural disasters is somewhat controllable. Buildings with special designs for earthquake protection are now available, and flood damage usually can be controlled. Computer rooms frequently are designed separately from the rest of the structure to minimize potential hazards. Wiring, air conditioning, and fire protection should be of special concern. Locks and physical deterrents should prevent most computer thefts.

The newest computer threat is computer viruses. A **computer virus** is a series of self-propagating program codes that are triggered by a specified time or

Table 7–1
Computer Disaster

Natural Disasters	Man-Made Disasters
Cold weather	Blackouts
Earthquakes	Fires
Floods	Gas leaks
Hot weather	Neighborhood hazards
Hurricanes	Nuclear attacks
Ice storms	Oil leaks
Ocean waves	Power failure
Severe dust	Power fluctuations
Snow	Radioactive fallout
Tornadoes	Structural failure

Table 7–2
Internal Computer Threats and Vulnerability

Type of Threat	Sources of Threats					
	I/O Operator	Supervisor	Programmer	System Engineer/ Technician	User	Competitor
Changing codes	X		X			
Copying files	X		X			
Destroying files	X	X	X		X	X
Embezzlement			X	X		X
Espionage	X	X	X			
Installing bugs			X	X		
Sabotage	X		X	X		X
Selling data	X	X	X		X	
Theft		X	X		X	X

Table 7–3
CBIS Components and
Security Problems

Input/Database	Process	Output	Transmission
Deleting data	Installing bugs	Selling output	Sending wrong data
Entering wrong data	Changing programs	Searching and using waste-paper	Sending incomplete data
Copying data	Erasing programs	Changing output Erasing output	Sending data to unauthorized users
Selling or changing data	Selling programs	Generating wrong output	

event within the computer system. When the program or the operating system containing the virus is used again, the virus latches onto another program and the cycle continues. The seriousness of computer viruses varies. They range from springing a joke on a user to completely destroying a computer program and data.

Computer viruses are very new in the United States; they have been around much longer in European countries. Virus infections also can be transmitted through a network. Probably the most dangerous type of virus infection is from a bulletin board, which can infect anyone who accesses the bulletin board. Experts feel that the greatest national risk would come from infecting large computers, such as those governing the air traffic control system, and the computers used in public safety and security, the Defense Department, or NASA. Computer viruses have been observed in many countries, including the United States, West Germany, Switzerland, Italy, Great Britain, and Israel. Computer viruses can be installed or programmed into a disk controller, hard disk, operating system, or simply in a floppy disk.

Table 7–3 summarizes different threats associated with different components of CBIS. Careful security planning may keep the computer hackers at bay.

SUMMARY

In this chapter we reviewed data communications and networking principles. Components of a network, types of networks, and network topologies were explained, and we looked at office automation and teleconferencing as two of the popular applications of networking. The chapter concluded with a brief discussion of computer security and computer threats.

REVIEW QUESTIONS

*These questions are answered in Appendix A.

1. What is data communication?
2. Why is data communication needed?
3. What are the major components of a communication system?
4. What is a modem?
5. Is a modem always needed in a communication system?
*6. What is modulation? Demodulation?
7. What are five major communication lines? Which line is the most secure? Which line is the least secure? Which costs the most? Which has the longest range?
8. What is an acoustic coupler?
9. What are three types of data-processing architectures? What are some of the advantages of each?

*10. What is distributed processing?

11. What is a local area network?

12. What is a wide area network?

13. What are some of the applications of a WAN?

*14. What are five major network topologies?

15. What is multiplexing? Why is it done?

16. What are three types of line configurations?

17. What is synchronous transmission? Asynchronous?

18. What is office automation? What are the ingredients of an automated office?

*19. What is teleconferencing? What are some of the advantages of teleconferencing?

20. What is a PBX?

21. What is an ISDN network?

*22. What are some of the applications of an ISDN?

23. What is computer security?

24. What are five examples of computer threats?

*25. What is a computer virus?

26. Do security risks increase in a distributed system? If yes, how? What can be done to avoid security loss?

27. What are some of the computer threats associated with each component of a CBIS? How are they prevented?

28. It has been estimated that a significant portion of the work force will work at home using communication systems by the year 2000. Discuss the pros and cons of "telecommuting."

29. Consult computer magazines and find out who are the major vendors of modems. Why is there such a price range for modems? What is the difference between an $80 modem and a $1,000 modem?

30. It has been said that fiber optics is the communication line of the future. Why is this statement true? Discuss.

31. Compare and contrast the five communication lines. What are the major advantages of each? Disadvantages of each?

32. Consult an organization in your area. What type of network system do they have? What are the applications of a LAN system in this organization?

33. Discuss the advantages and disadvantages of each network topology. Which application is the most suitable for each type? Discuss.

34. Consult an organization that has implemented an automated office. What are some of the unique advantages of an automated office? What functions are performed by an automated office? What equipment is used in an automated office?

35. How are we going to protect our computers? Can we really implement a tight security system? Consult the computer center of your school or an organization that you are familiar with. Have they had any problems with computer security? What type of security system is in place? Which is easier to implement, system security or physical security? Discuss.

KEY TERMS

Asynchronous

Centralized processing

Coaxial cable

Communication lines

Computer security

Computer virus

Concentration

Decentralized data processing

Distributed data processing

Fiber optics

Full-duplex

Half-duplex

Integrated Services
Digital Network
LAN
Microwave
Modem
Multiplexing

Office automation
Private branch exchange
(PBX)
Protocols
Satellite
Simplex

Synchronous
Teleconferencing
Topologies
WAN

ARE YOU READY TO MOVE ON?

Multiple Choice

1. An effective data communication system can improve the effectiveness of a CBIS by
   a. increasing the use of 4GLs
   b. incorporating NLP into the CBIS
   c. improving the flexibility of data collection and transmission
   d. increasing the complexity of data collection and transmission
   e. all of the above

2. A modem is used to
   a. convert analog signals to digital signals
   b. convert digital signals to analog signals
   c. synchronize the communication link
   d. both a and b
   e. all of the above

3. When choosing a communication line, which of the following should be considered:
   a. security of the line
   b. how much information can be transferred
   c. quality of transmission
   d. both b and c
   e. all of the above

4. The communication line that shows the most promise for future development is
   a. satellite
   b. fiber optics
   c. microwave
   d. coaxial cable
   e. telephone lines

5. A problem associated with decentralized data processing is
   a. lack of coordination between organizational units
   b. reduced costs of having multiple systems
   c. less duplication of data
   d. less duplication of efforts
   e. all of the above

6. Star, ring, bus, tree, and web are various types of
   a. strategic planning CBISs
   b. communication lines
   c. network topologies

    d. communication control units

    e. none of the above

7. "The breakdown of any node will not affect the operation of the entire system but, if the host computer goes down, the entire system is no longer operational" describes the

    a. star network

    b. ring network

    c. bus network

    d. tree network

    e. web network

8. A ring system

    a. is commonly used in a LAN system for resource sharing

    b. does not use a central host computer

    c. is more adaptable to computers with different powers

    d. has every node connected to every other node

    e. none of the above

9. Office automation includes all of the following technologies except

    a. electronic mail

    b. voice mail

    c. facsimile

    d. teleconferencing

    e. microgaphics

10. An ISDN network

    a. uses digital technology

    b. combines voice, data, and images

    c. is faster than current modems

    d. uses an ordinary telephone line

    e. all of the above

True/False

1. Data communication is the electronic transfer of data from one location to another.

2. The origin in a data communication system is called the sender and the destination is called the receiver.

3. Protocols are rules that govern a communication system and are used to synchronize the communication link.

4. Microwaves, satellites, and fiber optics can be used as communication lines but regular telephone lines cannot be used.

5. Only one communication device can use the communication line at a time.

6. A centralized data-processing system utilizes one central location for performing all data-processing tasks.

7. Asychronous communication sends each character as an independent message and may be more accurate than synchronous communication, where several characters are blocked together for transmission.

8. Communication line configurations include single, double, and half-double.

9. Remote data entry is more likely in a WAN system than a LAN system.

10. A computer virus is nothing more than a practical joke; it cannot really do any harm.

ANSWERS

Multiple Choice	True/False
1. c	**1.** T
2. d	**2.** T
3. e	**3.** T
4. b	**4.** F
5. a	**5.** F
6. c	**6.** T
7. a	**7.** T
8. b	**8.** F
9. d	**9.** T
10. e	**10.** F

Systems Analysis and Design

8

8-1

INTRODUCTION

This chapter reviews systems analysis and design principles. The life-cycle approach, one of the most commonly used methodologies for building a CBIS, is introduced. Different phases of this methodology, including problem definition, feasibility study, systems analysis, systems design, systems implementation, and the post-implementation audit are explained. We introduce new design methodologies, including prototyping, middle-out approach, and adaptive design. By analysis and synthesis of these different approaches, we introduce a "revised approach," which integrates the strong points of the earlier approaches. The chapter introduces CASE as the most recent technology used in the systems development process. We conclude with a series of guidelines for building a successful CBIS.

8-2

SYSTEMS ANALYSIS AND DESIGN

Systems analysis and **systems design** are two separate tasks performed by the systems analyst. There are two major objectives for systems analysis in a typical organization— identification of the objectives for the new system and identification of the operations and problems of the present system.

A systems analyst must identify all the objectives for the new system. This analysis may reveal that there is no need for the new system. However, many times a new system is recommended. The objectives of such a new system may be the elimination of errors in an order-entry system and expediting order processing. To achieve this goal, the analyst must identify the step-by-step operation of the present system and highlight the problems and bottlenecks associated with it.

In the systems design phase, two unique objectives usually are established:

- Preparation of a detailed system solution
- Outline of the tasks required by the user

A detailed solution may include writing a new program for the order-entry system or automating the current manual order-entry system. Tasks requested by the user may include a well-defined order-entry procedure for the warehouse manager or a weekly report of the sales performance of specific sales regions.

8-3

THE LIFE-CYCLE APPROACH

The **life-cycle approach** is the most popular methodology for systems analysis and design, particularly in EDP and MIS areas. This methodology includes a series of well-defined steps. Figure 8–1 illustrates the phases involved in the life-cycle approach.

8-3-1

Problem Definition

During the **problem-definition** stage, the user and the designer of the system try to define and understand the problem faced by the organization. This very important step must be undertaken with great care. It is possible to identify the symptoms of the problem instead of the problem itself.

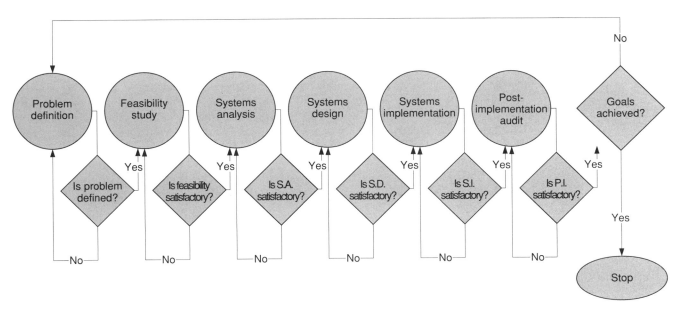

Figure 8–1
Phases Involved in the Life-Cycle Approach

The problem may have been identified internally or brought to the attention of the organization by customers, employees, or external agencies. The problem may have been identified and initiated by the user or top management (called demand pull). Or a problem may be caused by the change in the status of the computer technology (called technology push).

Problems in a typical business organization might include improper allocation of resources, an inaccurate billing system, an inefficient inventory system, an inaccurate budgeting system, or complaints from customers regarding the timeliness or quality of services. Some of these problems may be symptoms of larger problems. Sometimes problems are not as well-defined as these are. For example, the problem may be the improvement of competitiveness in the market place or employment of a new technology to analyze the organization's environment in a more thorough manner. Occasionally, problems are novel, nonrecurring, and unstructured, particularly those in the DSS environment.

Feasibility Study   8–3–2

During the **feasibility study** stage of the life cycle, the systems analyst, or a team of systems analysts, tries to investigate the feasibility of the solution proposed to resolve the problem. The study may include economic, technical, social, and time dimensions.

Economic feasibility is concerned with the cost or benefit of the system. For example, if the net gain of implementing an inventory system is $250,000, and the cost of implementation is $500,000, the system is not economically feasible. To conduct an economic feasibility study, the systems analyst team must identify all the costs and benefits of the proposed system. These costs and benefits can be both tangible and intangible. Tangible costs include costs of equipment, training, new employees, and so forth. Intangible costs include the social issues related to automation—for example, resistance to change, privacy, security, and employee turnover. We talk about social issues in Chapter 9. Benefits usually include all the cost savings of the new system.

The real challenge for the analyst is to assess intangible costs and benefits accurately. The analyst should attach a realistic monetary value to intangible costs and benefits, and then conduct an economic feasibility study.

To make the assessment of intangible benefits clearer, consider the following example. Suppose that one of the intangible benefits of a new system is improved customer service. One way to assign a monetary value to this benefit is to quantify the intangible benefit. Customer service means maintaining the present total sales and possibly increasing the total sales by a certain percentage. If improved customer service means 10 percent growth for a company with gross sales of $15 million, the benefit of the new system is worth $1.5 million in increased sales. If the company has a 20 percent net margin, this means a $300,000 net profit through improving customer service. The same type of analysis can be performed for the assessment of intangible costs.

Technical feasibility is concerned with the technical aspects of the new system. One way to investigate technical feasibility is to study the state of technology. A proposed solution may not be technically feasible because the technology does not exist. For example, a voice-activated monitoring system presently is not technically feasible.

Lack of technical feasibility also may stem from an organizational deficiency. A specific system may not be feasible because the organization lacks the expertise, time, or personnel required to implement the new system. This has been referred to as a lack of organizational readiness.

Social feasibility (sometimes called operational feasibility) investigates the proposed system within the context of social issues, such as employee replacement, privacy issues, turnover, and employee dissatisfaction. Some of the social issues can be addressed by design measures performed by the systems analyst team, such as on-going education and task force design. User education has always had a positive effect on user acceptance of the system. Involving a user representative in the design process is another design tool that minimizes the effect of the social issues of automation. However, some of these issues are an inherent part of any automation, and there is no way to eliminate such problems completely.

Finally, a feasibility study may be concerned with the **time factor.** Suppose that a system is feasible economically, technically, and socially, but it will not be ready within the time frame needed by an organization. The proposed system is not feasible from the time-factor viewpoint. Figure 8–2 illustrates the four dimensions of a feasibility study.

8–3–3

Systems Analysis

The third step in the life-cycle approach is systems analysis. In this phase, the systems analyst, or a team of analysts, specifically defines the problem and comes up with some possible alternatives for solving it. A variety of tools may be used during this phase, including interview, questionnaire, observation, form investigation and control, flowcharting, and data flow diagrams (DFDs).

Interviews are used to discover problem areas and user opinions regarding the implementation of the new system. This technique is usually effective but costly.

Questionnaires also attempt to identify problem areas. This tool is cheaper than conducting interviews; however, it is not as effective because some of the questions may be misinterpreted, and many of the questionnaires may not

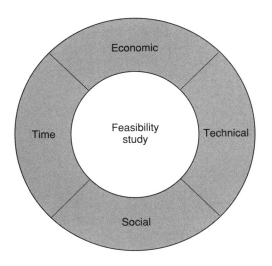

Figure 8-2
Different Dimensions of a Feasibility Study

be returned. This method is effective if the problem area is relatively well-defined and the return of the questionnaire is guaranteed.

Observation is sometimes used (particularly in a production environment) for discovering the problem area. However, workers do not always feel comfortable being watched and may perform differently while under supervision.

Form investigation and control is used to examine the effectiveness and efficiency of the existing forms. The current forms are analyzed to determine whether they contain the right information. Can any of the existing items be deleted? Should any new items be added?

Flowcharts are the most commonly used tools for both programming and systems design. They are used to illustrate the operation of the system under investigation. Two popular types of flowcharts are the programming flowchart and system flowchart. You use a **programming flowchart** when you develop a specific program. This tool helps the programmer to depict the logical flow of the program. How should data be read? What operation should take place? Has the end of data been reached? The **system flowchart** illustrates the entire operation of a system. For example, from which device should data be read and to what device should the output be displayed?

Figure 8-3 shows an example of a program flowchart. In this example, several records are read. When the computer reaches the end of the data, it stops. It checks whether the employee has worked more or less than 40 hours. If the hours are over 40, the employee receives overtime pay; otherwise, the employee receives regular pay. Next, exemptions and taxes are calculated. Finally, the net pay is calculated and printed and the process continues. Figure 8-4 shows the symbols used for flowcharting.

A **data flow diagram** depicts the operation of a system. This may include the flow of data, the input/output process, and error checking. Figure 8-5 illustrates a data flow diagram. In this example, a client's credit is checked. Based on the amount of the transaction and the client's credit limit, either the transaction is finalized, the database is updated, and a report is printed, or an error message is printed. In either case, the decision-maker is informed.

The output of the systems analysis phase is a clear problem definition, one or several alternatives, and some initial documentation relating to the operation of the new system.

Figure 8–3
A Program Flowchart

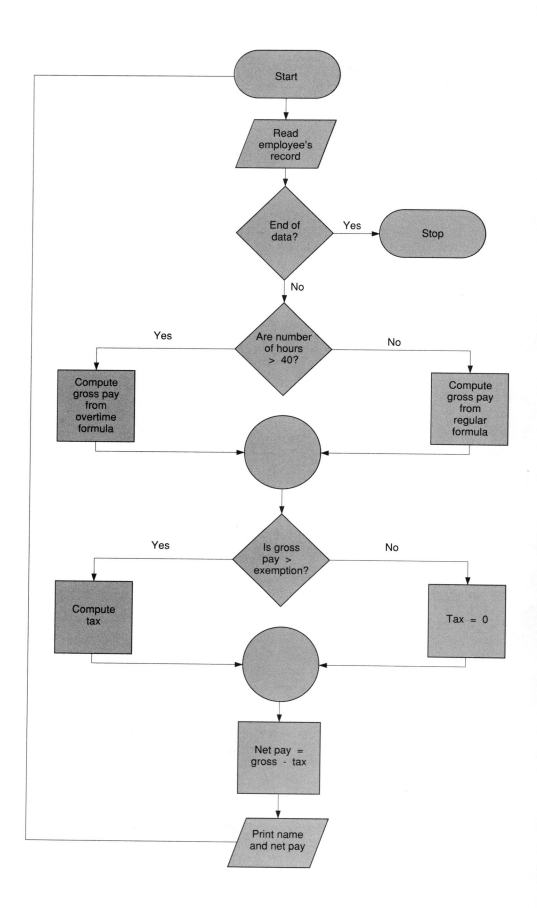

Figure 8–4
Symbols Used for Flowcharting

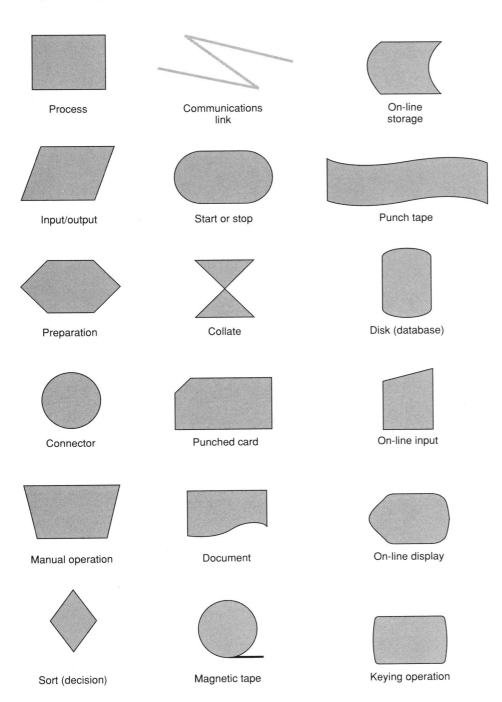

Process | Communications link | On-line storage

Input/output | Start or stop | Punch tape

Preparation | Collate | Disk (database)

Connector | Punched card | On-line input

Manual operation | Document | On-line display

Sort (decision) | Magnetic tape | Keying operation

Interviews, questionnaires, and observations are used to understand the problem better. Graphical tools such as flowcharts and data flow diagrams (DFDs) are used for highlighting the problem area, gaining a clear understanding of the input-process-output cycle, and eliminating the bottlenecks encountered throughout the entire system. Flowcharts usually show the logic involved in the system and highlight the detail by using special symbols. DFDs use bubbles and arrows to show the system process and highlight the overall system operations. These tools are very useful when pre-specifications can be done, but they may not be suitable if the problem under investigation is unstructured. Pre-

Figure 8–5
A Data Flow Diagram

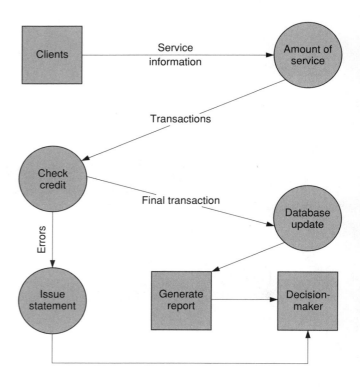

specification refers to a well-defined standard operating procedure for solving a problem. A good example would be designing a payroll system. There is always a well-defined procedure available for calculating an employee's paycheck.

8–3–4   Systems Design

During the systems design phase, the team of analysts chooses the alternative that is the most realistic and presents the greatest benefit to the organization. At this point, the details of the proposed solution are outlined. The output produced by the team is a document very similar to a blueprint for implementation, which includes file and database design, form and report design, documentation design, hardware configuration, software configuration, and general system specifications.

File and database design may include the logical view of the database (the way in which data appear to the user), file contents, data dictionary, and the file access method. Database principles were discussed in Chapter 6.

Form and report design should include the contents of the forms and reports, their general layout, and the frequency of their production. Documentation design includes a detailed document that highlights the step-by-step design procedure and all the activities involved. A detailed hardware configuration outlines the type of hardware that must be purchased or leased, including all the input, output, and memory devices. The software configuration should include a detailed program listing, documentation, and the specifics of commercial software. Finally, general system specifications include the overall operation of the new system, which will serve as a "cookbook" for the next phase of the life cycle.

Systems Implementation   8–3–5

During the implementation phase, the solution is transferred from paper to action. A variety of tasks take place while the implementation phase is underway:

- Acquiring the new equipment
- Hiring new employees
- Training new and old employees
- Physical planning and layout design
- Coding and testing
- Conversion planning and documentation

Acquisition of the new equipment may be done by purchasing, leasing from a vendor or a third party, or by upgrading existing equipment. In any case, the equipment must be in place before the life cycle can continue.

Hiring new employees may include hiring for any of the job titles discussed in the next chapter, and it also can be done by training existing employees.

When training new employees, you familiarize them with the operation of the system and the operation of the organization as a whole. This is a chance for these employees to get to know the operation of the system, its goals and objectives, and its place in the organization.

Physical planning and layout design are needed for the computer room and newly purchased equipment. This may include wiring, false floor design, air conditioning, humidity and dust control, and most important of all, a tight security system. These security measures should include both physical and system security to ensure that only authorized personnel can access the computer facilities.

Coding is the writing of all the programs designed in the systems design phase. These programs must be fully implemented and tested with various data to ensure accuracy.

Conversion marks the end of the implementation phase. When a system is ready to be converted, several options are available to the designer:

- Parallel conversion
- Phased-in, phased-out conversion
- Direct conversion
- Pilot conversion

Using the **parallel conversion** approach, the old and the new system run simultaneously for a short time to ensure that the new system operates properly. This, however, is a costly approach.

In the **phased-in, phased-out approach,** depending on the suitability of the system for such a conversion, each module of the new system is converted as the corresponding part of the old system is retired. This process continues until the entire system is converted. In accounting and finance, this approach may be very effective but it is not suitable for all applications.

Using the **direct conversion** (sometimes called crash) approach, the old system is stopped and the new system is implemented. This approach is risky, but the organization may save money by not running the old and new systems concurrently.

Finally, using a **pilot conversion** approach, the analyst develops the system and introduces it only to a limited area of the organization, such as a division or a department. If the system is working properly, it is installed in the rest of the organization. The installation may take place all at once or in several stages.

8–3–6   Post-Implementation Audit

The last phase in the life-cycle approach, the **post-implementation audit,** attempts to verify the suitability of the system after the implementation. The team of analysts collects data and talks with the users, customers, and others affected by the new system to make sure that the system is doing what it was designed to do.

If the system is not doing what it is supposed to do, immediate corrective action must take place. This monitoring mechanism must continue throughout the life of the system.

8–4

PROJECT CONTROL TECHNIQUES

To manage the implementation of a CBIS, the systems analyst usually uses project control techniques. These techniques are used to control the budget and the implementation time. Some of these techniques are PERT (Program Evaluation Review Technique), CPM (Critical Path Method), and Gantt Chart.

PERT or CPM is used to determine the critical path for the completion of a series of interrelated activities. The critical path includes all those activities that are extremely crucial for the completion of the project. If any of these activities are delayed, the entire project is delayed. Other activities that are not on the critical path are more flexible and can be delayed without delaying the project.

To establish a PERT/CPM network, the analyst must identify all the activities needed for the completion of the project, identify and establish a prerequisite list (which activities are prerequisites to subsequent activities), establish a PERT/CPM network, and calculate the critical path duration.

In figure 8–6 there are several paths that lead you from the beginning to the end of the project. Let us investigate them:

- $1\rightarrow2\rightarrow4\rightarrow6\rightarrow7 = 5 + 15 + 6 + 11 = 37$
- $1\rightarrow4\rightarrow6\rightarrow7 = 13 + 6 + 11 = 30$
- $1\rightarrow4\rightarrow5\rightarrow6\rightarrow7 = 13 + 9 + 10 + 11 = 43$
- $1\rightarrow3\rightarrow4\rightarrow5\rightarrow6\rightarrow7 = 7 + 10 + 9 + 10 + 11 = 47$
- $1\rightarrow3\rightarrow4\rightarrow6\rightarrow7 = 7 + 10 + 6 + 11 = 34$
- $1\rightarrow2\rightarrow4\rightarrow5\rightarrow6\rightarrow7 = 5 + 15 + 9 + 10 + 11 = 50$

In this example, the last path is the critical path because it takes the longest to be completed. While this path is being completed, the other paths will be completed as well. The activities in the other paths can be delayed for some time and the project will still be completed on time. However, all the activities on the last path must be completed on time if you want to finish the project on time.

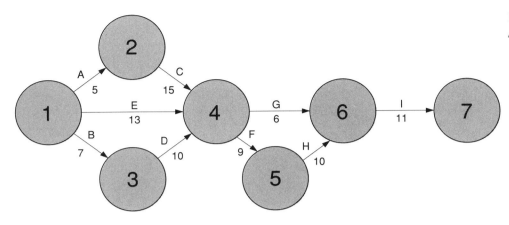

Figure 8–6
A PERT Network

Using the critical path, the analyst can establish a Gantt Chart. A Gantt Chart lists the completion time (sometimes called milestone) on the x-axis and all the activities on the y-axis. Using a Gantt Chart, the analyst can monitor the progress of the project and can see any delay in the daily operation of the project. If a delay is spotted, the systems analyst must use additional resources if the project is expected to be completed on schedule. Figure 8–6 illustrates a PERT network, and figure 8–7 illustrates a Gantt Chart.

8–5

NEW METHODOLOGIES

The life-cycle approach is a suitable methodology for systems analysis and design if a pre-specification can be made, but not when needs are continuously changing, particularly in the DSS environment. In these cases, design methodologies other than the life cycle are used.

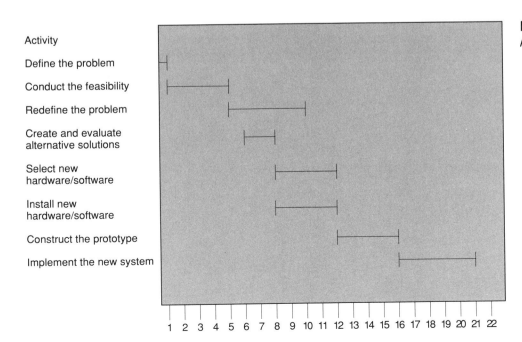

Figure 8–7
A Gantt Chart

8–5–1

Prototyping

Prototyping as a methodology for CBIS construction has gained popularity in recent years. Because constructing a complete system is time-consuming, difficult, and expensive, a prototype of the system is developed first. A prototype is usually a small version of the system that is large enough to highlight the system value to the user. Prototyping makes it easier for the user to suggest changes for the final CBIS. It also is the fastest way to put the CBIS into operation.

A prototype can serve as either a throwaway or an evolving system. A throwaway prototype is designed for illustration and to gain feedback. If the user does not like the prototype, it is thrown away. If the user is happy with the prototype, it may evolve into the final system or be used until a separate, full-featured CBIS is constructed. An evolving prototype starts from a small-scale system and evolves into the final system as new features are added and existing features are upgraded.

8–5–2

Middle-Out Methodology

To understand the **middle-out approach,** we first should explain top-down and bottom-up methodologies. In top-down design, the global view of a problem is identified. The problem is then divided into a series of subproblems, or modules. Each module is designed separately. Then these different pieces are put together. Top-down design has gained popularity for designing traditional computer-based information systems and has several advantages. It is easier to design, modify, and maintain the system.

Top-down design may not be always suitable for designing a CBIS, however. The major reason for its unsuitability to a CBIS environment is its long development process. It takes months or even years until a user sees the final product. By that time, the requirements may have changed. In addition, top-down methodology assumes pre-specification, which is not always the case.

Bottom-up methodology starts in a piecemeal fashion and may suffer from lack of direction. The solution offered to a subproblem may not be entirely suitable for a particular situation. This methodology may not keep in touch with the organizational needs of a particular setting.

Middle-out methodology begins close to the level of the problem, and it develops a process of generalizing (bottom-up) and specifying (top-down) at each stage of the problem-solving process.[1] In middle-out methodology, the prototype usually addresses one part of the problem under investigation. Later, several prototypes may be linked to solve the entire problem. This approach is justified because of the lack of understanding of all the dimensions (lack of structure) of the problem. With middle-out development, you should use a prototype that provides quick feedback on the suitability of the proposed solution.

---

[1]E. G. Hurts, Jr., D. N. Ness, T. J. Gambino, and T. H. Johnson, "Growing DSS: A Flexible Evolutionary Approach," *Building Decision Support Systems* by John L. Bennett (Reading, Mass.: Addison-Wesley Publishing Company, 1983), pp. 111–32.

Adaptive Design   8–5–3

Adaptive design advocates an evolving process in building a CBIS.[2] As a short-term solution, a CBIS may respond to the immediate needs of the user. Over the medium range, a CBIS may have to be modified and new features added to respond to the needs of the user. Over the long term, the CBIS may have to use a totally new technology in order to respond to the changing information needs of the user.

The entire computer field is a good example of the adaptive design process. Computers have evolved from first- through fourth-generation machines, and each generation uses a new technology that is more advanced than the earlier one. Fifth-generation computers are radically different from the fourth generation. 4GLs have been improving continuously. A CBIS that is designed using a 4GL has the potential to grow parallel to the 4GL. In other words, this process may provide an adaptive environment for the specific CBIS.

A REVISED APPROACH   8–6

We can combine the strong points of each of these approaches to systems analysis and design to develop a new approach. This new approach includes four steps as follows:

1. Problem definition
2. Formation of the task force
3. Construction of an on-line prototype
4. Evaluation

Problem Definition   8–6–1

In the problem-definition step, the system's objective must be defined using the following questions:

■ Why is the system going to be designed? What decision(s) will be affected? How will the organization use this system? Is the system really needed?

■ Who is going to use the system? Is it going to be used by one decision-maker or a group of decision-makers?

■ When will the system be operational? From now until the final implementation, how will decisions affected by the CBIS be made? How often will the system be used?

■ What kind of capabilities will be provided by the CBIS? How will these different capabilities be used, and how will the system provide these capabilities?

Formation of the Task Force   8–6–2

For the continued success of the CBIS, different users must have input into the construction and maintenance of their systems, and their views must be highly

---

[2]Peter G. W. Keen, "Adaptive Design for Decision Support Systems," *Data Base 12,* Nos. 1 and 2 (Fall), 1982, pp. 15–25.

valued. This issue is of considerable significance, particularly if the system is going to be used by more than one user.

The task force should include representatives from different user departments, top management, and technical staff. Preferably the task force should include the individuals presented in figure 8–8.

8–6–3

Construction of an On-Line Prototype

To show the user how the system will work, a simple prototype should be used. An on-line prototype gives the user a chance to see the system in action. In addition, the designer will discover the possible problems associated with the system. The process of prototype design and modification should continue until the user is satisfied with the system. When this occurs, construction of the final system can be started.

Figure 8–8
CBIS Task Force

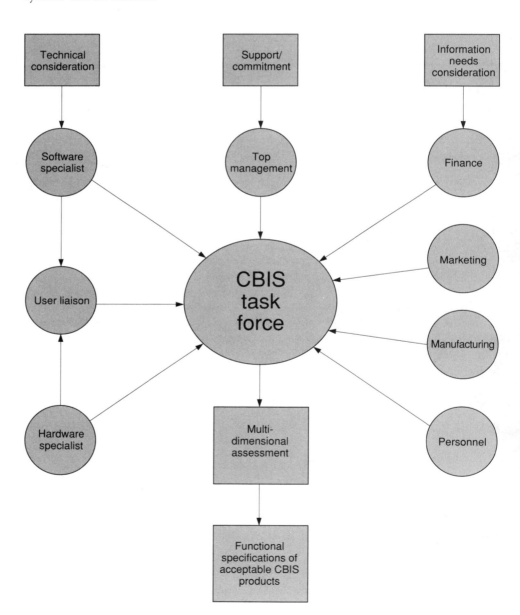

Evaluation

The evaluation of a CBIS is based on both the monetary and the non-monetary benefits generated by the system. The monetary effect of the system usually is easy to determine. However, non-monetary factors, such as the effect of the system on decision-making, decision implementation, the educational effect, and the system's overall effectiveness, are the most important concerns.

Based on the results of the evaluation, the process of modification either may be continued or halted temporarily until the user tries new system features or while new features are added to the system (see fig. 8–9). As this figure shows, all phases of the classic life-cycle approach are combined into one phase, and this

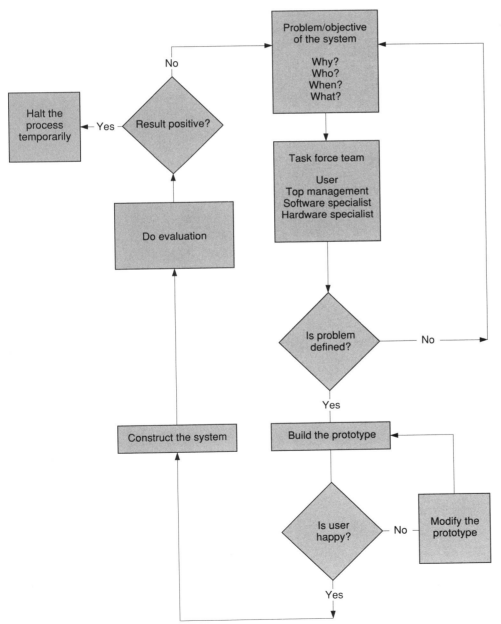

Figure 8–9
The Iterative Process of CBIS Design

phase continues in an iterative manner until the system is constructed. After construction of the system, the monitoring mechanism suggests any corrective action to guarantee the user's satisfaction.

8-7

CASE: COMPUTER-ASSISTED SOFTWARE ENGINEERING

CASE is one of the most recent tools used by systems analysts to automate parts of the application development process. **CASE tools** are a collection of computer programs similar to CAD (computer-aided design), which has been used by drafters and engineers for several years. The capabilities of CASE tools vary from product to product, but some of the general capabilities offered by a typical CASE tool include the following:

- Graphic tools such as data flow diagrams (DFDs), flowcharts, and structure charts to depict the entire system's operation graphically
- Dictionary tools designed to record the operation of the system in detail
- Prototyping tools for designing input and output format, forms, and screens
- Code generators to minimize or eliminate the programming efforts
- Project management tools to help control the time and budget of a project

Several CASE tools currently are available. Some of the most popular ones include Excelerator by Index Technology, Analyst/Designer Toolkit from Yourdon, System Developer's Prokit from McDonnell Douglas, and Information Engineering Facility from Texas Instruments.

CASE offers several advantages for systems analysis and design:

- You can spot design errors graphically.
- An analyst can design several alternatives. Addition and deletion are more manageable—there is no need to redraw the entire design after each change.
- CASE tools perform some of the repetitive tasks, freeing the analyst to concentrate on more important issues.
- Users can participate actively in the design process and express their opinions.
- CASE expedites prototyping.

8-8

BUILDING A SUCCESSFUL CBIS

To summarize the information in this chapter, we provide guidelines for designing a CBIS. These guidelines, summarized in table 8-1, may serve as a checklist.

Get top management involved
Get key users involved
Make users responsible for both the success and failure of the system
Establish a task force
Try to use existing hardware and software technologies
Develop the system in stages (modular design)
Use prototypes
Use commercial packages (if possible)
Define goals and objectives of the CBIS clearly
Identify that there is a need for the system
Provide training and education

Consider user requirements in the context of:
   feasibility (economic, technical, social, and time)
   simplicity (ease of use)
   reliability (to be up and running when it is needed)
   compatibility (to be compatible with the existing
      computer resources)

Establish effective communication both for motivation of the affected employees and for information transfer
Let decision-makers determine information usefulness

Table 8–1
Guidelines for Building a
Successful CBIS

SUMMARY

In this chapter the principles of systems analysis and design were discussed. The classic life-cycle approach for design and implementation of a CBIS was introduced. Because this methodology is not suitable for changing needs and lack of specifications, however, we introduced new methodologies, including prototyping, the middle-out approach, and adaptive design, that are suitable for changing needs. We synthesized all these approaches into one integrated approach called the revised approach, and we briefly explained CASE as a tool for system development. The chapter concluded with a series of guidelines for building a successful CBIS.

REVIEW QUESTIONS

*These questions are answered in Appendix A.

1. What is systems analysis and design?
2. What are the objectives of systems analysis? Of systems design?
3. What is the life-cycle approach?
*4. What are the steps involved in a life cycle?
5. What is a feasibility study?
6. What are the different dimensions of a feasibility study?
*7. What is social feasibility? Why is it important?
8. What are some of the activities performed in the systems analysis phase? In systems design?

9. What are different conversion methods?

10. Why is direct conversion risky?

11. What are two types of flowcharts?

12. Why are flowcharts used?

13. Why is a post-implementation audit needed?

14. What are the differences between the new methodologies and the traditional life-cycle methodology?

*15. What is a prototype?

*16. What is the middle-out approach?

17. What is adaptive design?

18. What are the steps involved in the revised approach?

*19. What is a task force? Who are the participants of a task force?

20. What is CASE technology?

21. What are the advantages of using CASE as a design tool?

22. What are some of the guidelines for building a CBIS?

23. Southern CRAFT, a manufacturer of wood products, is implementing a cost-control CBIS. What are the phases of systems design in this project as it applies to the life-cycle approach? What is the outcome of each phase? Conduct a feasibility study for the system. Which type of feasibility is the most important one in this particular case?

24. The president of a state university needs advice for construction of a student-monitoring CBIS. This system should help the president monitor all the students enrolled in different disciplines and display different graphs showing the number, age, nationality, and sex of the students in each discipline. The system also should generate exception reports regarding these four important variables. Apply systems analysis and design to this specific CBIS. Who should participate in the task force? What should the prototype do?

25. The corner grocery store is planning to design an order-entry system. Apply the systems analysis and design principle to this project. What does feasibility mean here? What is the difference between systems analysis and design?

26. How can project control tools such as PERT/CPM and Gantt Charts help you design an order-entry system for the corner grocery store? By using these techniques can you also control the budget? Discuss.

27. How do you build a prototype for the system in question 25? What is the purpose of the prototype?

28. Consult computer magazines and find out the latest on CASE tools. What are some of the advantages and disadvantages of CASE tools? Who are the major users of CASE tools? Is it justified to use these tools for small projects? Discuss.

KEY TERMS

Adaptive design	Observation	Problem definition
CASE tools	Parallel conversion	Programming flowchart
Data flow diagram	Phased-in, phased-out approach	Prototyping
Direct conversion	Pilot conversion	Questionnaire
Feasibility study	Post-implementation audit	System flowchart
Interview		Systems analysis
Life-cycle approach		Systems design
Middle-out approach		

Multiple Choice

1. Objectives for systems analysis include
   a. identification of the objectives of the new system
   b. identification of the operations and problems of the new system
   c. preparation of a detailed system solution
   d. both a and b
   e. all of the above

2. The most important phase in the life-cycle approach is:
   a. systems analysis
   b. systems design
   c. systems implementation
   d. problem definition
   e. none of the above

3. The first step in the life-cycle approach to systems design is the
   a. feasibility study
   b. problem definition
   c. systems analysis
   d. systems design
   e. systems implementation

4. The most commonly used tool in systems analysis is the
   a. questionnaire
   b. interview
   c. flowchart
   d. observation
   e. data flow diagram

5. Project control techniques used to manage the implementation of a CBIS include
   a. PERT
   b. Gantt Chart
   c. CPM
   d. both a and c
   e. all of the above

6. Nontraditional systems design methodologies include
   a. life-cycle approach
   b. middle-out
   c. top-down
   d. all of the above
   e. none of the above

7. Located at the heart of the revised approach to systems analysis and design is the
   a. task force
   b. problem definition
   c. on-line prototype
   d. evaluation
   e. none of the above

8. The nontraditional systems design approach that advocates an evolving process in building the CBIS is
   a. life-cycle approach
   b. middle-out methodology
   c. prototyping
   d. adaptive design
   e. bottom-up approach

9. The end of the implementation phase of the life-cycle approach to systems design is
   a. acquisition of new equipment
   b. hiring new employees
   c. conversion
   d. coding and testing
   e. physical planning and layout design

10. The most popular approach for systems analysis and design is
   a. bottom-up approach
   b. middle-out methodology
   c. prototyping
   d. adaptive design
   e. life-cycle approach

True/False

1. Systems analysis and systems design are basically the same task that the systems analyst performs.

2. Generally speaking, parallel conversion is more costly than other system conversion methods.

3. Dimensions of a system feasibility study include economic, social, technical, and time dimensions.

4. Details of the proposed solution are outlined in the systems implementation stage of the life-cycle approach.

5. Under a pilot conversion approach to system implementation, both the old and new systems are run simultaneously.

6. The life-cycle approach to systems design is not appropriate when needs are continuously changing and there is lack of pre-specification.

7. A task force should include representatives of all the affected users of the new system.

8. The iterative process of CBIS design ensures that the CBIS will function properly the first time through the process.

9. The design task force should include representatives from different user departments, top management, and technical staff.

10. The post-implementation audit phase of the life-cycle design approach occurs only once during the life of the system.

Multiple Choice	**True/False**	**ANSWERS**
1. a	**1.** F	
2. d	**2.** T	
3. b	**3.** T	
4. c	**4.** F	
5. e	**5.** F	
6. b	**6.** T	
7. a	**7.** T	
8. d	**8.** F	
9. c	**9.** T	
10. e	**10.** F	

CBIS and Society

9

9–1

INTRODUCTION

In this chapter, we define systems professionals and look at career opportunities in systems fields. Next, we present some of the negative issues associated with computers. By examining the history of computer development, we explore probable advances of the near future. We discuss computer performance, user profiles, artificial intelligence, and development in telecommunications, micro-computers, computers at home, and cost trends. This overview should provide you with an accurate perspective of the ever-increasing power and sophistication of computers in the years to come.

9–2

DEFINING SYSTEMS PROFESSIONALS

To design, implement, and use a computer-based information system, diverse expertise is needed. Specific duties and titles vary from organization to organization. In large organizations, jobs are more specialized; in medium and small organizations, one expert may perform different tasks. Generally speaking, at one end of the spectrum is the systems analyst, and at the other end is the user. Between these two individuals are many people who perform specific tasks. These positions include the following:

- Systems analyst. A **systems analyst,** sometimes called the agent of change, defines the information requirements of the user. The analyst interacts with the user at one end and with the data processing personnel at the other end in order to define the specific needs of the users. A systems analyst is similar to an architect—a general blueprint of the system is drawn by the analyst.

- Applications programmer. The applications programmer designs and codes the application programs. These programs may be in various application areas such as accounting, finance, and marketing, and may be written in COBOL, BASIC, or other computer languages.

- Systems programmer. The systems programmer maintains the system programs. These programs may include operating systems, compilers for different programs, and general input/output programs.

- Program librarian. The program librarian maintains a library of all the programs, the program documentation, and the listings of authorized users who can access these programs.

- Database administrator (DBA). A DBA is in charge of the design, maintenance, and operation of the database. Any modification in the database must be initiated by the DBA.

- Microcomputer specialist. A microcomputer specialist assists users through training, development of PC application programs, installation of commercial software, and customizing commercial software.

- Network specialist. The telecommunication, or network, specialist is in charge of all telecommunications activities. These may include connecting PCs to each other or connecting PCs to the mainframe, maintaining the network, and enforcing security and standards.

- Operator. An operator may perform different tasks and might be in charge of input/output devices, punch card operation, and mounting tapes and disks into tape and disk drives.

- Data entry clerk. The data entry clerk is in charge of data entry operations, which may include entering data by using a terminal or punching data by using punch card machines.
- Technician. A technician is usually in charge of the technical operation of the computer system, which may include repair and maintenance of disk drives, keyboards, and CRTs.
- User. The most important part of the entire cycle is the user. The entire data processing operation is focused around the user. The user utilizes the information provided by the CBIS for decision-making purposes. The systems analyst must make sure that the information needs of this individual are satisfied.

9–3 CAREER OPPORTUNITIES IN SYSTEMS FIELDS

Information systems professionals are some of the highest paid employees in the workplace. Some studies rank information systems professionals right after physicians and attorneys. Job opportunities in the information systems fields exist in both private and public sectors. The salary level varies with educational degree, number of years of experience, and type of organization.

Generally speaking, salaries in the information systems field vary from $24,000 (for a college graduate with no experience) to $100,000 for the director or vice president of an MIS department in a large organization.

The recommended degree is a bachelor's in information systems or computer science. However, a graduate with an associate degree can easily find a programming position. For systems analyst positions and directorships, a master's degree is recommended.

Throughout the country three different curriculums may be found in information systems: management information or computer information systems, computer science, and computer engineering. The first curriculum educates students in application programming such as COBOL; application analysis; and business operations, such as accounting, finance, and marketing. The second curriculum emphasizes scientific programming such as FORTRAN, PASCAL, C, and operating systems. The third curriculum focuses on the architecture of computers, microprocessors, and communication systems.

Current trends indicate that the demand for systems professionals should continue to grow. These jobs are challenging and highly paid.

9–4 NEGATIVE EFFECTS OF COMPUTERS

So far, we have discussed the positive effects of computer technology. No one can discount the positive impact that computers have had. However, some negative issues of the computerized environment deserve careful attention. These social and health issues are not so severe as to require banning computers, but these undesirable aspects should be addressed. To eliminate or reduce the negative effects, careful planning is required. Figure 9–1 illustrates these issues.

Computer Effects on the Workplace   9–4–1

There is no doubt that computers have eliminated some clerical jobs. At the same time, computers have created many new jobs for programmers, systems

Figure 9–1
CBISs in the Workplace

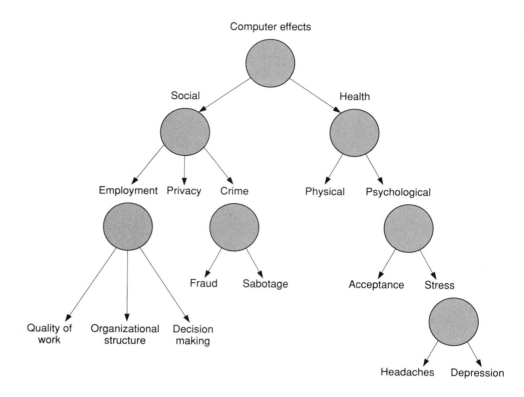

analysts, and technicians. Some argue that the jobs eliminated are clerical, while the jobs created are mostly technical and require extensive training. Others advocate that computers have reduced production costs and, therefore, have improved and increased the purchasing power of consumers, resulting in a stronger economy.

Computers definitely have a direct effect on the nature of jobs performed by different workers. Telecommuting, for example, will enable a significant portion of the workforce to perform their duties from their homes. Using telecommunications technology, a worker can use a personal computer and send and receive data to and from the main office. Computers have made some jobs more interesting by performing repetitive and boring tasks. As a result, computers have enabled typical workers to be more satisfied with their work.

Computers have created "job de-skilling" by performing technical tasks such as CAD (computer-aided design) for draftsmen. The job skill content decreases over time, such as with a machinist depending on computers to perform the technical aspects of his job. At the same time, computers have created "job upgrading" such as secretaries using computers to perform word processing tasks. One skilled worker may end up doing the job of several workers. For example, by using a word processor and a mail merge program, a secretary can generate thousands of letters, eliminating the need for additional secretaries. In job upgrading, the ideal case is to train some of the existing employees to perform the newly created jobs.

The effect of computers on the organizational structure may be varied. Computers can change the organizational structure of a company from a pyramid to a diamond structure. In a pyramid structure, three distinct layers of management exist: lower, middle, and upper. A diamond structure consists of only decision-makers and unskilled labor, eliminating middle management personnel. In this case, computers perform the jobs of middle managers. In another instance, computers may reinforce the existing structure (the pyramid) by providing timely and accurate information for the key decision-makers.

You have seen all along that computers can provide timely and accurate information that facilitates decision-making and, at the same time, creates a better control mechanism for the decision-makers. This may lead to a highly centralized organization.

Privacy Issues   9-4-2

The managers in some organizations are now able to monitor an employee's performance, number of errors made, speed of work, and time away from the desk by using computerized systems.

Much private data is left at doctors' offices, attorneys' offices, and financial institutions. This information will be entered into some computerized databases. The misuse and abuse of this information can have great consequences. Who should have access to this information and to what extent, is a difficult decision for MIS practitioners. Organizations should establish a tight security system.

Computer Crime   9-4-3

In November 1988, a virus attacked over 6,000 computer installations, bringing to the forefront the necessity of protecting computers from hackers, crackers, and computer criminals. At the present time, only 26 states have computer crime laws. Billions of dollars are stolen every year by computer criminals. Many organizations are reluctant to report their losses because they do not want to be recognized as vulnerable.

Computer fraud is the unauthorized use of computer data for personal gain. This includes transferring money from one account to another, or charging expenses to an account that did not use the service or product. Computer sabotage includes destruction, disruption, and disclosure of computer services. Computer criminals are those who modify, change, eliminate, hide, or use computer files for personal use. Computer criminals include insiders, extremists, and hackers. Hackers usually break into computer systems for personal satisfaction. Other computer criminals are after financial gain.

It is interesting to note that over 80 percent of computer crimes are committed by insiders. This presents an even more difficult challenge to protecting your computer facilities.

Health Issues   9-4-4

The health-related issues of computers, particularly video display terminals (VDTs), have been reported in recent years. There is no conclusive study to indicate that VDTs have caused health problems. However, there are many reported complaints. Work habits and how workers interface with VDTs do cause some physical problems. In general, health problems are not linked to the unit itself, but more likely they are associated with the environment in which computers are located. Static electricity, inadequate ventilation, poor lighting, dry atmosphere, inappropriate furniture, and few rest breaks are all possible causes of the problems.

Some of the health problems reported include eye and vision problems, such as fatigue, itching, and blurred vision; musculoskeletal problems, such as back strain and wrist pain; skin problems, such as rashes; reproductive problems, such as miscarriage; and stress-related problems, such as headaches and depression. The majority of these problems can be resolved by properly designing computer rooms.

The psychological problems associated with computer technology are primarily related to "resistance to change" attitudes— employees resist the new in favor of the old. This resistance is due to various reasons, among them economic concerns, uncertainty, and fear of losing their jobs.

9-5

A LOOK AT THE PAST

To present a relatively clear picture of the future of computers and CBISs, we must first look to the past. How did we get here? In the past 50 years the field of computers has progressed beyond all imagination. Observers in the field claim that computer technology has been unique in human history with respect to its impressive development. Still, some experts believe this is only the beginning and there is much to be seen in the near future.

9-6

HARDWARE TRENDS

We discussed hardware generations in Chapter 1. The summary of that information is presented in table 9-1.

9-7

SOFTWARE TRENDS

In parallel with hardware technology, software technology also has undergone major changes. We discussed these classes of software in Chapter 2. Table 9-2 summarizes this previous discussion.

Table 9-1
Hardware Trends

Generation	Date	Major Attribute	Example
First	1946–1956	Vacuum tubes	ENIAC
Second	1957–1963	Transistors	IBM 7094, 1401
Third	1964–1970	Integrated circuits	IBM 360, 370
Fourth	1971–1992	VLSI	Cray XMP, Cray II
Fifth	1992–?	Gallium arsenide	?

Table 9-2
Software Trends

Generation	Major Attribute
First	Machine language
Second	Assembly language
Third	High-level language
Fourth	Fourth-generation language (4GL)
Fifth	Natural language processing (NLP)

Generation	Speed
First	10 thousand ips
Second	200 thousand ips
Third	5 million ips
Fourth	30 to 100 million ips
Fifth	1 billion ips to 1 trillion ips

Table 9–3
Computer Performance

9–8
COMPUTER PERFORMANCE

Computer performance usually is measured in terms of the number of **instructions per second (ips)** performed by a computer. In the last 50 years the number of instructions processed per second has increased dramatically, as shown in table 9–3.

9–9
COMPUTER USERS

Computer users are no longer hard-core computer scientists. User-friendliness has become a reality, and computers are being used for diverse tasks in kindergarten classrooms and households. In the corporate world, the utilization of computers is unavoidable. Either through industry push or demand pull, computers have become an integral part of the corporate scene.

The typical user's general computer awareness has forced private and public organizations to improve their use of computer technology. A typical investment customer may ask for more detailed and sophisticated analysis when it comes to any business investment. A spreadsheet has become as popular as a calculator in any financial institution.

9–10
ARTIFICIAL INTELLIGENCE AND THE FIFTH-GENERATION PROJECT

Artificial intelligence was briefly discussed in Chapter 4. Development in AI technology, particularly in the areas of **expert systems (ES)** and **natural language processing (NLP),** undoubtedly will have a significant effect on the design and use of CBISs. Integration of ESs with CBISs promises a significant improvement in all aspects of CBIS operations. Further improvements in AI technology will have a direct effect on CBIS architecture.

NLP, by providing a free-format interface for typical CBIS users with minimum computer training, should improve and increase CBIS use significantly. NLP should enable a user to communicate in his or her natural spoken or written language. Computers should understand optical images such as pictures and symbols. The **fifth-generation project** in Japan has specified the following goals:[1]

- Listen when spoken to; then do what it is told
- Help program itself
- Sort through facts to find and use only what is pertinent

---

[1]Richard K. Miller, *Fifth Generation Computers* (Lilburn, GA: The Fairmount Press, 1987), p. 3.

- Translate foreign languages
- Treat images and graphs the same as words
- Learn from experience

Although these goals seem somewhat ambitious, we have already experienced progress in these areas.

In parallel with NLP, the hardware components of a CBIS also should be improved. Mice, touch technology, and joystick-type interfaces make it easier for a typical user to access a CBIS. At the same time, the quality of output devices (such as graphic terminals and laser printers) should be improved and they should be reasonably priced. This may make these systems more attractive to a typical CBIS user.

Development of **automatic programming** (or code generator), one branch of AI that advocates automating the software development cycle, would be a significant accomplishment. Automatic programming would make it easier to develop, maintain, and debug software.

9–11

DEVELOPMENT IN TELE-COMMUNICATIONS

In Chapter 7 we discussed distributed data processing and **telecommunications.** During the past 50 years, telecommunication technology has undergone major improvements. This branch of computer technology started with the telephone and teletype system as the first generation. The second generation consisted of digital transmission and **pulse-code modulation.** The third generation was propelled by several major technological breakthroughs, including satellite communications, microwaves, fiber optics, and packet switching.

Packet switching (also called value-added networks) offers alternative routes between a sender and receiver. This means there will be more than one route from point A to point B, resulting in more efficiency in the entire communication system. **Encryption** also has become commonly available. Using encryption, a data item is coded, and then sent through the communication channel. At the receiving point, it is decoded. Encryption increases the security of the transmitted data. With the fourth generation of telecommunication technology, the **integrated services digital network (ISDN)** has become prevalent. An ISDN provides transmission standardization and enables the user to combine voice, video, text, and image on one line. This technology requires further development.

In the fifth generation, we will see further development in networking and enhanced telecommunication systems and improvements in security and compatibility.

Improving the quality of telecommunication systems may have a direct effect on the CBIS database. A CBIS may be able to access a variety of internal and external databases with a fast turnaround time. At the same time, such an access will be provided at a reasonable cost and with a high degree of security.

9–12

MICROCOMPUTERS

We discussed the general capabilities of microcomputers in Chapter 3. Recent advancements and the projected growth of these computers will affect CBIS design and utilization. The total number of instructions performed by all microcomputers is already larger than the total number of instructions performed by mainframes, and it seems this trend will continue. In the last few years, microcomputers have undergone major improvement. The 8086 and 8088 chips are seriously challenged by the 80286, 80386, and 80486 series. Microcomputer processing speeds have improved from 4.7 to 25 MHz (megahertz) and will possibly go to 50 MHz, and the processor size has increased from 8 bits to 32 bits. A 80386-based microcomputer can physically address 4 **gigabytes** (billion bytes) of memory, and up to 64 **terabytes** (trillion bytes) by using the virtual-addressing technique, when the memory of a computer is partitioned. The entire application program does not need to be loaded in the memory for processing, providing an almost indefinite amount of memory to a user in a given situation.

Microcomputers started as **single-user** systems and are now becoming **multiuser** systems. **Single-tasking** is evolving into **multitasking**. Compact disk read-only memory (**CD ROM**) offers mass-storage capability; one of these disks is capable of storing almost 550 **megabytes** (million bytes) of data. The CD ROM, in conjunction with laser beams, can scan a disk very rapidly.

CP/M, the major operating system for older PCs, has been almost replaced by **MS-DOS and PC-DOS**. Some manufacturers, such as AT&T, have moved to the **UNIX** operating system. IBM and Microsoft are selling a new operating system for personal computers called OS/2. Soon, a $100,000 computer will make the Cray, a $5,000,000 computer, almost obsolete. This new super minicomputer will perform at 10 **mips (million instructions per second)**. Experts have predicted an interesting outlook for microcomputers by the turn of the century. These computers will have many features, including the following:[2]

- Parallel processing power
- High storage capacity
- Read-write optical disks
- Very high resolution CRTs or flat-panel LCDs (liquid crystal displays)
- Hard copy output on typeset-quality color laser printers
- Combined communication of data, voice, and video on the same line
- A truly user-friendly interface
- CD ROM database access
- Multitasking and multiprocessing
- Processing speed of 30 million or more instructions per second
- Gallium arsenide chips instead of silicon
- Communication speed of over 19,200 bits per second (bps)
- Relatively few compatibility problems

9–13
COMPUTERS AT HOME

The advancement of computers, improved user-friendliness, and general computer awareness should significantly increase computer use by ordinary people. Improvement in telecommunication systems will make telecommuting a reality. In the not too distant future, a large portion of the work force may work at home and perform their jobs through telecommunication systems. The office of the future could be your kitchen. Via personal computers, workers at home

---

[2]Reed McManus, "In Pursuit of Tomorrow's PC," *PC World*, May, 1987, pp. 260–273.

should be able to send and receive work assignments from a central office. This approach has its advantages and disadvantages; however, it is a reality and is gaining popularity.

A massive job shortfall has been projected by the year 2010 due to the advanced applications of computers in areas such as engineering, construction, transportation, finance, government, manufacturing, trade, and services. Jobs are changing, which means education and job training need to change as well. It is not clear exactly how these changes will affect CBISs, but it is almost certain that CBISs will be a part of this transformation.

Computer development also may change the traditional arrangement at home. For example, voice synthesis and voice-recognition systems used in conjunction with robotics may control appliances such as smoke alarms and heating systems. Homes may be radically different in the future, possibly containing furniture that moves by itself and robots that listen and respond. Teleshopping also may become a reality by incorporating other senses, such as touch, smell, and taste, into the telecommunication system.[3]

These developments in computer technology may bring a significant portion of handicapped individuals into the active workforce. Patients with damaged spinal nerves causing paralyzed limbs are able to walk and ride bicycles by using attached electrodes and specially designed equipment. Using the Kurzweil reading machine, which scans typed materials and reads them back through a synthesizer, blind workers can hear and react to typed materials. The Versabraille computer enables blind students to write letters or take notes. There are several braille keyboards on the market now. These keyboards are designed for individuals with limited muscle control. Also there are keyboards that can be activated by eye movement. All of these indicate a significant change in the workforce and more applications of computers in the home.

9–14

COST TRENDS

The cost of hardware and software continues to decrease, while the quality and quantity of both are expected to increase. Cost decreases, quality improvement, and improved user-friendliness should make CBISs more attractive to organizations regardless of their size and type of operation.

9–15

WHAT IT ALL MEANS TO YOU

By examining some of the important factors surrounding computers, it is possible to make some predictions. Although it is very difficult to provide a long-range projection, we can make a prediction. By the mid-1990s, the status of the fifth-generation computer will be more clear, and a more decisive trend for the future can be ascertained. These trends are as follows:

1. The cost of hardware and software will continue to decline, meaning that it will be cheaper to process 1 byte of information in the future than it is today. This should make computers a more affordable alternative to all organizations regardless of their size and financial status.

---

[3]Edward Cornish, "Did You Hear the One About the Human Who . . .?" *ComputerWord*, November 1986, pp. 28–29.

2. AI technology and its related fields will continue to grow. This enhancement will make computers easier to use.

3. User awareness and computer literacy will improve.

4. Networking technology should improve. Issues of compatibility are becoming more manageable. Quality of communication should improve as voice, data, and images are integrated. This development should further promote distributed processing, thereby enhancing telecommuting.

5. Microcomputers will continue to improve in power and quality. This will make computers more powerful and affordable.

SUMMARY

This chapter reviewed systems professionals and career opportunities in systems fields. The discussion touched on the effect of computers in the workplace, and security, privacy, and computer crime issues. The chapter provided an outlook for several dimensions of CBIS technology. The dimensions discussed include hardware, software, computer performance, users, artificial intelligence, telecommunications, microcomputers, and computers at home. Our predictions should provide a clearer picture of CBIS technology; they also should tell you what to expect from this dynamic field in the near future.

REVIEW QUESTIONS

*These questions are answered in Appendix A.

*1. Who are systems professionals?

2. What are the responsibilities of a systems analyst?

3. What is the outlook for career opportunities in the information systems field? What are the salary ranges?

4. What are some of the negative issues of computer technology?

5. What are some of the effects of computers on the workplace?

6. What is de-skilling? Upgrading?

*7. How have computers caused de-skilling? Upgrading?

*8. What are privacy issues?

9. What is computer crime? Who are computer criminals?

10. What are some of the health-related issues? How can they be resolved?

11. What is resistance to change? How can this be minimized?

12. How many generations of computers have we seen? What is a distinguishing feature of each generation?

13. What is the main difference between the third and the fourth generation in hardware? Software? Telecommunications?

*14. What are different generations of software technology? What is a 4GL? How is a 4GL different from a traditional language like COBOL?

15. How has computer performance improved? How do you measure computer performance?

16. What is an IPS?

17. How would you describe a future computer user?

18. It has been said that the user's computer literacy will increase. Why is this claim true?

19. AI should enhance computer operation. How is this true?

*20. NLP should make the use of computers easier for a typical user. Why is this true?

21. What are the specific goals of the fifth-generation project? Are these goals realistic? Discuss.

22. Telecommunications also should improve, both in quality and quantity, in the future. Discuss.

23. What is an integrated services digital network? Is this a major factor in telecommunications of the future? Why? Discuss.

24. In what aspects will microcomputers improve?

25. What is a multitasking computer?

*26. What are some of the features of the future microcomputers?

27. What will the status of computers be in private homes in the future? What is teleshopping? Telecommuting?

28. Consult MIS journals to find out what job opportunities exist in the MIS field. Who are some of the employers of MIS professionals? What is the career path in the MIS field?

29. Consult MIS journals to find out more about the negative effects of computer technologies in general. Can we control them? Are these effects significant enough to justify the abandonment of computer use? Discuss.

30. Why are privacy issues so important in a computerized environment? What does privacy mean here? How can privacy be protected? Who are computer criminals?

31. Compare and contrast all the computer generations. What has happened from one generation to the next? What are the promises of the fifth generation?

32. How will AI revolutionize computer design and use? Is AI really something new? Is AI a reality? Discuss.

33. Consult computer/MIS literature to find out the latest on ISDNs. What is offered by ISDNs that is not found in earlier communication technologies? Will ISDNs have anything to do with telecommuting? Discuss.

KEY TERMS

Artificial intelligence	Megabytes	Programmer
Automatic programming	Microcomputer	Pulse-code modulation
CD ROM	Mips (million instructions per second)	Single-tasking
Encryption		Single user
Expert systems (ES)	MS-DOS and PC-DOS	Systems analyst
Fifth-generation project	Multitasking	Telecommunications
Gigabytes	Multiuser	Terabytes
Instructions per second (ips)	Natural language processing (NLP)	UNIX
Integrated services digital network (ISDN)	Packet switching	

ARE YOU READY TO MOVE ON?

Multiple Choice

1. Computers in the workplace have
   a. not created any jobs
   b. not eliminated any jobs
   c. reduced production costs
   d. not had a direct effect on the nature of jobs performed
   e. increased production time

2. Although many companies are installing computer systems and computerized databases, they sometimes do not reveal their purpose to the workers because

   a. the workers would not understand computers

   b. these systems can be used to monitor employee efficiency without the employee's knowledge.

   c. these systems have nothing to do with the workers

   d. the workers are not affected

   e. all of the above

3. Most computer crimes are committed by

   a. insiders

   b. extremists

   c. hackers

   d. MIS students

   e. none of the above

4. In general, physical problems associated with VDTs are more likely associated with

   a. the VDT unit

   b. the computer unit

   c. the person operating the equipment

   d. the environment in which the computers are located

   e. none of the above

5. An attribute of fourth-generation computers is

   a. integrated circuits

   b. vacuum tubes

   c. transistors

   d. telecommunications

   e. very large scale integration

6. A major attribute of the so-called fifth generation of computers is

   a. parallel processing

   b. serial processing

   c. gallium arsenide technology

   d. both a and b

   e. both a and c

7. NLP should improve and increase the utilization of a CBIS significantly by

   a. providing a free-format interface

   b. standardizing user input to a few sets of commands

   c. minimizing training

   d. both a and c

   e. both b and c

8. Packet switching offers

   a. alternative communication routes

   b. alternative I/O paths

   c. alternative hardware/software combinations

   d. alternative user input options

   e. alternative user output options

9. Trends in the advancement of computer technology and fifth-generation computers include

   a. an increase in hardware and software costs

    b. a decrease in improvements in networking technology

    c. an increase in AI technology

    d. a decrease in the importance of microcomputers

    e. all of the above

10. Telecommuting describes

    a. the use of computers to get street maps for navigation

    b. working at home and performing one's job through telecommunication systems

    c. video conferencing

    d. E-mail

    e. office automation

True/False

1. Computers have improved our way of life dramatically; there are no negative effects.

2. Computers can change the organizational structure of a company from a pyramid to a diamond structure.

3. MIS practitioners must decide who should have access to confidential information and to what extent in order to prevent misuse.

4. Because computers are so complex, computer criminals cannot do much damage.

5. There is no conclusive study to indicate that VDTs have caused health problems.

6. Psychological problems associated with computer technology are primarily associated with the desire to change and not being allowed to do so.

7. Computer performance, as measured in terms of the number of instructions performed per second, has increased dramatically over the years.

8. Development in AI technology should not have a significant impact on the future design and implementation of CBISs.

9. Encryption is done to increase the security of transmitted data.

10. Microcomputer technology has grown dramatically in the past but has now reached its limits and cannot improve any further.

ANSWERS	**Multiple Choice**	**True/False**
	1. c	**1.** F
	2. b	**2.** T
	3. a	**3.** T
	4. d	**4.** F
	5. e	**5.** T
	6. e	**6.** F
	7. d	**7.** T
	8. a	**8.** F
	9. c	**9.** T
	10. b	**10.** F

Appendix A
Information Systems Literacy

A–1

WHAT'S HAPPENING INSIDE YOUR COMPUTER: NUMBER SYSTEMS

In grade school you learned a number system called the decimal system. In this system, there are 10 digits (0 through 9) and the base is 10. As an example, consider the number 15. You can break it down into five sets of 1s and one set of 10, as follows:

$$15 = (5 * 10^0) + (1 * 10^1) = 5 + 10 = 15$$

However, this is not the system used by computers. Computers either use base 2 (binary), base 8 (octal) or base 16 (hexadecimal).

A computer switch can be either on or off, so many times the computer uses base 2 to represent numbers as combinations of voltage on (1) or voltage off (0).

To show you how numbers are presented in a binary system, consider the number 8. To find the binary representation of the number 8, divide 8 by 2, getting a remainder of either 0 or 1, as follows:

	Quotient	Remainder
8/2	4	0
4/2	2	0
2/2	1	0
1/2	0	1

If you arrange the remainders in reverse order, you have the binary representation of the decimal number 8. So the number 8 in base 10 is equal to 1000 in base 2. You can easily get back to the original number (8) by multiplying from right to left as follows:

$$0 * 2^0 + 0 * 2^1 + 0 * 2^2 + 1 * 2^3 = 8$$

Base 8 (octal) is very similar to base 2 with one difference. In this base, there are 8 digits (0 through 7). Let's convert the number 22 from base 10 to base 8:

	Quotient	Remainder
22/8	2	6
2/8	0	2

So the number 22 in base 10 is the same as 26 in base 8. To reverse the process, do the following:

$$6 * 8^0 + 2 * 8^1 = 6 + 16 = 22$$

which is 6 sets of ones and 2 sets of eight.

The hexadecimal system is very similar to the base 2 or base 8 systems. In this base there are 16 digits (0 through 15). To eliminate the confusion, the digits 10 through 15 are represented by the letters A through F. Let's convert the number 50 from base 10 to base 16.

	Quotient	Remainder
$50/16$	3	2
$3/16$	0	3

The number 50 in base 10 converts to 32 in base 16. To reverse the process, do the following:

$$2 * 16^0 + 3 * 16^1 = 2 + 48 = 50$$

which is 2 sets of ones and 3 sets of sixteen.

This same method can be followed for converting a number from one base to any other base. For example, what is the equivalent of 37 from base 8 to

Table A–1
Numbers 1 through 25 in
Four Number Systems

Decimal	Binary	Octal	Hexadecimal
0	0	0	0
1	1	1	1
2	10	2	2
3	11	3	3
4	100	4	4
5	101	5	5
6	110	6	6
7	111	7	7
8	1000	10	8
9	1001	11	9
10	1010	12	A
11	1011	13	B
12	1100	14	C
13	1101	15	D
14	1110	16	E
15	1111	17	F
16	10000	20	10
17	10001	21	11
18	10010	22	12
19	10011	23	13
20	10100	24	14
21	10101	25	15
22	10110	26	16
23	10111	27	17
24	11000	30	18
25	11001	31	19

base 16? To do this, we first must convert 37 from base 8 to base 10 and then convert this new number from base 10 to base 16:

$$7 * 8^0 + 3 * 8^1 = 7 + 24 = 31$$

	Quotient	**Remainder**
$^{13}/_{16}$	1	15
$^1/_{16}$	0	1

Remember, number 15 in base 16 is represented by the character F, so now you know that 37 in base 8 is the same as 1F in hexadecimal.

Table A−1 shows the numbers 1 through 25 in four different number systems. Try to verify this table.

A–2
INFORMATION SYSTEMS GLOSSARY

accounting software Software that performs accounting tasks, such as general ledgers and accounts payable.

acoustic coupler A device used with a telephone line for sending and receiving computer messages.

adapter cards Cards used to attach a particular option to the system unit.

adaptive design A methodology that advocates an evolving process in building a CBIS.

ALU (arithmetic logic unit) A part of the computer that performs arithmetic and logical operations.

analog computer A computer that works on a continuous process, such as pressure or temperature.

arithmetic operations Addition, subtraction, multiplication, and division used to process data.

artificial intelligence A series of related technologies that try to reproduce human-thought behavior, including thinking, speaking, feeling, and reasoning.

ASCII format The American Standard Code for Information Interchange uses a 7-bit presentation divided into zone and digit parts. The zone part uses different combinations of 0's and 1's. For numbers, the zone part is always 011 and the digit part is a combination of 0's and 1's, except for zero itself.

assembly language Uses a series of short codes, or mnemonics, to represent data or instructions to the computer.

asynchronous A mode of transmission where each character is sent through a channel as an independent message. Each message is one character long. The character is preceded by a start bit and ends with a stop bit.

automatic programming Automates the software development cycle. Makes it easier to develop, maintain, and debug software.

bar code An input device that uses laser light to read codes.

BASIC (beginner's all-purpose symbolic instruction code) A high-level computer language used by the majority of microcomputers.

batch processing Data are sent to the computer on a periodic basis.

binary system A number system that uses two digits (0 and 1) and the base is 2.

built-in functions or formulas Already available within the application program. The program directly calculates these formulas. The user will provide only the values needed by the function.

C A high-level computer language known for its power to exercise full control over the existing hardware.

CD ROM (compact disk read only memory) A permanent device on which information is recorded. It is similar to an audio compact disk and it can be duplicated.

centralized processing Uses one central location for performing the entire data-processing task.

CGA (color graphics adapter) A monitor that displays 320-by-200 pixels.

coaxial cable A communication line used to connect the sender to the receiver.

COBOL (common business oriented language) A high-level computer language used mostly for business applications.

communication control unit (CCU) A microcomputer or minicomputer serving as a front-end processor in a network.

communication lines Connect the sender to the receiver.

communications software Used with a modem to connect the user with the information available in public and private databases.

compact disk A storage device that offers mass storage capability.

computer A machine that accepts data as input, processes data without human interference using a set of stored instructions (programs), and outputs information.

computer-aided design (CAD) Software used for drafting and design purposes.

computer-based information system (CBIS) An organized integration of hardware/software technologies and human elements designed to produce timely, integrated, accurate, and useful information for decision-making purposes.

computer file An electronic document specified by a unique name.

computer program Instructions written in a language understood by a computer.

computer security Measures taken to keep computer hardware and software protected from controllable, partially controllable, and uncontrollable threats.

computer virus A series of self-propagating codes that are triggered by a specified time or event within the computer system.

concentration An advanced version of multiplexing. For example, a 6,400 bps line may be shared by four 3,200 slower lines.

constants Constants always have fixed values.

control unit Tells the computer what to do and how to do it.

CP/M (control program microcomputer) An operating system for PCs. Used to be the major operating system.

CPM (critical path method) A project management tool to control the duration of a CBIS.

CPU (central processing unit) The heart of the computer. It is divided into the ALU and the control unit.

CRT (cathode ray tube) An output device—a screen similar to a TV screen.

cursor A special character that indicates the user's present position on the computer screen or acts as an indicator (pointer) to focus attention to a specific point on the display monitor.

data Raw facts entered into the computer.

database A collection of related data stored in a central location.

database administrator (DBA) The person who designs and implements databases.

database machine A dedicated DBMS that serves as a back-end processor to the main computer system.

database management system (DBMS) A series of computer programs that creates, stores, maintains, and accesses a database.

database software   A computer program that performs database applications.

data communications   The electronic transfer of data from one location to another.

data flow diagram (DFD)   A graphic tool that depicts the operation of a system.

data model   A procedure for creating and maintaining a database.

data representation   Computers use a special format to represent data. Every character, number, symbol, and so forth, is represented as a binary number in the memory of the computer. Two common formats are ASCII and EBCDIC.

data tablet   An input device with small pad and a pen. Menus generated by the user on the pad can be transferred to the computer.

decentralized processing   A decentralized arrangement where each office, department, or division has its own computer.

decimal system   A number system that uses 10 digits (0 through 9) and the base is 10.

decision support system (DSS)   A computer-based information system consisting of hardware, software, and the human element designed to assist decision-makers at any organizational level. The emphasis is on semistructured and unstructured tasks.

desktop publishing software   Software used to produce professional-quality documents (with or without graphics).

digital computer   Works on numbers (discrete process).

direct conversion (crash conversion)   The old system is stopped and the new system implemented.

disk drive   A device used to read and store data and information.

disk operating system   A collection of programs that run the entire operation of your microcomputer.

distributed data processing (DDP)   Has centralized control and at the same time maintains decentralized operations. The processing power is distributed among several locations.

EBCDIC format (extended binary coded decimal interchange code)   Uses an 8-bit presentation divided into two 4-bit presentations. The first half is the zone half and the second half is the digit half.

economic order quantity (EOQ)   The order amount that minimizes the total cost of inventory.

EGA (enhanced graphics adapter)   A monitor that displays 640-by-350 resolution in 16 colors.

electromechanical data processing   With this processing, data must be in machine-readable form. This processing improves speed and accuracy compared to mechanical data processing.

electronic data processing (EDP)   Using computers to expedite data processing. Usually applied to structured tasks.

electronic mail (E-mail)   With E-mail, messages are delivered electronically.

encryption   A security measure that mixes up characters and forms codes to prevent access to unauthorized users.

EPROM (erasable programmable read only memory)   Memory that can be programmed and erased and programmed again.

erasable optical disk   Information can be recorded and erased repeatedly. Used for high-volume storage and updating.

executive information system (EIS)   EIS delivers only information critical to a decision-maker and is user- or problem-driven.

expert systems   Systems that mimic human expertise in a particular discipline in order to solve a specific problem in a well-defined area.

FAX (facsimile)   Sends hardcopy documents from one location to another through an ordinary telephone line.

feasibility study   The system analyst or a team of system analysts try to investigate the feasibility of the solution proposed to resolve the problem.

fiber optics   A communication line with high-quality transmission, high throughput, and high security. Major communication means of the future.

fifth-generation project   A project in Japan that is trying to get a computer to listen when spoken to, then repeat what it's told, program itself, translate foreign languages, and several other goals.

financial information systems   Provide financial information to finance executives in a timely manner.

financial planning software   This software works with large amounts of data and performs diverse financial analyses.

flat-file model   A file or series of files containing a series of records and fields. No relationships exists among the files.

floppy disk   A disk made of plastic material coated with magnetic material. Used to store data.

flowchart   A graphical tool used for outlining a computer program.

FORTRAN (formula translator)   A high-level computer language used mostly for scientific applications.

fourth-generation language (4GL)   A computer language that is nonprocedural and more forgiving than previous languages and that uses "macro codes." A very powerful language.

full duplex   A line configuration in which communications can take place in both directions at the same time.

function   A built-in formula within the computer software that performs various calculations.

gallium arsenide   Material used to build the main memory of the fifth-generation computers.

Gantt chart   A project-management tool used to control the implementation of a CBIS.

gigabyte   1 billion bytes.

graphics software   Presents data in a graphic format.

half-duplex   Line configuration where communication takes place in both directions but not at the same time.

hard copy   Output printed by a printer.

hard disk   A storage device connected to the computer. Stores large amounts of information.

hardware trend   The developments of computer hardware. There are five generations of computer hardware. Computers today are faster, more reliable, and easier to program and maintain.

heuristics   General rules. Basic knowledge available in a discipline.

hexadecimal system   Base 16. A number system that uses digits 0 through 9 and letters A through F. A is equal to 10, B is equal to 11, and so forth.

hierarchical model   A data model made up of nodes and branches connected by common fields. This model resembles an upside-down tree.

high-level languages   The third generation of computer languages. They are user- and application-oriented and easier to learn than the earlier generations of languages.

information   Processed facts that are used for decision-making purposes. What the computer outputs.

information systems life cycle (ISLC)   The four stages of introduction, growth, maturity, and decline in every computer-based information system.

input device   Device used to enter data into the computer (a keyboard or mouse, for example).

instructions per second (ips)   Computer performance is measured in terms of the number of instructions (calculations) performed per second.

integrated circuits   Third generation of computer memory. Also called chip technology.

intersection operation   A DBMS function that generates the intersection of two relations in a third relation containing a common tuple (row).

interview   A tool for fact finding used by systems analysts. By talking to people, the analysts can discover problem areas and obtain opinions regarding the implementation of the new system.

ISDN (integrated services digital network)   A communication system that combines voice, data, and images on the same line.

join operation   A DBMS function that combines two or more files, tables, or relations within one database on a common field to generate the third file, table, or relation.

joy stick   An input device to access a computer-based information system.

keyboard   An input device similar to a typewriter. It has certain keys not available in a typical typewriter.

kilobyte   1,024 bytes.

LAN (local area network)   This network system typically limits its operations to a certain geographical area and is usually owned by one company.

laser printer   Output device used for high-quality printed output.

life-cycle approach   A methodology for systems analysis and design, particularly in EDP/MIS areas. Includes a series of well-defined steps.

light pen   An input device similar to a conventional pen connected to the terminal with a cable. It is used mostly for drafting and design purposes.

logical operation   Compares two numbers or characters to find which is larger or smaller.

logistic information system   An information system that provides information for managing all the machinery and equipment in an organization.

machine language   A computer language that uses a series of 0's and 1's to represent data or instructions to the computer.

main memory devices   The main memory of a computer system made of semiconductor, or bubble memory.

management information system   An information system that produces timely, accurate, and useful information for middle management on a scheduled basis. Same as CBIS.

manual data processing   An information system that processes data manually.

manufacturing information system   An information system that produces timely information regarding total inventory costs, order amounts, and quantity of orders.

mechanical data processing   Mechanical devices are used to improve speed and accuracy of data processing. An improvement over manual data processing.

megabyte   Approximately one million bytes.

megahertz (MHz) A unit of measurement equal to one million electrical cycles per second. A way to measure a microcomputer processing speed.

microcomputer Smallest type of computer in terms of memory, size, speed, and sophistication.

micrographics The process of reducing texts and graphs to a fraction of their size and storing them on film.

microwave A communication line with short-range waves used for short-range communication.

middle-out approach A system-design methodology that begins close to the level of the problem at hand, and then develops a process of generalizing and specifying at each stage of the problem-solving process. Advocates the use of a prototype.

miniaturization Computers have become smaller in size; therefore, more data and information can be stored in a smaller space.

MIPS (millions of instructions per second) A measure of computer performance.

modem A device which converts digital signals into analog signals that can be transferred over a regular telephone line. It also converts analog signals to digital before the signal enters to the computer.

mouse An input device to draw, write, and choose options from the menu. An interface method to make it easier for users to access a computer.

MS-DOS/PC-DOS The major operating systems for PCs. PC-DOS is used by IBM, and MS-DOS is used in IBM compatibles.

multiplexing A relatively fast line is divided into several slower lines so many terminals can use one single line.

multitasking Computers doing more than one task at a time.

multiuser More than one user using a computer system at the same time.

natural language processing (NLP) A computer language that is supposed to enable a computer user to communicate with the computer in his/her native language.

network model A data model in which records and fields are linked by fields that are not related. One-to-many or many-to-many relationships are possible.

network topologies Different architectures for a network system. They include star, ring, bus, tree, and web networks.

non-numeric data Alphanumeric data, including any type of valid character.

numeric data Any combination of digits 0 through 9. These can be integers (whole numbers) or real (with decimal points) numbers.

observation A system design methodology that includes observing workers and workflow to discover the problem area.

octal system Base 8. A number system that uses eight digits (0 through 7).

office automation A series of related technologies to make office operation more effective. They include word processing, electronic mail, electronic message distribution, and so forth.

operating system A series of computer programs that manages the computer's resources.

optical disk A storage device that stores large amounts of data in a very small space.

optical technology A type of storage device still in the beginning stages of development. Storage devices using this technology are revolutionizing the computer field by allowing large amounts of data to be stored in a very small space.

OS2 A new operating system for PCs used by IBM and Microsoft Corporation.

output device Devices used to output data and information from a computer.

packet switching   Offers alternative routes between a sender and receiver. Offers more than one route from point a to point b.

parallel conversion   A conversion methodology where the old system and the new system run simultaneously for a short time in order to ensure that the new system operates properly.

parallel processing   Multiple central processing units in a computer.

Pascal   A high-level computer language named for Blaise Pascal. It is known for its structure and portability.

PBX (private branch exchange) network   A computer system that performs telephone signal switching.

permanent area   Work stays in this area until it is erased.

personnel information system   An information system that provides information to assist decision-makers in the personnel department to carry out their tasks in a more effective way.

PERT (program evaluation review technique)   A project management tool used to control the development process of a CBIS.

phased-in, phased-out conversion   A conversion methodology where as each module of the new system is converted, the corresponding part of the old system is retired. This process continues until the entire system is converted.

pilot conversion   A conversion methodology where the analyst introduces the system to a limited section of the organization and enhances the system to work for the rest of the organization.

pixel   The smallest picture element that a device can display on-screen. Displayed images are made up of pixels.

post-implementation audit   Attempts to verify the suitability of the system after the implementation. The analyst team collects data and talks with users, customers, and others affected by the new system to make sure that the system is doing what it is designed to do.

primary memory   Main memory that is a part of the central processing unit.

priority of operations (order of precedence)   The order in which the computer performs arithmetic operations from the highest priority to the lowest are:

1. Expression inside parentheses.
2. Exponentiation.
3. Multiplication and division.
4. Addition and subtraction.
5. Proceed from left to right when there are more than two operations with the same priority.

problem definition   The user and the designer of the system try to define and understand the problem faced by the organization.

programmer   The person who designs and codes the application programs and maintains the system programs.

programming flowchart   A graphical tool that assists the programmer in depicting the logical flow of the program.

project management software   A software that assists the user to control both time and budget in performing a complex project.

projection operation   A special case of a general query operation that may generate a subset of the fields.

PROM (programmable read only memory)   This memory can be programmed by a special device, but once programmed it cannot be erased.

prototyping   A methodology for CBIS construction. A small-scale version of the system under investigation that is significant enough to highlight the value of the system to the user.

pulse code modulation   Second generation of telecommunications.

query operation   Searches the database for specific information that meets a particular condition.

questionnaire   A system-design methodology that asks many questions to identify the problem areas.

RAM (random access memory)   The main memory of the computer. It is volatile: if there is a power failure, the information in this memory will be lost.

relational model   A data model that uses a mathematical construct of rows and columns of data. Relations can be linked by the common field.

revised approach   Integrates problem definition, formation of the task force, construction of an on-line prototype, and evaluation in one integrated approach. This methodology is implemented by an iterative process.

robot   A machine that is used in manufacturing. It usually has a fixed arm and sometimes has limited vision. It is controlled by a computer and a program.

ROM (read only memory)   A prefabricated chip that stores some general-purpose instructions or programs.

satellite   A communication line that collects satellite waves and covers a broad geographical range but is not completely secure. Used for long-range communication.

secondary memory   Auxiliary memory used for mass data storage. Includes magnetic tape, magnetic disk, and optical disk.

semistructured tasks   Tasks not as well-defined by standard operating procedures as structured tasks are.

simplex   Communication that takes place in only one direction.

single tasking   Computers doing one task at a time.

single user   A computer that can be used by one person at a time.

soft copy   Output presented on a CRT.

sort operation   Puts the database in a specific order.

spreadsheet software   A computer software that manipulates a matrix (table) of data.

structured tasks   A well-defined standard operating procedure that exists for the execution of structured tasks.

synchronous   A mode of transmission in which several characters are blocked together for transmission. At the beginning and end of each block there are empty bits.

system flowchart   A graphical device that illustrates the entire operation of a system.

systems analysis   The system analyst or a team of analysts specifically define the problem and determine possible alternatives for solving it.

systems analyst   The person who defines the information requirements of the user and interacts with the user at one end and with the data processing personnel at the other end to define the specific needs of the users.

systems design   A team of analysts tries to choose the alternative that is the most realistic and presents the highest payoff to the organization. The details of the proposed solution are outlined.

systems implementation   The solution is transferred from paper into action. Acquisition of new equipment, hiring of new employees, training employees, physical planning and layout design, coding and testing, and conversion planning and documentation take place.

systems professionals   A group of experts working in the MIS field that includes programmers, systems analysts, technicians, and so forth.

task force design   Includes representatives from different user departments, top management, and technical staff. There should be a continuous discussion among the task force representatives until the users' needs are precisely defined.

telecommunications   The use of computers, phone lines, and electronics to allow several people to communicate at the same time from different locations.

telecommuting   Working at home, sending and receiving work assignments through a personal computer.

teleconferencing   An interactive electronic communication among several people in several locations.

teletype   One of the first types of telecommunications.

temporary area   Any work in this area will disappear if the computer is turned off. Same as RAM.

terabyte   Approximately one trillion bytes.

touch technology   This technology enables the user to choose options from the computer by placing his finger on the choice. An interface that makes it easier for a user to access a CBIS.

transaction processing   A transaction is processed as soon as it occurs.

transistors   Second generation of computer memory.

twisted pair (telephone line)   Communication lines used to connect the sender to the receiving end.

unix operating system   Operating system used by companies such as AT&T. It is a multitasking operating system.

unstructured tasks   These are unique in nature, are mostly nonrecurring, and have no standard operating procedure that pertains to their implementation.

user   Utilizes the information provided by the computer-based information system for decision-making purposes.

user-defined functions or formulas   A combination of computer addresses designed to perform a certain task.

vacuum tubes   First generation of computer memory. They were bulky, unreliable, and generated excessive amounts of heat.

variables   Valid computer addresses that hold different values. A variable holds one value at any one time.

very large scale integration (VLSI)   Putting more than 100,000 transistors on one semiconductor chip.

VGA (video graphics array)   Video display of 640-by-480 resolution in 16 colors and 320-by-200 resolution in 256 colors.

virtual addressing   A method of apparently extending the computer's RAM.

voice mail   Sending and receiving messages through a telephone line.

voice recognition system   An input device uses voice digitizer in order to transfer the user's voice to the computer.

WAN (wide area network)   A network system that has no geographical limit.

wild card   Characters such as an asterisk and a question mark that can represent any other character(s).

word processing software   Generates documents, makes deletions and insertions, and cuts and pastes electronically.

WORM disk (write once, read many)   A permanent device on which information can be recorded once but cannot be altered. It cannot be duplicated.

A–3

ANSWERS TO SELECTED REVIEW QUESTIONS

Chapter 1

2. A computer program is a series of instructions that tells a computer what to do.

8. Accuracy and speed.

14. Comparison operations are called logical operations. For example, has the employee worked over 40?

16. We have seen four generations and are beginning to see the fifth generation.

19. Because everything inside the computers is represented in binary format.

Chapter 2

1. Keyboard. Because it has been around for years.

4. Ambiguity in our native language, idioms, the different frequencies of different voices, several meanings for the same word, and so forth.

6. Semiconductor and bubble memory.

11. Speed, quality, noise, and cost.

16. Machine, assembly, high-level, 4GL, and natural language processing (NLP). Machine language is closest to the computer's language and NLP is closest to human language.

19. Because COBOL handles non-numeric data very well, it generates nice looking output and numerous business programs have already been written in COBOL.

Chapter 3

2. Disk drive and keyboard.

6. Floppy and hard disks.

12. It varies. It starts at 256 or 512.

16. Keep it in a dust-free environment. Protect it against excessive heat and humidity. Provide a constant electrical current.

21. Every application program provides an editing feature so you can edit your mistakes. Or, in the worst case, you can retype your mistakes.

26. Priority of operations or precedence of operations refers to the order in which a computer handles calculations. The order is as follows:

- Expressions inside parentheses have the highest priority
- Exponentiation (raising to power) has the next highest priority
- Multiplication and division have the third highest priority
- Addition and subtraction have the fourth highest priority
- When there are two or more operations with the same priority, operations proceed from left to right

Chapter 4

3. EDP, MIS, DSS, and EIS.

6. EDP→data, MIS→information, and DSS→decision.

9. LAN, WAN, E-mail, facsimile, voice mail, and so forth.

15. There are numerous applications of expert systems and they are steadily increasing. Some of the current applications include medicine, geology, computer design, and chemistry. R1/XCON, DIPMETER ADVISOR, and MYCIN are some examples.

21. Manpower, materials, machineries, and money.

Chapter 5

3. Financial ratios can be misleading. Financial statements can be manipulated to generate desirable financial ratios that may not reflect the true picture of the financial strength of a company.

9. Annual sales
Ordering cost
Single unit cost
Percentage of inventory value allotted for
Carrying costs

14. Price, promotion, place, and product.

17. Input data include personal data, skill data, and job market data. Output data include recruitment analysis, scheduling assignment, work force planning, and affirmative action statistics.

20. Strategic planning is concerned with the long-term goals of an organization. For example, introduction of a new product, new marketing campaign, new plant, and so forth.

Chapter 6

3. Designing and implementing a database, establishing security measures, documenting the database, and so forth.

7. A data model is a procedure for creating and maintaining a database. The popular data models are relational, hierarchical, and network.

13. Union compatibility means that two relations (tables) must include the same type and the same number of fields.

16. A distributed database should increase the responsiveness of a CBIS by providing localized access. The user receives data in an immediate mode.

20. Database machines improve the efficiency of database processing by devoting an entire CPU to the database tasks. This should improve the overall data processing operations by freeing the main computer from database processing and devoting its entire processing power to other data processing tasks.

Chapter 7

6. Modulation means conversion of digital signals to analog signals. Demodulation means conversion of analog signals to digital signals.

10. Distributed processing is a type of data processing where processing power is distributed over several locations. This may include distribution of databases, input/output devices, CPUs, and so forth.

14. Star, bus, web, hierarchy, and ring.

19. Teleconferencing enables two or more decision-makers to communicate with each other through communication channels. The main advantage of a teleconferencing

system is that a decision-maker can participate in various decision-making processes without leaving the office. Cost savings is another major advantage of a teleconferencing system.

22. ISDN is used wherever voice, data, and images are combined and transmitted over the same line. ISDN has numerous applications in an automated office. These may include networking, E-mail, message distribution, and so forth.

25. A computer virus is a series of self-propagating program codes that are triggered by a specified time or event within the computer system.

Chapter 8

4. There are six steps:

   1. problem definition
   2. feasibility study
   3. systems analysis
   4. systems design
   5. systems implementation and
   6. post-implementation audit

7. Social feasibility studies the acceptance level of the new system by the employees. It also investigates the intangible cost of the new system. This may include employees' satisfaction, turnover, and resistance to change.

15. A prototype is a small-scale version of the new system. It is significant enough in order to highlight the major operations of the new system.

16. Middle-out approach combines top-down and bottom-up methodologies into a single approach and studies the problem at hand. It starts with a prototype and improves the prototype in successive stages of development.

19. Task force is a group that includes the representatives of various users in an organization. It usually includes representatives from top management, accounting, marketing, production, and personnel departments.

Chapter 9

1. There are many job titles in the MIS field. Programmers, systems analysts, operators, DBAs, and technicians are a few examples.

7. When computers take over drafting and design tasks, this causes de-skilling. When computers perform repetitive word processing and clerical tasks, this causes upgrading.

8. Privacy issues are concerned with unauthorized access to personal information. This may include financial information, health information, and so forth.

14. They started as machine language, assembly language, high-level language, 4GL, and natural language processing. A 4GL language (fourth-generation language) is more forgiving. It is non-procedural, more powerful, and easier to learn and use than previous computer languages.

20. Because a fully operational NLP will allow a user to issue a command in his/her native language. No typing is required.

26. Multitasking, large main and secondary memories, higher speed, and lower costs.

Appendix B
A Quick Trip with MS- and PC-DOS

B-1

INTRODUCTION

In this appendix, we explain the basics of the disk operating system (DOS). We define the differences between internal and external DOS commands, and explain how you use system time and date. We review file specifications in the DOS environment and discuss how to use the DIR command. Important keys are highlighted, and you learn how to create a data disk using the FORMAT command. We also review the different versions of MS- and PC-DOS. The appendix concludes with a table summarizing most of the important DOS commands.[1]

B-2

TURNING ON YOUR PC

When you access a personal computer, it is either on or off. If the computer is off, put the DOS disk into drive A and turn on the computer (DOS comes with the computer). This procedure is called a **cold boot** (boot means starting the computer).

If the computer is already on, insert the DOS disk into drive A and press Ctrl-Alt-Del (press all three keys simultaneously). This procedure is called a **warm boot**. A warm boot is faster than a cold boot because the computer does not check its memory when you do a warm boot.

When the computer is booted, it prompts you for the current date. Enter the date in the format requested (mm-dd-yy) and press Enter. Next, the computer requests the current time. Enter the time in the correct format (hh:mm:ss) and press Enter. Remember that DOS operates on a 24-hour clock. This means that 2:30 p.m., for example, is entered as 14:30.

You should see the A> prompt, which indicates that the necessary portions of DOS have been loaded into random-access memory (RAM) and drive A is the default drive. Default means that this is the drive the computer will use unless you indicate otherwise. If DOS is installed on your hard disk (which is usually drive C), your default drive will be C.

You can avoid entering the date and time by pressing Enter at the prompts. Your PC will then use the default date and time when saving files. However, it is a good habit to enter the correct date and time each time you start your computer. That way you know your files will be saved with the current time and date stamps. The correct date and time help you determine the most or least recent versions of your files in a directory. (A directory is a listing of all your files.)

If you forget to enter the current date and time at boot-up, you can enter this information at any time with the DATE and TIME commands. At the A> prompt, type *DATE* and press Enter. The computer prompts you to enter the current date in the format mm-dd-yy. Type the date and press Enter. To enter the current time, type *TIME* at the A> prompt and press Enter. You are prompted to enter a new time in the format hh:mm:ss. Then press Enter. The computer holds this information in memory and updates it automatically until you turn off your computer. Some computers have a battery-operated clock on

---

[1]For a detailed discussion of DOS commands, see *Information Systems Literacy and Software Productivity Tools: DOS* by Hossein Bidgoli (Macmillan, 1991).

their motherboard, which keeps the time and date current even when the computer is turned off.

Internal commands (sometimes called memory-resident commands) are those commands that are loaded into the computer at boot-up. You can use internal commands without the DOS disk in a drive. CLS (clear screen) is an example of an internal DOS command. If you type *CLS* and press Enter, your screen is cleared.

External commands (sometimes called non-memory-resident commands) are those commands that you can execute only when the DOS disk is in a drive. These commands are sometimes called DOS utilities. They are separate programs stored on the DOS disk. DISKCOPY (disk copy), for example, is an external DOS command. You can find a listing of most of these commands at the end of this appendix.

B–3
DOS PROMPTS

Depending on how you start your computer, you will see different prompts. If you have a hard disk and you boot your system from it, your prompt will probably be C>. The prompt indicates the current default drive. The computer uses the default drive unless you specify a different one. Changing the default drive is an easy task. For example, if the default drive is A (indicated by the A> prompt) and you want to change it to drive B, at the A> prompt, type *B:* and press Enter. You prompt should now be B>. To change it back, type *A:* and press Enter. You can customize the DOS prompt with the PROMPT command.

B–4
DOS FILE SPECIFICATIONS

DOS files follow the same general naming conventions as other software. A DOS file name can be up to eight characters long and can contain the digits 0 through 9, as well as special characters, such as an underscore (_) and a pound sign (#). Usually, you should avoid using special symbols.

File extensions can be up to three characters long, and they follow the same conventions as file names. Important file extensions in the DOS environment include the following:

- BAK—Backup files are generated by some word processing, spreadsheet, and database management programs. BAK files are backup copies of original files.
- BAT—Batch files are text files that the user generates. Batch files contain DOS commands that are executed when you type the name of the file.
- COM—Command files can be executed by typing the name of the file.
- EXE—Like COM files, you run executable files by typing the file name.
- SYS—System files can be used only by DOS.

B–5
THE DIR COMMAND

If you type *DIR* and press Enter, you will receive a listing of your current directory. It will resemble the listing shown in figure B–1. At the top of this

Figure B–1
A Directory Listing

```
DIR

 Volume in drive A is MSDOS_330A
 Directory of  A:\

ANSI     SYS     1647    3-01-88    8:00a
APPEND   EXE     5794    3-01-88    8:00a
ASSIGN   COM     1530    3-01-88    8:00a
ATTRIB   EXE    10656    3-01-88    8:00a
CHKDSK   COM     9819    3-01-88    8:00a
COMMAND  COM    25308    3-01-88    8:00a
COMP     COM     4183    3-01-88    8:00a
COUNTRY  SYS    11254    3-01-88    8:00a
DISKCOMP COM     5848    3-01-88    8:00a
DISKCOPY COM     6264    3-01-88    8:00a
DISPLAY  SYS    11259    3-01-88    8:00a
DRIVER   SYS     1165    3-01-88    8:00a
EDLIN    COM     7495    3-01-88    8:00a
EXE2BIN  EXE     3050    3-01-88    8:00a
FASTOPEN EXE     3888    3-01-88    8:00a
FDISK    COM    48983    3-01-88    8:00a
FIND     EXE     6403    3-01-88    8:00a
FORMAT   COM    11671    3-01-88    8:00a
GRAFTABL COM     6136    3-01-88    8:00a
GRAPHICS COM    13943    3-01-88    8:00a
JOIN     EXE     9612    3-01-88    8:00a
KEYB     COM     9041    3-01-88    8:00a
LABEL    COM     2346    3-01-88    8:00a
MODE     COM    15440    3-01-88    8:00a
MORE     COM      282    3-01-88    8:00a
NLSFUNC  EXE     3029    3-01-88    8:00a
PRINT    COM     9011    3-01-88    8:00a
RECOVER  COM     4268    3-01-88    8:00a
SELECT   COM     4132    3-01-88    8:00a
SORT     EXE     1946    3-01-88    8:00a
SUBST    EXE    10552    3-01-88    8:00a
SYS      COM     4725    3-01-88    8:00a
TREE     COM     3540    3-01-88    8:00a
        33 File(s)    19456 bytes free

A>
```

figure, you can see that the volume in drive A is MSDOS-3.30A, which is the internal name for this disk. You can use the LABEL command to change the volume names of your disks.

The DIR command displays the name of each file, the file extension, the size of the file in bytes, and the date and time at which the file was created. At the end of the listing, you see the number of files in the current directory and the number of bytes available on the disk.

You can use the DIR command with wild card characters. DOS accepts the asterisk (*) and the question mark (?) as wild cards. These characters substitute for other characters in the file name or extension. The ? substitutes for only one character; the * can substitute for one or more characters. For example, if you type

DIR PLAN?.MON

DOS lists all the files that begin with PLAN and end with .MON, such as PLAN1.MON, PLAN2.MON, or PLANA.MON. If you type

DIR *.MON

DOS lists all the .MON files, such as LETTER.MON, 123.MON, or CHART_1.MON.

B-6
USING DIR WITH SWITCHES

You can use the DIR command with different switches (parameters) to provide different types of listings. The /W switch lists your files in a wide format. Only the file names and extensions are listed. For example, we generated the wide listing of our drive A shown in figure B-2 by placing our DOS disk in drive A and typing *DIR/W*.

When you use the /P switch, DOS pauses when a directory listing fills your screen and waits for you to press a key before it continues listing files. In figure B-3, we used the DIR/P command to display the directory of drive A.

You can use the DIR command to list files on any drive, regardless of whether it is the current drive. For example, if your current drive is A and you want to see a listing of drive B, type

DIR B:

Remember to include at least one space between the DIR command and the drive name.

B-7
IMPORTANT KEYS IN THE DOS ENVIRONMENT

Figure B-4 shows a typical PC keyboard. Several keys perform special tasks in the DOS environment. Table B-1 lists these keys and their functions.

```
DIR/W

 Volume in drive A is MSDOS_330A
 Directory of  A:\

ANSI      SYS    APPEND   EXE    ASSIGN   COM    ATTRIB   EXE    CHKDSK   COM
COMMAND   COM    COMP     COM    COUNTRY  SYS    DISKCOMP COM    DISKCOPY COM
DISPLAY   SYS    DRIVER   SYS    EDLIN    COM    EXE2BIN  EXE    FASTOPEN EXE
FDISK     COM    FIND     EXE    FORMAT   COM    GRAFTABL COM    GRAPHICS COM
JOIN      EXE    KEYB     COM    LABEL    COM    MODE     COM    MORE     COM
NLSFUNC   EXE    PRINT    COM    RECOVER  COM    SELECT   COM    SORT     EXE
SUBST     EXE    SYS      COM    TREE     COM
        33 File(s)      19456 bytes free

A>
```

Figure B-2
A Wide Directory Listing

Figure B-3

Pausing a Directory Listing

```
DIR/P

 Volume in drive A is MSDOS_330A
 Directory of  A:\

ANSI      SYS       1647    3-01-88    8:00a
APPEND    EXE       5794    3-01-88    8:00a
ASSIGN    COM       1530    3-01-88    8:00a
ATTRIB    EXE      10656    3-01-88    8:00a
CHKDSK    COM       9819    3-01-88    8:00a
COMMAND   COM      25308    3-01-88    8:00a
COMP      COM       4183    3-01-88    8:00a
COUNTRY   SYS      11254    3-01-88    8:00a
DISKCOMP  COM       5848    3-01-88    8:00a
DISKCOPY  COM       6264    3-01-88    8:00a
DISPLAY   SYS      11259    3-01-88    8:00a
DRIVER    SYS       1165    3-01-88    8:00a
EDLIN     COM       7495    3-01-88    8:00a
EXE2BIN   EXE       3050    3-01-88    8:00a
FASTOPEN  EXE       3888    3-01-88    8:00a
FDISK     COM      48983    3-01-88    8:00a
FIND      EXE       6403    3-01-88    8:00a
FORMAT    COM      11671    3-01-88    8:00a
GRAFTABL  COM       6136    3-01-88    8:00a
GRAPHICS  COM      13943    3-01-88    8:00a
JOIN      EXE       9612    3-01-88    8:00a
KEYB      COM       9041    3-01-88    8:00a
LABEL     COM       2346    3-01-88    8:00a
Strike a key when ready . . .
MODE      COM      15440    3-01-88    8:00a
MORE      COM        282    3-01-88    8:00a
NLSFUNC   EXE       3029    3-01-88    8:00a
PRINT     COM       9011    3-01-88    8:00a
RECOVER   COM       4268    3-01-88    8:00a
SELECT    COM       4132    3-01-88    8:00a
SORT      EXE       1946    3-01-88    8:00a
SUBST     EXE      10552    3-01-88    8:00a
SYS       COM       4725    3-01-88    8:00a
TREE      COM       3540    3-01-88    8:00a
      33 File(s)        19456 bytes free

A>
```

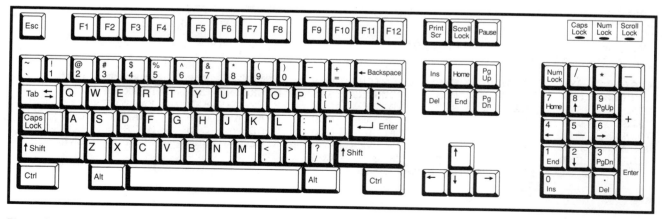

Figure B-4

A PC Keyboard

Key	Description
Ctrl-Alt-Del	Warm boots your system. Equivalent to turning your computer off, and then on.
Ctrl-C or Ctrl-Break	Cancels a command while it is being executed.
Ctrl-PrtSc or Ctrl-P	Sends a copy of each line on-screen to the printer as it is displayed. This command is a toggle; it remains in effect until you press it again.
Shift-PrtSc (or PrtSc on enhanced keyboards)	Sends a copy of the entire screen to the printer. This command is not a toggle.
Ctrl-S or Ctrl-Num Lock	Pauses the directory listing for viewing.
F1 function key	Displays one character of the previous command with each press. Useful for editing a DOS command.
F3 function key	Displays the previous command. Useful for repetitive tasks.
Esc	Erases the current command or statement.

B–8

THE FORMAT COMMAND

Before you can use a new disk on your computer, it must be formatted. To format a disk, place the DOS disk into drive A, type

FORMAT A:

and press Enter. Remove the DOS disk, insert the disk to be formatted into drive A, and press Enter. When DOS is finished formatting the disk, you are asked if you want to format another. If you answer yes, you are prompted to insert another disk. If you answer no, the DOS prompt reappears.

When you format a disk, DOS checks it for defective spots and tells you whether the disk is usable. The FORMAT command also divides a disk into tracks and sectors, and creates a File Allocation Table (FAT). The FAT tells DOS where the data are stored on the disk.

When you format a disk, everything on it is erased. Make sure that the disk you are formatting is either brand new or contains files that you no longer need.

Figure B–5 shows what your screen looks like when you have completed formatting a disk in drive A. You also can format a disk in a different drive. For

```
A>FORMAT A:
Insert new diskette for drive A:
and strike ENTER when ready

Format complete

    362496 bytes total disk space
    362496 bytes available on disk

Format another (Y/N)?N
A>
```

Figure B–5
Formatting a Disk in Drive A

example, if you have your DOS disk in drive A, you can format a disk in drive B by typing

FORMAT B:

B–9

DIFFERENT VERSIONS OF MS- AND PC-DOS

PC-DOS is used with the IBM computer, and MS-DOS is used with IBM-compatible computers. Both versions have evolved through several levels. Major versions are numbered 1.0, 2.0, 3.0, and so forth. Minor revisions are numbered 1.01, 2.2, 3.02, and so on. The current version is 5.0. Each new version has added new commands and corrected the bugs in previous versions. Versions 3.1 and later include commands for a LAN (Local Area Network).

Versions of MS- and PC-DOS are upwardly compatible, which means that all the commands in earlier versions are available in later versions. To a typical microcomputer user, PC-DOS and MS-DOS are almost identical. To find out which version of DOS you are using, type *VER* and press Enter. Figure B–6 illustrates this process. As you can see, our version of DOS is 3.3. All commands discussed in this book work with all versions of DOS unless otherwise specified.

B–10

BATCH AND AUTOEXEC FILES

Batch files contain a series of DOS commands that are executed as if you typed them individually. These files are helpful when you must perform repetitive operations. A batch file can have any standard name and the extension must always be BAT. Batch files can be any length, and you can include any valid command or statement. To generate a batch file, you can use EDLIN (the DOS line editor) or any word processing program.

For simple files, you can use a version of the copy command as follows:

```
COPY CON MYFILE.BAT
command or statement
command or statement
command or statement
```

You must press Enter after each command or statement in your batch file. To end a batch file, press Ctrl-Z or the F6 function key. To execute a batch file, insert the disk containing the file into your default drive and type the name of the file.

Figure B–6

Displaying the DOS Version Number

```
A>VER

MS-DOS Version 3.30

A>
```

Enter the following batch file at the A> prompt, pressing keys as indicated:

COPY CON HELLO.BAT (Enter)
DIR (Enter)
CLS (Enter)
BASICA (Enter)(Ctrl-Z)

If you type *HELLO* at the A> prompt, you will see a directory of that drive, the screen will clear, and BASICA will be loaded into RAM (assuming that the disk in drive A contains BASICA).

The only limitation with using the COPY CON command is that you cannot edit your batch file. You must recreate the entire file or import the file created by COPY CON into EDLIN or a word processing program to make changes.

To stop execution of your batch file, press Ctrl-Break.

You can have your batch file execute automatically when you start your computer system by naming it AUTOEXEC.BAT. DOS always looks for this file first. You can use this file to create custom menus for your system, to load a particular program that you use frequently, or anything else you want to have done automatically when you first turn on your computer.

Table B–2 lists some DOS commands and their functions. In this table, we assume that you are working from the A> prompt. A means drive A, B means drive B, ext stands for any valid file extension, and filename stands for any valid file name.

Command	Function
ATTRIB +R filename.ext	Makes a file a read-only file (Release 3 and higher)
ATTRIB -R filename.ext	Removes the read-only status (Release 3 and higher)
CHDIR (CD)	Changes the current directory or displays the current path
CHKDSK	Displays amount of free disk space or the amount of free memory on your computer
CHKDSK B:	Displays amount of free disk space in drive B
CLS	Clears the screen
COMP A:filename.ext B:filename.ext	Compares two files
COPY filename.ext B:	Copies filename.ext to drive B
COPY B:filename.ext	Copies filename.ext to drive A
COPY *.ext B:	Copies all files with the ext extension from A to B
COPY B:*.ext	Copies all files with the ext extension from B to A
COPY *.* B:	Copies all files from A to B

Table B–2
Important DOS Commands

Command	Function
COPY B:*.*	Copies all files from B to A
COPY filename1.ext filename2.ext	Copies a file from A to A with a different name
COPY filename1.ext B:filename2.ext	Copies a file from A to B with a different name
COPY B:filename1.ext filename2.ext	Copies a file from B to A with a different name
COPY CON B:filename.BAT	Creates a batch file in drive B
Ctrl-Alt-Del	Resets system (warm boot)
DATE	Sets system date
DEL filename.ext	Erases filename.ext from A
DEL B:filename.ext	Erases filename.ext from B
DEL B:filename.*	Erases filename with any extension from B
DEL B:*.ext	Erases files with the same extension from B
DIR	Displays directory of A
DIR B:	Displays directory of B
DIR/P	Pauses while displaying directory of A
DIR B:/P	Pauses while displaying directory of B
DIR/W	Displays directory of A in wide format
DIR B:/W	Displays directory of B in wide format
DIR | SORT	Displays a sorted directory of A
DIR B: | SORT	Displays a sorted directory of B
DISKCOPY A: B:	Copies disk in A to disk in B
DISKCOMP	Compares two disks, track by track and sector by sector to determine whether the contents are identical
ERASE filename.ext	Erases filename.ext on A
ERASE B:filename.ext	Erases filename.ext on B
ERASE *.ext	Erases all files with same extension on A
ERASE B:*.ext	Erases all files with same extension on B
FORMAT	Formats disk in A
FORMAT B:	Formats disk in B
FORMAT/V	Formats disk in A with volume label
FORMAT B:/V	Formats disk in B with volume label
LABEL	Creates, changes, or deletes a volume label
MKDIR (MD)	Creates a subdirectory
PATH	Searches a specified directory for a program that cannot be found in current directory
PROMPT	Customizes DOS system prompt
RENAME filename1.ext filename2.ext	Renames a file on A

Command	Function
RENAME B:filename1.ext filename2.ext	Renames a file on B
RMDIR (RD)	Removes a subdirectory
Shift-PrtSc (PrtSc on enhanced keyboards)	Prints the screen
SYS	Places operating system files (IBM.DOS and IBMBIO.COM) on the disk specified
TIME	Sets system time
TREE	Displays structure of current directory
TYPE filename.ext	Displays contents of filename.ext
TYPE B:filename.ext	Displays contents of filename.ext on B
VER	Displays DOS version
VERIFY	Checks data just written to disk to be sure the data has been recorded correctly
VERIFY ON/VERIFY OFF	Sets verify status
VOL	Displays volume label of disk (if label exists)

SUMMARY

This appendix reviewed simple DOS operations. We explained the difference between internal and external DOS commands, and we discussed the types of DOS prompts and file name specifications. You learned how to use the DIR command with various switches and how to format a disk using FORMAT.

Appendix C
BASIC Programming

C–1

INTRODUCTION

In this appendix we provide a quick review of BASIC programming. We review the steps in the program-development life cycle and discuss flowcharting. Several commonly used BASIC commands are explained, including LIST, RUN, REM, READ-DATA, FOR-NEXT, GOTO, IF-THEN, and IF-THEN-ELSE. We also touch on arrays, tables, and subroutines.

C–2

STEPS IN THE PROGRAM-DEVELOPMENT LIFE CYCLE

To use BASIC or any other application software as a programming language, you should follow the steps presented in figure C–1.

The problem definition step is very important. In the logic design step, you use a series of tools to come up with a "road map" for your attack on the problem. The flowchart is one of the most commonly used techniques for logic design. In the coding stage, you select a suitable programming language and code the problem.

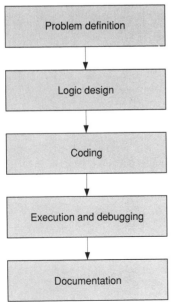

Figure C–1
Steps in the Program-
Development Life Cycle

When the program is fully coded, you execute it to see whether it runs correctly. If it doesn't, you must find your mistakes and correct them. The process of finding errors is called debugging. When the program is fully debugged, the programmer should provide further explanation for the operation of the program. This process is called documentation.

C–3

DEFINING A FLOWCHART

A flowchart is a pictorial representation of all the steps involved in a program. It shows what must be accomplished. There are two different types of flowcharts: a program flowchart and a system flowchart. In this appendix, we discuss the program flowchart.

A flowchart makes the logic of a program more understandable to both the programmer and the user of a program, reduces the complexity of large programs by dividing them into smaller sections, and is a valuable tool for documentation.

Flowchart Symbols

A series of standard symbols are used for preparing a flowchart. The most commonly used symbols are as shown in figure C–2. These symbols include the following:

> Terminal (START, END, or STOP)
> Process (X+Y, X*Y, X/Y, and so on)
> Input/Output (READ or PRINT)
> Decision (X>Y, X=Y, and so on)
> Connector (connecting two different parts of a flowchart)

In figure C–3, you see a flowchart template. We will show the applications of most of these symbols in this appendix.

Figure C–2
Selected Flowcharting Symbols

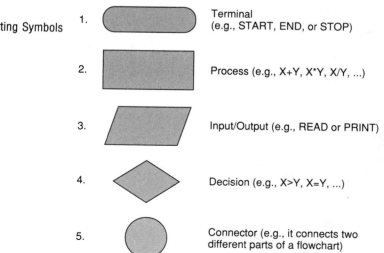

1. Terminal (e.g., START, END, or STOP)

2. Process (e.g., X+Y, X*Y, X/Y, ...)

3. Input/Output (e.g., READ or PRINT)

4. Decision (e.g., X>Y, X=Y, ...)

5. Connector (e.g., it connects two different parts of a flowchart)

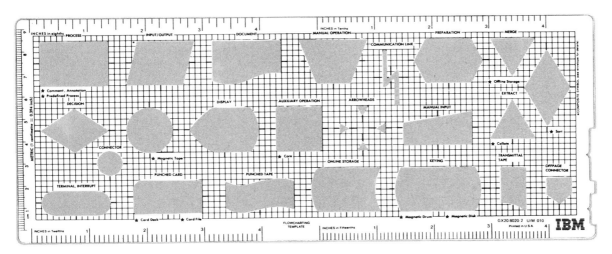

Figure C–3
Flowchart Template (Courtesy of IBM Corporation)

Flow Direction

All the symbols presented in the flowchart template are connected by using straight lines called flow lines. Arrows are used to indicate the direction of flow. Usually, the flow is from left to right and from top to bottom. Figure C–4 shows a flowchart for reading a group of student names and printing them. Figure C–5 shows a flowchart to read 10 numbers from a data line and to print their average.

C–4

LOADING BASIC

If you are using an IBM type computer, the BASIC language is stored on your DOS disk. Insert your DOS disk into drive A and, at the A> prompt, type BASICA. This will load BASICA, which is more powerful than regular BASIC. This version of BASIC is sometimes called GW-BASIC, IBM BASIC, or Microsoft BASIC. If you have another type of computer, ask your instructor to tell you how to get BASIC started. When you see the OK prompt, it means you have successfully started the BASIC language. You are now able to issue any BASIC command.

For a detailed discussion of BASIC, see *Information Systems Literacy and Software Productivity Tools: DOS* by Hossein Bidgoli (Macmillan, 1991).

C–5

BASIC LINE NUMBERS

Any BASIC program must have line numbers. The range of line numbers differs from system to system, but a range between 1 and 30,000 is usually acceptable. Line numbers show the sequence in which a BASIC program is to be executed. Each line number must be different, and you should number your program lines in increments of 5, 10, or 15 to allow for later insertions.

Figure C–4
Flowchart for Reading and Printing Student Names

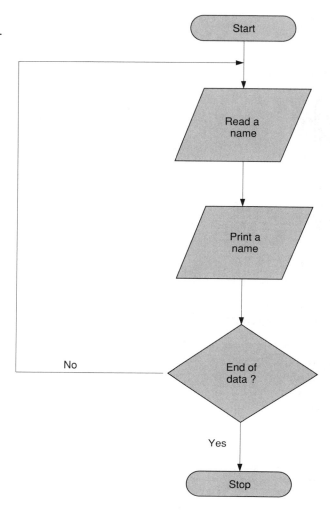

C–6

SOME BASIC COMMANDS

The END Statement

Any BASIC program should have an END statement, which is given the last
(largest) line number in your program. The END statement terminates the
BASIC program. Any line number after the END statement is ignored by the
computer.

The REM Command

REM (REMARK) is used for documentation purposes. When your computer
sees a line that begins with REM, it ignores anything on that line, so you use the
line to enter a description of what the program does. For example, you might
enter

    10 REM This program calculates weekly checks.

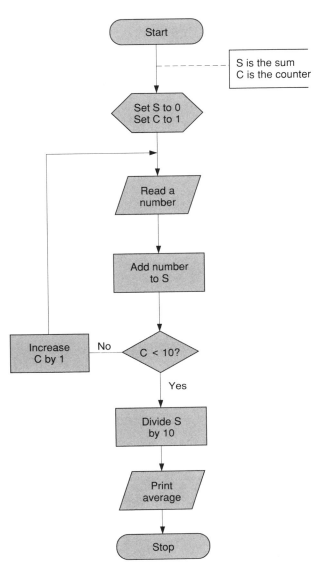

Figure C-5
Flowchart for Reading Numbers
and Printing the Average

The PRINT Command

The PRINT statement is used to print the result of a calculation. For example,
if you use the statement

    PRINT 2+2

the computer will respond with

4

  You can use PRINT in order to print literals such as data enclosed in
quotes. For example:

    PRINT "This is a computer"

The computer responds with

```
This is a computer
```

You can also use the ? (question mark) in place of the PRINT command. For example:

```
?"We are learning BASIC"
```

The computer responds with

```
We are learning BASIC
```

When you generate a listing of your program by using the LIST command explained later, all ? (question marks) will be replaced automatically by the PRINT command.

The RUN Command

The RUN command tells BASIC to execute your program. The BASIC compiler checks for errors and, if there are none, it prints whatever it has been asked. When the program is executed, the computer responds with OK, which means your program has been executed and the computer is waiting for the next command.

The AUTO Command

After starting BASIC, the AUTO command automatically generates line numbers for you as you enter your program. To use this feature, simply type *AUTO* and press Enter. To get out of the AUTO mode, press Ctrl-Break. The Ctrl-Break keys are also used to stop the execution of a program. You can use the AUTO command to generate line numbers beginning with any number, using any increment. For example, if you type *AUTO 1000,* your program will be numbered as follows:

```
1000
1010
1020
1030
```

and so forth (BASIC uses the default increment of 10). You can also change the increment. For example, you can type *AUTO 5000,50* to number your program as follows:

```
5000
5050
5100
5150
```

The LIST Command

You can use the LIST command in several ways. If you type *LIST* and press Enter, you will see a listing of the current file. You can use the LIST command to display just one line or several lines of your program. For example, if you type *LIST 5050,* the computer will display the line beginning with line number 5050. If you type

    LIST 5050,5150

the computer will display lines 5050 and 5150 of your program. If you type

    LIST 5000-5100

you will get a listing of all the lines from 5000 to 5100.

Use the LLIST command to send the listing of your program to your printer.

The DELETE and NEW Commands

If you want to delete a line, you have two options. You can type the line number of the line you want to delete and press Enter or you can type *DELETE* followed by the line number. For example,

    DELETE 500

will delete line 500. With the DELETE command, you can delete a series of line numbers or even the entire program. If you type

    DELETE 500-2000

all the lines in this range will be deleted.

Use the NEW command to delete the entire current file. In other words, the NEW command erases the RAM memory. Just type NEW and press Enter. To erase the screen, you can either use the CLS command or press Ctrl-Home.

The SAVE Command

To transfer a temporary file (the file in RAM) to secondary storage (to your disk—floppy or hard), you must use the SAVE command. For example, to save the current file, JACK, to the disk in drive A, you would type

    SAVE "A:JACK

The computer saves your program with the file name JACK.BAS. The BAS extension is automatically added by the BASIC language during the saving process. It is used to identify all your BASIC files.

To retrieve this program, type

    LOAD "A:JACK

The computer responds with OK, which means that it has been able to find the program called JACK. In most computer systems, a file name can be up to eight characters long. It can contain numbers or symbols such as a hyphen or a pound sign (#). Avoid spaces in the file names and get in the habit of using meaningful names.

The KILL Command

To delete a permanent file, you must use the KILL command. To erase a file from the disk in drive A, you would, for example, type

KILL "A:JACK.BAS

and press Enter. Remember, you must include BAS.

The RENUM Command

The RENUM command changes the sequence of line numbers. You can use any sequence of line numbers you want. Suppose, for example, that your current program is as follows:

```
1000 PRINT "SUE"
1010 PRINT "BASIC"
1020 PRINT "COBOL"
1030 PRINT "COMPUTER"
1040 END
```

If you type *RENUM*, press Enter, and then type *LIST* and press Enter, you will see the following:

```
10 PRINT "SUE"
20 PRINT "BASIC"
30 PRINT "COBOL"
40 PRINT "COMPUTER"
50 END
```

You can use the RENUM command in order to specify the starting line number and the increment, and specify from which line number of the program this new numbering should begin. For example:

RENUM 5000, 110, 15

will start from line 110 of your program and renumber it to 5000, and continues with increments of 15.

If you type *RENUM 5000*, your program will be as follows:

```
5000 PRINT "SUE"
5010 PRINT "BASIC"
5020 PRINT "COBOL"
5030 PRINT "COMPUTER"
5040 END
```

The FILES Command

To see a listing of all the files that you have saved on your disk, you must use the FILES command. If you use FILES by itself, you will see a listing of the files on your default drive. If you use FILES "C:, for example, you will see a listing of all the files on your C drive.

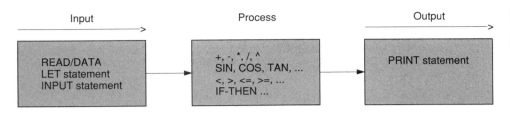

Figure C–6
Interaction of BASIC Commands
with the Black Box

Most of these commands can be executed by using the function keys F1-F10. Look at the bottom of your screen to see which key is used for what command.

C–7
BASIC AS A BLACK BOX

Figure C–6 shows examples of common commands used in the input-process-output cycle of a BASIC program.

It is possible to have a program that does not include the entire cycle: programs with only input and output, or programs with only output. However, for all practical purposes, a program should include the entire cycle.

C–8
THE ASSIGNMENT STATEMENT (THE LET STATEMENT)

The assignment statement is one way of assigning a value to a variable. In some computers, you must use the LET statement; however, the majority of computers do not need LET in the assignment statement. To assign the value 50 to the variable A, you can use either of the following:

LET A=50

or

A=50

Understanding this simple statement is very important. When you assign a value to a variable, you have generated a location inside the computer; the address of this location is A, and the value in this address is 50. You must remember that a particular address can hold only one value at a time. A new value replaces the old one. The following diagram shows how the assignment statement is presented in the computer:

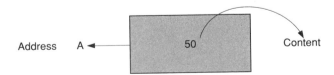

Program 1: An Example of the Assignment Statement

Figure C–7 illustrates this program.

Figure C—7

The LET Statement

```
100     REM SOME EXAMPLES OF THE ASSIGNMENT STATEMENT.
110     REM
120     REM ******* VARIABLE TABLE
130     REM          NUM1 = INPUT VARIABLE
140     REM          NUM2 = INPUT VARIABLE AND TOTAL
150     REM
160     REM ******* INITIALIZATION SECTION
170     LET NUM1 = 10
180     LET NUM2 = 10
190     LET NUM1 = 25
200     REM
210     REM ******* PROCESS SECTION
220     LET NUM2 = NUM1 + NUM2
230     REM
240     REM ******* OUTPUT SECTION
250     PRINT "THE FINAL VALUE OF NUM2 IS =";NUM2
260     END
Ok
RUN
THE FINAL VALUE OF NUM2 IS = 35
Ok
```

In line 170, the value of NUM1 is equal to 10. In line 190, this value is replaced by 25, so the final value of NUM1 is 25. In line 220, the final values of NUM1 and NUM2 are added together and the result is stored in address NUM2. The following diagram shows this process.

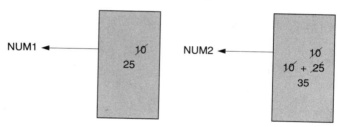

Program 2: The LET Statement as an Accumulator

Figure C—8 illustrates this program.

Figure C—8

LET Statement as an Accumulator

```
100     REM THIS PROGRAM SHOWS THE APPLICATION OF THE LET
110     REM STATEMENT AS AN ACCUMULATOR.
120     REM
130     REM ******* VARIABLE TABLE
140     REM          A = INPUT VARIABLE AND ACCUMULATOR
150     REM          B = INPUT VARIABLE AND ACCUMULATOR
160     REM
170     REM ******* INITIALIZATION SECTION
180     LET A = 10
190     LET B = 20
200     LET A = A + 1
210     LET B = B + 20
220     REM
230     REM ******* OUTPUT SECTION
240     PRINT "THE NEW VALUES OF A AND B ARE = ",A,B
250     END
Ok
RUN
THE NEW VALUES OF A AND B ARE =          11          40
Ok
```

In algebra, A=A+1 and B=B+20 does not make any sense. There is no way for a variable to equal itself plus one. Nor can a variable equal itself plus 20. But, in computer programming, this expression has a quite different meaning. Line 200 simply means to take the old value of A, which is 10, add one to it, and store the result in the same address. Line 210 instructs the computer to use the old value of B, which is 20, add 20 to it, and store it in the same address.

C−9
SIMPLE NUMERIC VARIABLES

In GW-BASIC, a variable name can be up to 40 characters. A variable name can be any letter of the alphabet, A through Z, or any valid character. Avoid spaces in variable names. Try to use meaningful names.

C−10
NUMERIC CONSTANTS

Variables, as the name indicates, can change in value. For example, the value of the variable A can change throughout a program several times.

A numeric constant has a fixed value throughout a program. A numeric constant can have a sign (positive or negative), must not contain commas, and, for large numbers, must be expressed in scientific notation.

C−11
SCIENTIFIC NOTATION (''E NOTATION'')

Usually, very large or very small numbers are presented in E notation. Most computers can also output these numbers in scientific notation. The following are some examples of E notation:

2987	$=2.987E+3$	$=29.87E+2$
0.00223466899	$=.223466899E-2$	$=22.3466899E-4$
10000000000	$=1E+10$	$=1000E+6$
2000	$=2E+3$	$=20E+2$
0.0002	$=2E-4$	$=20E-5$

C−12
THE NON-NUMERIC (STRING) VARIABLES

The variables used in a BASIC program are not always numeric. For example, in a payroll program, the number of hours, the pay rate, and the tax rate are numeric—they consist of the digits zero through nine. However, the employee's name and address are not numeric. These variables are called non-numeric or string variables.

To distinguish a numeric variable from a non-numeric variable, a $ is placed at the end of the variable name. All other rules for numeric variable names are the same. Whenever non-numeric data value is assigned to a non-numeric variable, you must enclose it in double quotation marks.

C-13

THE READ AND DATA STATEMENTS

The second method of sending data to the computer is by using the READ and DATA statements. This method is usually used whenever there are a great deal of data to be entered into the computer. Figure C–9 shows an example of this method of sending data to the computer.

READ and DATA must be used together. You can place your DATA statements anywhere in the program. Usually, experienced programmers put the data either at the top or at the bottom of the program (before the END statement). That way the data are easier to find for future modification.

C-14

THE INPUT STATEMENT

The third method of sending data to the computer is by using the INPUT statement. This command enables a programmer to use the computer in an interactive mode. You use this statement so that the computer will accept input from the keyboard. This method is useful for running the same program with different data, for example, a program for calculating the G.P.A. of different students in a computer class. The program is the same, but the data are different for each student. This method is also useful whenever the data part of a program does not need to be included in the program.

Figures C–10 and C–11 are examples of how to use the INPUT statement.

Figure C–9
Using READ and DATA Statements

```
100     REM THIS PROGRAM CALCULATES THE AVERAGE OF 4 NUMBERS.
110     REM
120     REM ******* VARIABLE TABLE
130     REM          NUM1 = VARIABLE 1
140     REM          NUM2 = VARIABLE 2
150     REM          NUM3 = VARIABLE 3
160     REM          NUM4 = VARIABLE 4
170     REM          SUM = THE SUM OF THE NUMBERS
180     REM          AVERAGE = THE AVERAGE OF THE NUMBERS
190     REM
200     REM ******* INITIALIZATION SECTION
210     READ NUM1, NUM2, NUM3, NUM4
220     REM
230     REM ******* PROCESS SECTION
240     SUM = NUM1+NUM2+NUM3+NUM4
250     AVERAGE = SUM/4
260     REM
270     REM ******* OUTPUT SECTION
280     PRINT "THE AVERAGE OF THE 4 NUMBERS IS =";AVERAGE
290     REM
300     REM ******* DATA SECTION
310     DATA 100, 200, 50, 250
320     END
Ok
RUN
THE AVERAGE OF THE 4 NUMBERS IS = 150
Ok
```

```
100     REM THIS PROGRAM ACCEPTS 3 NUMBERS FROM THE KEYBOARD
110     REM AND COMPUTES THEIR SUM.
120     REM
130     REM ****** VARIABLE TABLE
140     REM           NUM1, NUM2, NUM3 = INPUT VARIABLES
150     REM           SUM = SUM OF THE THREE INPUT VARIABLES
160     REM
170     REM ****** INITIALIZATION SECTION
180     PRINT "YOU TELL ME ANY 3 NUMBERS, AND I WILL TELL YOU THEIR SUM."
190     PRINT "THE 3 NUMBERS MUST BE SEPARATED BY COMMAS."
200     INPUT NUM1, NUM2, NUM3
210     REM
220     REM ****** PROCESS SECTION
230     LET SUM = NUM1+NUM2+NUM3
240     REM
250     REM ****** OUTPUT SECTION
260     PRINT "THE SUM OF THE THREE NUMBERS IS = ";SUM
270     END
Ok
RUN
YOU TELL ME ANY 3 NUMBERS, AND I WILL TELL YOU THEIR SUM.
THE 3 NUMBERS MUST BE SEPARATED BY COMMAS.
? 10,20,30
THE SUM OF THE THREE NUMBERS IS =   60
Ok
```

Figure C–10
An Application of the INPUT Statement

```
100     REM THIS PROGRAM ACCEPTS THE RADIUS OF A CIRCLE FROM
110     REM THE KEYBOARD AND COMPUTES ITS AREA.
120     REM
130     REM ****** VARIABLE TABLE
140     REM           PI = VALUE OF PI (3.1416)
150     REM           RADIUS = INPUT VARIABLE (RADIUS OF A CIRCLE)
160     REM           AREA = AREA OF THE CIRCLE
170     REM
180     REM ****** INITIALIZATION SECTION
190     LET PI = 3.1416
200     PRINT "WHAT IS THE RADIUS OF THE CIRCLE"
210     INPUT RADIUS
220     REM
230     REM ****** PROCESS SECTION
240     LET AREA = PI*RADIUS*RADIUS
250     REM
260     REM ****** OUTPUT SECTION
270     PRINT "THE AREA OF THE CIRCLE IS =";AREA
280     END
Ok
RUN
WHAT IS THE RADIUS OF THE CIRCLE
? 5
THE AREA OF THE CIRCLE IS = 78.54
Ok
```

Figure C–11
Another Application of the
INPUT Statement

C–15

BUILT-IN FUNCTIONS

In BASIC and many other software programs, a series of operations and calculations are readily available in the language or software. For example, for calculating the natural logarithm of a number you don't need to do any extra coding. You can just use X=LOG(W) to store the natural logarithm of W in address X. The most commonly used built-in functions are summarized in table C–1.

C–16

THE PRINT COMMAND—A SECOND LOOK

The PRINT command enables a programmer to receive the output from the computer. You can use the PRINT command in three different ways. The following programs show the different applications of this command. Figures C–12 to C–15 show some examples of the PRINT command. Figure C–16 shows the flowchart for the program displayed in Figure C–15.

Table C–1
Built-In Functions in BASIC

SIN(X)	Sine of X, angle measured in radians
COS(X)	Cosine of X, angle measured in radians
TAN(X)	Tangent of X, angle measured in radians
COT(X)	Cotangent of X, angle measured in radians
ATN(X)	Arctangent of X, angle measured in radians
EXP(X)	e (2.718 . . .) is raised to the power X
LOG(X)	Natural logarithm of X (X must be positive)
ABS(X)	Absolute value of X
SQR(X)	Square root of X (X must be positive)
INT(X)	The greatest integer less than or equal to X
RND(X)	Generates random numbers between 0 and 1
SGN(X)	Generates 1 for positive numbers, −1 for negative numbers, and 0 for zero

(X is called the argument of the function. Consult documentation for the specific software to determine the correct format for the argument—radians or degrees.)

Figure C–12
Printing Numeric Constants

```
100    REM THE FIRST APPLICATION OF THE PRINT STATEMENT.
110    REM
120    REM ****** VARIABLE TABLE
130    REM          THERE ARE NO VARIABLES IN THIS PROGRAM.
140    REM
150    REM ****** OUTPUT SECTION
160    PRINT 2
170    PRINT 4
180    PRINT 2+4
190    END
Ok
RUN
 2
 4
 6
Ok
```

```
100    REM THE SECOND APPLICATION OF THE PRINT STATEMENT.
110    REM
120    REM ****** VARIABLE TABLE
130    REM           THERE ARE NO VARIABLES IN THIS PROGRAM.
140    REM
150    REM ****** OUTPUT SECTION
160    PRINT "THIS IS PROGRAM NUMBER 2."
170    PRINT "THIS IS A PAYROLL REPORT."
180    PRINT "I ENJOY MY COMPUTER CLASS!"
190    END
Ok
RUN
THIS IS PROGRAM NUMBER 2.
THIS IS A PAYROLL REPORT.
I ENJOY MY COMPUTER CLASS!
Ok
```

Figure C–13
Printing Titles or String Constants

C–17

FORMATTING THE OUTPUT WITH COMMAS OR SEMICOLONS

Using the semicolon as a delimiter produces a more compact output than using the comma. There are five standard zones in one line. The semicolon increases the number of zones in a line. This number depends upon the size of a particular number or field. Figures C–17 and C–18 show this process.

C–18

COMMAS AND SEMICOLONS AFTER VARIABLES

You use a comma or a semicolon after a variable in a PRINT statement to keep the printer on the same line until all the printing zones have been filled. Again, the semicolon produces a more compact output. Figure C–19 shows this process.

```
100    REM THE THIRD APPLICATION OF THE PRINT STATEMENT.
110    REM THIS IS PROBABLY THE MOST IMPORTANT APPLICATION OF
120    REM THE PRINT STATEMENT.
130    REM
140    REM ****** VARIABLE TABLE
150    REM           NUM1, NUM2 = INPUT VARIABLES
160    REM           NUM3 = SUM OF NUM1 AND NUM2
170    REM
180    REM ****** INITIALIZATION SECTION
190    LET NUM1 = 5
200    LET NUM2 = 10
210    REM
220    REM ****** PROCESS SECTION
230    LET NUM3 = NUM1+NUM2
240    REM
250    REM ****** OUTPUT SECTION
260    PRINT "*****************************"
270    PRINT "** THE SUM OF NUM1+NUM2 =";NUM3;"**"
280    PRINT "*****************************"
290    END
Ok
RUN
*****************************
** THE SUM OF NUM1+NUM2 = 15 **
*****************************
Ok
```

Figure C–14
Printing the Results of Calculations.

Figure C–15

Performing the Four Basic Arithmetic Operations on Variables A and B

```
100     REM THIS IS ANOTHER EXAMPLE OF THE PRINT STATEMENT.
110     REM
120     REM ****** VARIABLE TABLE
130     REM          NUM1, NUM2 = INPUT VARIABLES
140     REM          MULT = PRODUCT OF NUM1 AND NUM2
150     REM          DIV = RESULT OF NUM1 DIVIDED BY NUM2
160     REM          SUBT = RESULT OF NUM1 MINUS NUM2
170     REM          ADD = RESULT OF NUM1 PLUS NUM2
180     REM
190     REM ****** INITIALIZATION SECTION
200     LET NUM1 = 10
210     LET NUM2 = 5
220     REM
230     REM ****** PROCESS SECTION
240     LET MULT = NUM1*NUM2
250     LET DIV = NUM1/NUM2
260     LET SUBT = NUM1-NUM2
270     LET ADD = NUM1+NUM2
280     REM
290     REM ****** OUTPUT SECTION
300     PRINT "**************** RESULTS *****************"
310     PRINT "THE MULTIPLICATION OF NUM1 BY NUM2 IS = ";MULT
320     PRINT "THE DIVISION OF NUM1 BY NUM2 IS = ";DIV
330     PRINT "THE SUBTRACTION OF NUM2 FROM NUM1 IS = ";SUBT
340     PRINT "THE ADDITION OF NUM1 AND NUM2 IS = ";ADD
350     PRINT "*****************************************"
360     END
Ok
RUN
**************** RESULTS ****************
THE MULTIPLICATION OF NUM1 BY NUM2 IS =  50
THE DIVISION OF NUM1 BY NUM2 IS =  2
THE SUBTRACTION OF NUM2 FROM NUM1 IS =   5
THE ADDITION OF NUM1 AND NUM2 IS =   15
****************************************
Ok
```

There are five standard zones in each line. Therefore, in each line you can print up to five variables (if the length of a field does not exceed the length of a zone). The extra variables will be printed in the next line. The statement:

100 PRINT A,B,C,D,E,F,G

results in the printing of the first five values in the five standard zones; the sixth and seventh values are printed in the first and second zones beneath the first and second values.

Commas and semicolons can be used together in the same line. The following statements show this process:

10 PRINT A,B,C;D,E
20 PRINT A ,A ,A ;A ,A

C–19

RELATIONAL COMPARISONS

One of the advantages of computers is the amazing speed with which they make relational comparisons. Table C–2 lists the various symbols used for comparison operations.

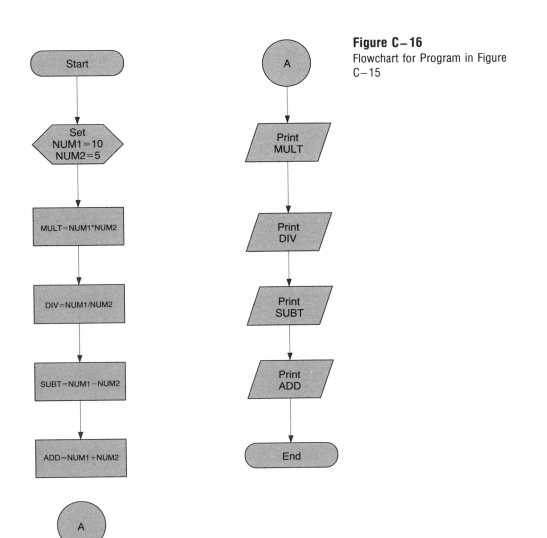

Figure C–16
Flowchart for Program in Figure C–15

```
100    REM A SEMICOLON PROVIDES MORE COMPACT OUTPUT THAN A COMMA.
110    REM
120    REM ****** VARIABLE TABLE
130    REM        NUM1, NUM2, NUM3, NUM4, NUM5 = INPUT VARIABLES
140    REM
150    REM ****** INITIALIZATION SECTION
160    LET NUM1 = 1
170    LET NUM2 = 2
180    LET NUM3 = 3
190    LET NUM4 = 4
200    LET NUM5 = 5
210    REM
220    REM ****** OUTPUT SECTION
230    PRINT NUM1,NUM2,NUM3,NUM4,NUM5
240    PRINT NUM1;NUM2;NUM3;NUM4;NUM5
250    END
Ok
RUN
 1              2              3              4              5
 1   2   3   4   5
Ok
```

Figure C–17
Using Commas and Semicolons as Delimiters

219

```
100     REM THIS IS ANOTHER EXAMPLE OF SEMICOLONS AND
110     REM COMMAS AS DELIMITERS.
120     REM
130     REM ****** VARIABLE TABLE
140     REM          WORD1$, WORD2$, WORD3$ = INPUT STRING VARIABLES
150     REM
160     REM ****** INITIALIZATION SECTION
170     LET WORD1$ = "THIS IS"
180     LET WORD2$ = "A COMPUTER"
190     LET WORD3$ = "CLASS"
200     REM
210     REM ****** OUTPUT SECTION
220     PRINT WORD1$,WORD2$,WORD3$
230     PRINT WORD1$;WORD2$;WORD3$
240     END
Ok
RUN
THIS IS         A COMPUTER       CLASS
THIS ISA COMPUTERCLASS
Ok
```

Figure C–18
Using Commas and Semicolons between String Variables

```
100     REM THIS EXAMPLE SHOWS THE EFFECT OF A COMMA AFTER A VARIABLE.
110     REM
120     REM ****** VARIABLE TABLE
130     REM          NUM1, NUM2, NUM3 = INPUT VARIABLES
140     REM
150     REM ****** INITIALIZATION SECTION
160     LET NUM1 = 1
170     LET NUM2 = 2
180     LET NUM3 = 3
190     REM
200     REM ****** OUTPUT SECTION
210     PRINT NUM1,
220     PRINT NUM2,
230     PRINT NUM3
240     PRINT NUM1;
250     PRINT NUM2;
260     PRINT NUM3
270     END
Ok
RUN
 1              2               3
 1   2   3
Ok
```

Figure C–19
Using Commas and Semicolons after Variables

Table C–2
Relational Symbols

Symbol	Meaning	BASIC Symbol	Example
$=$	equal to	$=$	$A+B=C+D$
$<$	less than	$<$	$A+B<C+D$
$>$	greater than	$>$	$A+B>C+D$
$\leq$	less than or equal to	$<=$	$X+H<=Q+R$
$\geq$	greater than or equal to	$>=$	$X+W>=Q+R$
$\neq$	not equal to	$<>$	$M+N<>Q+R$

Relational comparisons are the key element in using computers as decision-makers.

C-20

THE GOTO (GO TO) STATEMENT

This command will be used whenever a programmer wants to change the normal sequence of a program unconditionally. Figures C–20 to C–22 show this process.

When you run Figure C–20, nothing is printed. Control is transferred from line 210 to line 230, and the computer never considers line 220 as part of the program.

C-21

THE IF-GOTO, IF-THEN, AND IF-THEN-ELSE STATEMENTS

These statements enable a programmer to branch based on a condition. Figures C–23 to C–25 show this process.

Line 210 of Figure C–24 checks for the end of the data items. This checking is called flagging. You should always put a fictitious data item at the end of the data. When the computer reads this item, it knows it has reached the end of the data, and the program is terminated. Because you cannot know whether the computer has reached the end of the data, you must check for this situation. The flag can be any data item, but it is a good practice to make it an unusual data item—a G.P.A. of less than 0, for example.

Figures C–23 and C–24 show the IF-THEN and IF-GOTO statements perform the same function; a programmer can use either of these, based on personal preference.

Figure C–26 shows the flowchart for the program in Figure C–25.

```
100     REM THIS PROGRAM SHOWS THE WAY IN WHICH THE GOTO STATEMENT
110     REM WORKS.  IT SIMPLY CHANGES THE NORMAL SEQUENCE OF THE
120     REM PROGRAM.
130     REM
140     REM ****** VARIABLE TABLE
150     REM          NUM1 = INPUT VARIABLE
160     REM
170     REM ****** INITIALIZATION SECTION
180     LET NUM1 = 5
190     REM
200     REM ****** OUTPUT SECTION
210     GOTO 230
220     PRINT NUM1
230     END
Ok
RUN
Ok
```

Figure C–20
Using the GOTO Statement

Figure C–21
Another Application of the GOTO Statement

```
100     REM THIS PROGRAM GENERATES AN ENDLESS LOOP.
110     REM
120     REM ****** VARIABLE TABLE
130     REM          WORD1$ = INPUT STRING VARIABLE
140     REM
150     REM ****** INITIALIZATION SECTION
160     LET WORD1$ = "JACK"
170     REM
180     REM ****** OUTPUT SECTION
190     PRINT WORD1$
200     GOTO 190
210     END
JACK
JACK
JACK
JACK
JACK
JACK
JACK
JACK
JACK
JACK
JACK
JACK
JACK
JACK
JACK
JACK
JACK
JACK
^C
Break in 190
Ok
```

Figure C–22
Read a Variable from a DATA Line and Print the Contents

```
100     REM THIS PROGRAM READS A VARIABLE FROM A DATA LINE AND
110     REM PRINTS ITS CONTENT.
120     REM
130     REM ****** VARIABLE TABLE
140     REM          NUM1 = INPUT VARIABLE
150     REM
160     REM ****** OUTPUT SECTION
170     READ NUM1
180     PRINT NUM1
190     GOTO 170
200     REM
210     REM ****** DATA SECTION
220     DATA 5, 10, 15
230     END
Ok
RUN
 5
 10
 15
Out of DATA in 170
Ok
```

```
100     REM THIS PROGRAM SELECTS THE SMALLEST NUMBER AMONG THREE.
110     REM
120     REM ****** VARIABLE TABLE
130     REM          NUM1, NUM2, NUM3 = INPUT VARIABLES
140     REM
150     REM ****** INITIALIZATION SECTION
160     READ NUM1,NUM2,NUM3
170     REM
180     REM ****** PROCESS SECTION
190     IF NUM1<NUM2 THEN GOTO 230
200     IF NUM2<NUM3 THEN GOTO 270
210     PRINT "THE SMALLEST NUMBER AMONG 5, 10 AND 15 =";NUM3
220     GOTO 310
230     IF NUM1<NUM3 THEN GOTO 250
240     GOTO 210
250     PRINT "THE SMALLEST NUMBER AMONG 5, 10 AND 15 =";NUM1
260     GOTO 310
270     PRINT "THE SMALLEST NUMBER AMONG 5, 10 AND 15 =";NUM2
280     REM
290     REM ****** DATA SECTION
300     DATA 15, 10, 5
310     END
Ok
RUN
THE SMALLEST NUMBER AMONG 5, 10 AND 15 = 5
Ok
```

Figure C-23
Select the Smallest Number

```
100     REM THIS PROGRAM PRINTS THE NAME OF THE STUDENTS WITH A
110     REM GPA OF 3.5 OR BETTER.
120     REM
130     REM ****** VARIABLE TABLE
140     REM          GPA = GRADE POINT AVERAGE
150     REM          STUDENT$ = STUDENT NAME
160     REM
170     REM ****** INITIALIZATION SECTION
180     READ GPA, STUDENT$
190     REM
200     REM ****** PROCESS SECTION
210        IF GPA = -1 THEN GOTO 360
220        IF GPA >= 3.5 THEN GOTO 260
230     GOTO 180
240     REM
250     REM ****** OUTPUT SECTION
260     PRINT STUDENT$;" HAS A GPA OF";GPA
270     GOTO 180
280     REM
290     REM ****** DATA SECTION
300     DATA 3.00, JACK
310     DATA 3.60, SUE
320     DATA 3.90, PAT
330     DATA 1.80, DENISE
340     DATA 2.20, CHARLIES
350     DATA -1, FLAG
360     END
Ok
RUN
SUE HAS A GPA OF 3.6
PAT HAS A GPA OF 3.9
Ok
```

Figure C-24
Read Five Students' Names and G.P.A.s from a DATA Line and Print the Names of Students with a G.P.A. of 3.50 or Greater

223

```
100     REM THIS PROGRAM IS AN EXAMPLE OF INTERACTIVE PROGRAMMING.
110     REM YOU CAN INPUT ANY NUMBER FROM THE KEYBOARD, AND THE
120     REM COMPUTER WILL TELL YOU WHETHER YOUR NUMBER IS NEGATIVE,
130     REM ZERO OR POSITIVE.
140     REM
150     REM ******* VARIABLE TABLE
160     REM          NUMBER = INPUT VARIABLE
170     REM          ANSWER$ = REPEAT PROGRAM STRING VARIABLE
180     REM
190     REM ******* INITIALIZATION SECTION
200     PRINT "YOU TELL ME A NUMBER, I WILL TELL YOU"
210     PRINT "WHETHER IT IS ZERO, NEGATIVE, OR POSITIVE."
220     PRINT
230     INPUT "WHAT IS YOUR NUMBER";NUMBER
240     PRINT
250     REM
260     REM ******* PROCESS SECTION
270     IF NUMBER < 0 THEN 320
280     IF NUMBER = 0 THEN 340
290     GOTO 360
300     REM
310     REM ******* OUTPUT SECTION
320     PRINT "THE NUMBER YOU ENTERED IS NEGATIVE."
330     GOTO 400
340     PRINT "THE NUMBER YOU ENTERED IS ZERO."
350     GOTO 400
360     PRINT "THE NUMBER YOU ENTERED IS POSITIVE."
370     PRINT
380     REM
390     REM ******* TERMINATION SECTION
400     INPUT "WOULD YOU LIKE TO TRY AGAIN?  ANSWER WITH Y OR N";ANSWER$
410     IF ANSWER$ = "Y" OR ANSWER$ = "y" THEN GOTO 230
420     IF ANSWER$ <> "N" AND ANSWER$ <> "n" THEN GOTO 400
430     END
Ok
RUN
YOU TELL ME A NUMBER, I WILL TELL YOU
WHETHER IT IS ZERO, NEGATIVE, OR POSITIVE.

WHAT IS YOUR NUMBER? -7

THE NUMBER YOU ENTERED IS NEGATIVE.
WOULD YOU LIKE TO TRY AGAIN?  ANSWER WITH Y OR N? Y
WHAT IS YOUR NUMBER? 9

THE NUMBER YOU ENTERED IS POSITIVE.

WOULD YOU LIKE TO TRY AGAIN?  ANSWER WITH Y OR N? Y
WHAT IS YOUR NUMBER? 0

THE NUMBER YOU ENTERED IS ZERO.
WOULD YOU LIKE TO TRY AGAIN?  ANSWER WITH Y OR N? N
Ok
```

Figure C–25
Interactive Programming with an IF-THEN Statement

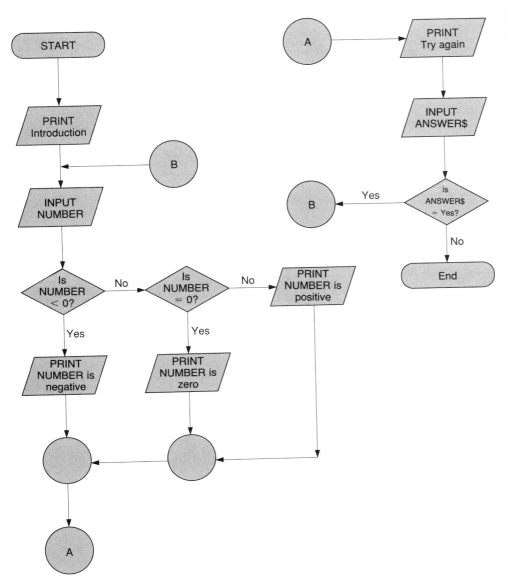

Figure C-26
Flowchart for Program in Figure
C-25

The IF-THEN-ELSE command can make your coding more compact. For example, in Figure C-25, you can replace lines 280 and 290 with the following line:

IF NUMBER=0 THEN 340 ELSE 360

In lines 410 and 420 of Figure C-26, we have used the OR and AND commands, which you have not seen before. These commands are used for OR/AND conditions. In an AND comparison, all conditions must be correct. In an OR comparison, at least one condition must be correct.

C−22

THE FOR-NEXT STATEMENT

You use the FOR-NEXT statement to perform an operation or a series of operations for a fixed number of times. Figures C−27 to C−30 show this process.

    As we see in these four programs, the FOR-NEXT loop is used for doing some operations for a fixed number of times. In the program in Figure C−27, lines 210 through 230 constitute the FOR-NEXT loop. When this process is done four times, the loop is terminated and line 240, which is the last line of the program, is encountered.

    You can use a step value in a FOR-TO statement. The starting, ending, and step values can be any numbers, positive, negative, or zero (however, a zero step value generates an endless loop). The program in Figure C−30 demonstrates the looping process.

```
100     REM THIS PROGRAM WILL PRINT THE NAME "JACK" IN FIVE
110     REM DIFFERENT PRINT ZONES USING THE FOR-NEXT LOOP STRUCTURE.
120     REM
130     REM ****** VARIABLE TABLE
140     REM          NAM$ = STRING VARIABLE (JACK)
150     REM          COUNTER = FOR-NEXT LOOP COUNTER VARIABLE
160     REM
170     REM ****** INITIALIZATION SECTION
180     LET NAM$ = "JACK"
190     REM
200     REM ****** PROCESS SECTION
210     FOR COUNTER = 1 TO 4
220        PRINT NAM$,
230     NEXT COUNTER
240     END
Ok
RUN
JACK          JACK          JACK          JACK
Ok
```

Figure C−27
One Application of the FOR-NEXT Loop

Figure C−28
Another Application of the FOR-NEXT Loop

```
100     REM THIS PROGRAM WILL PRINT THE SQUARES OF THE NUMBERS
110     REM 1 THROUGH 5 USING THE FOR-NEXT LOOP STRUCTURE.
120     REM
130     REM ****** VARIABLE TABLE
140     REM          COUNTER = FOR-NEXT LOOP COUNTER VARIABLE
150     REM
160     REM ****** PROCESS SECTION
170     FOR COUNTER = 1 TO 5
180        PRINT COUNTER^2,
190     NEXT COUNTER
200     END
Ok
RUN
 1            4             9             16            25
Ok
```

```
100     REM THIS PROGRAM PRINTS THE SUM OF NUMBERS 1 THROUGH 10
110     REM INCLUSIVE.
120     REM
130     REM ****** VARIABLE TABLE
140     REM          TOTAL = SUM OF ALL THE NUMBERS
150     REM          COUNTER = FOR-NEXT LOOP COUNTER VARIABLE
160     REM
170     REM ****** INITIALIZATION SECTION
180     LET TOTAL = 0
190     REM
200     REM ****** PROCESS SECTION
210     FOR COUNTER = 1 TO 10
220        LET TOTAL = TOTAL + COUNTER
230     NEXT COUNTER
240     REM
250     REM ****** OUTPUT SECTION
260     PRINT "THE SUM OF THE NUMBERS 1 THROUGH 10 =";TOTAL
270     END
Ok
RUN
THE SUM OF THE NUMBERS 1 THROUGH 10 = 55
Ok
```

Figure C–29

Print the Sum of Numbers 1 through 10 Using a FOR-NEXT Loop

```
10      REM THERE ARE 3 LOOPS IN THIS PROGRAM.   CAN YOU FIND THEM?
20      REM
30      REM ****** VARIABLE TABLE
40      REM          COUNTER1 = FOR-NEXT LOOP COUNTER VARIABLE
50      REM          COUNTER2 = FOR-NEXT LOOP COUNTER VARIABLE
60      REM          COUNTER3 = FOR-NEXT LOOP COUNTER VARIABLE
70      REM
80      REM ****** PROCESS SECTION
90      FOR COUNTER1 = 1 TO 2 STEP .5
100        PRINT "A COMPUTER IS AN INTERESTING DEVICE"
110      NEXT COUNTER1
120      REM
130      PRINT
140      FOR COUNTER2 = 6 TO 2 STEP -2
150        PRINT "BASIC IS EASY"
160      NEXT COUNTER2
170      REM
180      PRINT
190      FOR COUNTER3 = -1 TO 7 STEP 2
200        PRINT "LOOP",
210      NEXT COUNTER3
220      END
Ok
RUN
A COMPUTER IS AN INTERESTING DEVICE
A COMPUTER IS AN INTERESTING DEVICE
A COMPUTER IS AN INTERESTING DEVICE

BASIC IS EASY
BASIC IS EASY
BASIC IS EASY

LOOP            LOOP            LOOP            LOOP            LOOP
Ok
```

Figure C–30

Example of a FOR-NEXT Loop with Step

227

C–23

NESTED LOOPS

There are many occasions when you may want to use one loop inside another. This is called nested looping. Whenever you are using a nested loop, the inner loop must be completely inside the outside loop—nested loops cannot cross each other. Figures C–31 and C–32 are some examples of nested loops.

C–24

THE STOP STATEMENT

The STOP statement terminates a BASIC program. This statement is very similar to the END statement, but there are several differences. A BASIC program can have only one END statement, but it can have several STOP statements, and the END statement must be at the end of the program, but the STOP statement can be anywhere. The STOP statement causes the computer to skip over statements and go to the last line, the END statement. The following two programs are identical:

```
10 PRINT "ANDREW"        10 PRINT "ANDREW"
20 STOP                  20 GOTO 40
30 PRINT "JACK"          30 PRINT "JACK"
40 END                   40 END
```

Both of these programs generate the following output:

```
ANDREW
```

Remember, the program with STOP also generates the error message:

```
Break in 20
```

Figure C–31

Print a 5-by-15 Square of Stars by Using Nested Loops

```
100     REM THIS PROGRAM PRINTS A 5 BY 15 SQUARE OF STARS.
110     REM
120     REM ****** VARIABLE TABLE
130     REM          ROW = FOR-NEXT LOOP COUNTER VARIABLE
140     REM          COLUMN = FOR-NEXT LOOP COUNTER VARIABLE
150     REM
160     REM ****** PROCESS SECTION
170     FOR ROW = 1 TO 5
180        FOR COLUMN = 1 TO 15
190           PRINT "*";
200        NEXT COLUMN
210        PRINT
220     NEXT ROW
230     END
Ok
RUN
***************
***************
***************
***************
***************
Ok
```

```
100      REM THIS PROGRAM USES A TOTAL ACCUMULATOR TO ADD TOGETHER
110      REM THE VALUES OF FOR-NEXT LOOP VARIABLES AT SUCCESSIVE
120      REM POINTS THROUGH THE EXECUTION OF THE PROGRAM, AND
130      REM PROVIDES A RUNNING DISPLAY OF THE TOTAL.
140      REM
150      REM ****** VARIABLE TABLE
160      REM          TOTAL = TOTAL ACCUMULATOR
170      REM          COUNTER1 = FOR-NEXT LOOP COUNTER VARIABLE
180      REM          COUNTER2 = FOR-NEXT LOOP COUNTER VARIABLE
190      REM
200      REM ****** INITIALIZATION SECTION
210      LET TOTAL = 0
220      REM
230      REM ****** PROCESS SECTION
240      FOR COUNTER1 = 1 TO 5 STEP 2
250         FOR COUNTER2 = -6 TO -10 STEP -2
260            LET TOTAL = TOTAL+COUNTER1+COUNTER2
270            PRINT TOTAL
280         NEXT COUNTER2
290      NEXT COUNTER1
300      END
Ok
RUN
-5
-12
-21
-24
-29
-36
-37
-40
-45
Ok
```

Figure C–32
Another Example of Using Nested Loops

C–25

THE TAB FUNCTION

The TAB function is used for spacing within an output line. The general format of this function is as follows:

PRINT TAB(expression);(data to be printed)

This function causes the computer to print the next data field at the column indicated by the value of the expression. Figure C–33 shows this process.

Line 160 tells the computer to skip the first 9 columns and to start printing at column 10. Line 170 tells the computer to skip the first 17 columns and to start printing at column 18.

Whenever you use the TAB function, you must consider two exceptions: if the value of the expression is less than the current position of the character, the TAB function ignores the current line and prints the results in the next line; and if the expression results in a value greater than the last position in the line, the TAB function will print in the last possible positions in the line.

```
100     REM THIS PROGRAM SHOWS THE WAY IN WHICH THE TAB FUNCTION WORKS.
110     REM
120     REM ****** VARIABLE TABLE
130     REM           THERE ARE NO VARIABLES IN THIS PROGRAM.
140     REM
150     REM ****** OUTPUT SECTION
160     PRINT TAB(10);"COMPUTERS"
170     PRINT TAB(18);"ARE INTERESTING"
180     END
Ok
RUN
          COMPUTERS
                  ARE INTERESTING
Ok
```

Figure C–33
Using the TAB Function

C–26

THE PRINT USING STATEMENT

This statement is used for formatting a line or a series of lines of output. These commands are very helpful in producing an exact output. You can use the PRINT USING statement with integer, decimal, exponential, and alphanumeric fields.

Integer Field

An integer field PRINT USING statement is used for printing integer numbers. Each digit of an integer field is indicated by a pound sign (#); you must use a pound sign for the sign of the number as well. The number of pound signs must be at least equal to the width of the field. Figures C–34, C–35, and C–36 show this process.

When you execute Figure C–34, the specified values are printed in a right-justified format. Because this format is for an integer field, the decimal parts of numbers are rounded. In this program, 5267 is printed in columns 1 to

Figure C–34
PRINT USING for Integer Fields

```
100     REM THIS PROGRAM WILL PRINT THREE NUMBERS
110     REM USING THE PRINT USING STATEMENT.
120     REM
130     REM ****** VARIABLE TABLE
140     REM           NUM1, NUM2, NUM3 = INPUT VARIABLES
150     REM
160     REM ****** INITIALIZATION SECTION
170     LET NUM1 = 5267
180     LET NUM2 = 918.99
190     LET NUM3 = 5011.44
200     REM
210     REM ****** OUTPUT SECTION
220     PRINT USING "####    ####    ####";NUM1,NUM2,NUM3
230     END
Ok
RUN
5267    919    5011
Ok
```

```
100    REM THIS PROGRAM WILL PRINT TWO NUMBERS
110    REM USING THE PRINT USING STATEMENT.
120    REM
130    REM ****** VARIABLE TABLE
140    REM          NUM1, NUM2 = INPUT VARIABLES
150    REM
160    REM ****** INITIALIZATION SECTION
170    LET NUM1 = 9999
180    LET NUM2 = 9999
190    REM
200    REM ****** OUTPUT SECTION
210    PRINT USING "#### ###";NUM1,NUM2
220    END
Ok
RUN
9999 %9999
Ok
```

Figure C–35
Insufficient Format Width in the Integer Field

4; 918.98 is rounded to 919 and printed in columns 8 to 10 (columns 5, 6, and 7 are skipped); and 5011.44 is rounded to 5011 and printed in columns 13 to 16 (columns 11 and 12 are skipped).

In Figure C–35, we specified only three places for variable NUM2, which is not adequate. The computer displays a percent sign (%) to indicate the insufficient format width. Figure C–36 illustrates the use of the dollar sign ($). If you use two dollar signs ($$), the dollar sign will be floated. Using one dollar sign will not float the sign.

Decimal Fields

The decimal field format is very similar to the integer field format. The only difference is that a decimal point separates the integer part from the decimal part. Figure C–37 shows this process.

Exponential Fields

The exponential field is similar to the decimal field, except that it is followed by four carets (^^^^). These carets provide the required spaces for the exponent. See Figure C–38. The exclamation sign is displayed by the computer to indicate single-precision format.

```
100    REM THIS PROGRAM WILL PRINT TWO NUMBERS USING
110    REM THE PRINT USING STATEMENT WITH CURRENCY FORMAT.
120    REM
130    REM ****** VARIABLE TABLE
140    REM          NUM1, NUM2 = INPUT VARIABLES
150    REM
160    REM ****** INITIALIZATION SECTION
170    LET NUM1 = 9999
180    LET NUM2 = 9999
190    REM
200    REM ****** OUTPUT SECTION
210    PRINT USING "$$#### $$####";NUM1,NUM2
220    END
Ok
RUN
 $9999   $9999
Ok
```

Figure C–36
A Dollar Sign as Part of the Output

```
100    REM THIS PROGRAM WILL PRINT FOUR NUMBERS USING THE PRINT
110    REM USING STATEMENT CARRYING THE DECIMAL TO DIFFERENT LENGTHS.
120    REM
130    REM ****** VARIABLE TABLE
140    REM          NUM1, NUM2, NUM3, NUM4 = INPUT VARIABLES
150    REM
160    REM ****** INITIALIZATION SECTION
170    LET NUM1 = -999.99
180    LET NUM2 = -300.43
190    LET NUM3 = -11.019
200    LET NUM4 = 999.99
210    REM
220    REM ****** OUTPUT SECTION
230    PRINT USING "####.## ####.#### ###.## ###.####";NUM1,NUM2,NUM3,NUM4
240    END
Ok
RUN
-999.99 -300.4300 -11.02 999.9900
Ok
```

Figure C–37
PRINT USING for Decimal Fields

Alphanumeric Fields

Figure C–39 illustrates an example of an alphanumeric field.

The string is left-justified within the field, and the rest of the field is blanked out. If the string is longer than the length of the field specified, it is truncated.

```
100 REM THIS PROGRAM WILL PRINT FOUR NUMBERS USING
110 REM THE PRINT USING STATEMENT WITH EXPONENTIAL FORMAT.
120 REM
130 REM ****** VARIABLE TABLE
140 REM NUM1, NUM2, NUM3, NUM4=INPUT VARIABLES
150 REM
160 REM ****** INITIALIZATION SECTION
170    NUM1=1296540!
180    NUM2=.0000489
190    NUM3=-764692!
200    NUM4=11.96721
210 REM
220 REM ****** OUTPUT SECTION
230    PRINT USING "##.##^^^^   ##.###^^^^   ##.##^^^^   #.##^^^^";NUM1,NUM2,NUM3,
NUM4
290 END
Ok
RUN
 1.30E+06    4.890E-05   -7.65E+05    0.12E+02
Ok
```

Figure C–38
PRINT USING for Exponential Fields

```
100    REM THIS PROGRAM WILL PRINT STRING DATA USING
110    REM THE PRINT USING STATEMENT.
120    REM
130    REM ****** VARIABLE TABLE
140    REM          WORD1$ = STRING VARIABLE
150    REM          WORD2$ = STRING VARIABLE
160    REM
170    REM ****** INITIALIZATION SECTION
180    LET WORD1$ = "BASIC"
190    LET WORD2$ = "ABCDEWELL"
200    REM
210    REM ****** OUTPUT SECTION
220    PRINT USING "\                 \";WORD1$,WORD2$
230    END
Ok
RUN
BASIC           ABCDEWELL
Ok
```

Figure C-39
PRINT USING for Alphanumeric
Fields

C-27
SUBSCRIPTED VARIABLES

So far, we have discussed only simple numeric variables. But, by using the subscripted variables, you can increase the number of variables to a very large number. The general form of subscripted variables in BASIC is as follows:

A(I)
B(J)
W9(T)

In this example, A, B, and W9 are called subscripted variables or arrays. These arrays stand for a family of variables, all of which are referred to by A, B, or W9, but with different subscripts. For example, "I" can be any positive integer from 1 to 100,000, or an even larger number.

You must keep in mind that A, A1, and A(1) are three different variables. A and A1 are both from the family of simple numeric variables. A(1) is a subscripted variable and is from the family of subscripted variables.

C-28
THE DIM STATEMENT

Before using an array, the size of the array must be defined. You define the size with the DIM statement. In most systems, an array up to size 10 doesn't need to be dimensioned, but it's a good practice to dimension any array. The following program segment shows different types of DIM statements:

```
10 DIM A(100),B(50)
20 DIM A$(70),B$(40)
```

In line 10, 152 addresses are reserved in arrays A and B— 101 addresses in A and 51 addresses in B. In line 20, we have reserved 112 addresses in the string arrays A\$ and B\$. For example, A(10) simply means:

```
A(0)     |___ 0 ___|
A(1)     |___ 0 ___|
A(2)     |___ 0 ___|
A(3)     |___ 0 ___|
A(4)     |___ 0 ___|
A(5)     |___ 0 ___|
A(6)     |___ 0 ___|
A(7)     |___ 0 ___|
A(8)     |___ 0 ___|
A(9)     |___ 0 ___|
A(10)    |___ 0 ___|
```

A(0) through A(10) are the names of the addresses; the addresses contain zeros. In some versions of BASIC, the starting address is 1, not 0. For example, A(10) creates only 10 addresses, from A(1) to A(10). In IBM BASIC, by using the OPTION BASE command, you can start the first address at 0 or 1. For example, if you type

OPTION BASE 1

your starting address will be 1, not 0.

C–29
STORING DATA IN AN ARRAY

You can use the three common methods of sending data to the computer (READ/DATA, LET statements, and INPUT statements) to fill an array. Figures C–40 to C–42 show these processes by filling an array of size 5 with the numbers 10, 20, 30, 40, and 50.

The program in Figure C–42 asks for the numbers for the array from the keyboard.

C–30
RETRIEVING THE CONTENTS OF AN ARRAY

When an array is filled, you can use the PRINT statement to retrieve its contents. Figure C–43 fills an array of size 11 with the numbers 2, 4, 6, 8, 10, 12, 14, 16, 18, 20, and 22, and then retrieves its contents.

C–31
SEQUENTIAL SEARCH

Sometimes you are interested in the value of a particular member of an array. One way of finding the value is by using the sequential search algorithm. You simply compare a particular value with all the members of the array until the

```
100     REM THIS PROGRAM FILLS AN ARRAY OF SIZE 5
110     REM BY USING THE READ AND DATA STATEMENT COMBINATION.
120     REM
130     REM ******* VARIABLE TABLE
140     REM           COUNTER = FOR-NEXT LOOP CONTROL VARIABLE
150     REM
160     REM ******* ARRAY TABLE
170     REM           A(5) = A FIVE-ELEMENT INPUT DATA ARRAY
180     REM
190     REM ******* INITIALIZATION SECTION
200     DIM A(5)
210     REM
220     REM ******* PROCESS SECTION
230     FOR COUNTER = 1 TO 5
240        READ A(COUNTER)
250     NEXT COUNTER
260     REM
270     REM ******* DATA SECTION
280     DATA 10,20,30,40,50
290     END
Ok
RUN
Ok
```

Figure C–40
Using READ and DATA Statements

desired value is found. Suppose that the G.P.A.s of 11 students in a computer class have been stored in array G. You want to search this array to see if there is any person with a G.P.A. of 2.2. Figure C–44, an algorithm for sequential search, performs this search using the following sample data:

2.90,3.60,2.88,3.60,4.00,1.50,1.75,3.20,2.20,4.00,3.75

If more than one person has a G.P.A. of 2.20, the computer prints the first one encountered. You can generalize this program by redefining the DIM statement.

```
100     REM THIS PROGRAM FILLS AN ARRAY OF SIZE 5 BY THE ASSIGN-
110     REM MENT STATEMENT.
120     REM
130     REM ******* VARIABLE TABLE
140     REM           THERE ARE NO VARIABLES IN THIS PROGRAM.
150     REM
160     REM ******* ARRAY TABLE
170     REM           A(5) = A FIVE-ELEMENT INPUT DATA ARRAY.
180     REM
190     REM ******* INITIALIZATION SECTION
200     DIM A(5)
210     LET A(1) = 10
220     LET A(2) = 20
230     LET A(3) = 30
240     LET A(4) = 40
250     LET A(5) = 50
260     END
Ok
RUN
Ok
```

Figure C–41
Using the LET (Assignment) Statement

```
100     REM THIS PROGRAM FILLS AN 5-ELEMENT ARRAY CALLED SALES
110     REM USING AN INPUT STATEMENT WITHIN A FOR-NEXT LOOP STRUCTURE.
120     REM
130     REM ****** VARIABLE TABLE
140     REM          COUNTER = FOR-NEXT LOOP CONTROL VARIABLE
150     REM
160     REM ****** ARRAY TABLE
170     REM          SALES(5) = A FIVE-ELEMENT INPUT DATA ARRAY
180     REM
190     REM ****** INITIALIZATION SECTION
200     DIM SALES(5)
210     REM
220     REM ****** PROCESS SECTION
230     FOR COUNTER = 1 TO 5
240        INPUT SALES(COUNTER)
250     NEXT COUNTER
260     END
Ok
RUN
? 2
? 5
? 7
? 10
? 12
Ok
```

Figure C-42
Using the INPUT Statement

```
100     REM THIS PROGRAM FILLS AN 11-ELEMENT ARRAY CALLED ROOM
110     REM AND DISPLAYS ITS CONTENTS.
120     REM
130     REM ****** VARIABLE TABLE
140     REM          COUNTER1 = FOR-NEXT LOOP CONTROL VARIABLE
150     REM          COUNTER2 = FOR-NEXT LOOP CONTROL VARIABLE
160     REM
170     REM ****** ARRAY TABLE
180     REM          ROOM(11) = AN 11-ELEMENT INPUT DATA ARRAY
190     REM
200     REM ****** INITIALIZATION SECTION
210     OPTION BASE 1
220     DIM ROOM(11)
230     REM
240     REM ****** PROCESS SECTION
250     FOR COUNTER1 = 1 TO 11
260        READ ROOM(COUNTER1)
270     NEXT COUNTER1
280     REM
290     REM ****** OUTPUT SECTION
300     REM THIS PART OF THE PROGRAM RETRIEVES THE ARRAY'S CONTENTS.
310     FOR COUNTER2 = 1 TO 11
320        PRINT ROOM(COUNTER2);
330     NEXT COUNTER2
340     REM
350     REM ****** DATA SECTION
360     DATA 2,4,6,8,10,12,14,16,18,20,22
370     END
Ok
RUN
 2   4   6   8   10   12   14   16   18   20   22
Ok
```

Figure C-43
Fill an Array and Retrieve Its Contents

```
100     REM THIS IS AN ALGORITHM FOR SEQUENTIAL SEARCH.
110     REM
120     REM ****** VARIABLE TABLE
130     REM         COUNT = FOR-NEXT LOOP CONTROL VARIABLE
140     REM
150     REM ****** ARRAY TABLE
160     REM         GPA(11) = AN 11-ELEMENT ARRAY CONTAINING ARRAY VALUES
170     REM
180     REM ****** INITIALIZATION SECTION
190     PRINT "****** G.P.A.   REPORT ******"
200     DIM GPA(11)
210     REM
220     REM ****** PROCESS SECTION
230     FOR COUNT = 1 TO 11
240        READ GPA(COUNT)
250        IF GPA(COUNT) = 2.2 THEN GOTO 300
260     NEXT COUNT
270     REM
280     REM ****** OUTPUT SECTION
290     PRINT "THERE IS NOBODY WITH A GPA OF 2.20!   SORRY" : GOTO 340
300     PRINT "STUDENT NO";COUNT;"HAS A GPA OF 2.20."
310     REM
320     REM ****** DATA SECTION
330     DATA 2.90,3.60,2.88,3.60,4.00,1.50,1.75,3.20,2.20,4.00,3.75
340     END
Ok
RUN
****** G.P.A.   REPORT ******
STUDENT NO 9 HAS A GPA OF 2.20.
Ok
```

Figure C-44
An Algorithm for Sequential Search

C-32
SORTING

Whenever some numeric or non-numeric data are stored in an array, they can be sorted either in ascending or in descending order. Sorting is always performed based on key values.

There are many applications of sorting procedures. For example, you can sort students based on their G.P.A.s, on their last names, or on their social security numbers. You can sort the names of sales people in a store based on their sales performance.

There are several different kinds of sorting routines. The method discussed in this appendix is called a bubble sort. When the execution of the program is completed, the smallest or the largest number has been "bubbled" to the top. The bubble sort routine is a relatively slow procedure, but is probably the easiest kind of sort. Figure C-45 presents a general algorithm for a bubble sort routine.

```
100 REM THIS PROGRAM PERFORMS A BUBBLE SORT IN ASCENDING ORDER.
110 REM N IS THE SIZE OF THE ARRAY. X IS THE NAME OF THE ARRAY AND
120 REM T IS A TEMPORARY ADDRESS.
130 FOR K=1 TO N-1
140    FOR J=K+1 TO N
150       IF X(K)<=X(J) THEN 200
160       T=X(K)
170       X(K)=X(J)
180       X(J)=T
190    NEXT J
200 NEXT K
210 END
```

Figure C–45

Bubble Sort Algorithm

```
100     REM THIS PROGRAM SORTS 5 NUMBERS INTO ASCENDING ORDER.
110     REM
120     REM ****** VARIABLE TABLE
130     REM          COUNT1 = FOR-NEXT LOOP CONTROL VARIABLE
140     REM          COUNT2 = FOR-NEXT LOOP CONTROL VARIABLE
150     REM          COUNT3 = FOR-NEXT LOOP CONTROL VARIABLE
160     REM          COUNT4 = FOR-NEXT LOOP CONTROL VARIABLE
170     REM
180     REM ****** ARRAY TABLE
190     REM          ARRAY(5) = A 5-ELEMENT INPUT DATA ARRAY
200     REM
210     REM ****** INITIALIZATION SECTION
220     DIM ARRAY(5)
230     REM
240     REM ****** PROCESS SECTION
250     FOR COUNT1 = 1 TO 5
260        READ ARRAY(COUNT1)
270     NEXT COUNT1
280     REM
290     REM ****** DATA SECTION
300     DATA 18,40,31,25,10
310     REM
320     REM THE SORTING ROUTINE BEGINS.
330     PRINT "THE FOLLOWING NUMBERS ARE SORTED IN AN ASCENDING ORDER"
340     FOR COUNT2 = 1 TO 4
350        FOR COUNT3 = COUNT2+1 TO 5
360           IF ARRAY(COUNT2)<=ARRAY(COUNT3) THEN GOTO 400
370           LET TEMP = ARRAY(COUNT2)
380           ARRAY(COUNT2) = ARRAY(COUNT3)
390           ARRAY(COUNT3) = TEMP
400        NEXT COUNT3
410     NEXT COUNT2
420     REM ****** OUTPUT SECTION
430     REM THIS SEGMENT OF THE PROGRAM PRINTS THE SORTED ARRAY.
440     FOR COUNT4 = 1 TO 5
450        PRINT TAB(25);ARRAY(COUNT4)
460     NEXT COUNT4
470     END
Ok
RUN
THE FOLLOWING NUMBERS ARE SORTED IN AN ASCENDING ORDER
                         10
                         18
                         25
                         31
                         40
Ok
```

Figure C–46

Sort the Numbers 18, 40, 31, 25, and 10 in Ascending Order

Let's trace this program to see how a bubble sort routine works. Lines 340 to 410 are the sort routine. Before we start this routine, the array ARRAY appears as follows:

ARRAY(1) ┌ _ _ 18 _ _ _ ┐
ARRAY(2) │ _ _ 40 _ _ _ │
ARRAY(3) │ _ _ 31 _ _ _ │
ARRAY(4) │ _ _ 25 _ _ _ │
ARRAY(5) └ _ _ 10 _ _ _ ┘

When we are done with the first iteration, the smallest number will be on the top of the array; in this case 10 has bubbled to the top, as follows:

COUNT2=1   COUNT3=2   TEMP=18   ARRAY(1)=10
              COUNT3=3   ARRAY(5)=18
              COUNT3=4
              COUNT3=5

ARRAY(1) ┌ _ _ 10 _ _ _ ┐
ARRAY(2) │ _ _ 40 _ _ _ │
ARRAY(3) │ _ _ 31 _ _ _ │
ARRAY(4) │ _ _ 25 _ _ _ │
ARRAY(5) └ _ _ 18 _ _ _ ┘

When we are finished with the second iteration, the second smallest number will be in the second position from the top; in this case, 18 has come up to the second position, as follows:

COUNT2=2   COUNT3=3   TEMP=40   ARRAY(2)=31
                                        ARRAY(3)=40
              COUNT3=4   TEMP=31   ARRAY(2)=25
                                        ARRAY(4)=31
                                        ARRAY(2)=18
              COUNT3=5   TEMP=25   ARRAY(5)=25

ARRAY(1) ┌ _ _ 10 _ _ _ ┐
ARRAY(2) │ _ _ 18 _ _ _ │
ARRAY(3) │ _ _ 40 _ _ _ │
ARRAY(4) │ _ _ 31 _ _ _ │
ARRAY(5) └ _ _ 25 _ _ _ ┘

When we are done with the third iteration, the third smallest number will be in the third position from the top; in this case, 25 has come up to the third position, as follows:

COUNT2=3   COUNT3=4   TEMP=40   ARRAY(3)=31   ARRAY(1) ┌ _ _ 10 _ _ _ ┐
                                        ARRAY(4)=40   ARRAY(2) │ _ _ 18 _ _ _ │
              COUNT3=5   TEMP=31   ARRAY(3)=25   ARRAY(3) │ _ _ 25 _ _ _ │
                                        ARRAY(5)=31   ARRAY(4) │ _ _ 40 _ _ _ │
                                                         ARRAY(5) └ _ _ 31 _ _ _ ┘

When we are finished with the fourth iteration, the fourth smallest number will be in the fourth position from the top; in this case, 31 has come to the fourth position, as follows:

COUNT2=4   COUNT3=5   TEMP=40   ARRAY(4)=31   ARRAY(1) | 10 |
                                        ARRAY(5)=40   ARRAY(2) | 18 |
                                                         ARRAY(3) | 25 |
                                                         ARRAY(4) | 31 |
                                                         ARRAY(5) | 40 |

After this iteration, the last number will be on the bottom and the sorting routine will be completed. In a bubble sort, the number of iterations is always $n - 1$, where n is the size of the array. Remember, in GW-BASIC you can replace lines 160, 170, and 180 in Figure C–45 with a SWAP command. You can type:

SWAP X(J),X(K)

This will make the SORT process more efficient and easier to understand. However, both methods work fine.

C–33

DEFINING A TABLE

A table or a two-dimensional array is a group of memory locations similar to a grid of boxes arranged in rows and columns, as shown below:

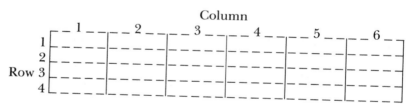

As with one-dimensional arrays, the size of a table must be defined in the DIM statement. The DIM statement always defines the number of rows and the number of columns. For example,

DIM A(5,3), D(4,4)

defines two tables. Table A has five rows and three columns, and table D has four rows and four columns (assuming that we start from address 1,1 and not 0,0). In the DIM statement, the first number enclosed in parentheses refers to the number of rows, the second number refers to the number of columns.

There are a great number of examples of tables in real-life practice. For example, a shoe company may record its inventory in a table. The rows of the table might represent the different sizes of the shoes and the columns might represent the different colors of the shoes. For example, row 1, column 1 may indicate the number of shoes of size 7 and color white. Row 12, column 5 may indicate the number of shoes of size 9 and color brown, and so on.

A college could maintain its students' records in a table. The rows of the table might represent different names and the columns might represent the ages, majors, G.P.A.s, and so on, of the students. For example, row 1 may indicate all the information related to John Brown, column 10 may include all the students' G.P.A.s, and so forth.

C–34
IDENTIFICATION OF THE DIFFERENT ELEMENTS OF A TABLE

As mentioned earlier, the DIM statement defines the size of a table. An element of a table is referred to by its unique address in the table. For example, DIM X(4,5) defines a 4-by-5 table as follows (assuming that we start from address 1,1 and not 0,0):

Column

X(1,1) means row 1 column 1
X(3,5) means row 3 column 5

We should keep in mind that these are just addresses in the computer, but at the present time their contents are zeros.

C–35
FILLING AND RETRIEVING A TABLE

The three common methods of sending data into the computer (READ-DATA statements, LET statements, and INPUT statements) can be used to fill a table. However, using nested loops and the READ-DATA statements is probably the most efficient way of filling a table. You can use the PRINT statement to retrieve the contents of a table.

Suppose that the Fan-Fan Company has three branches that are active in four different regions. The following data are the total sales for the past 12 months of three different branches. Each line of data shows the total sales of a branch in four different regions:

    Branch 1, 15000, 20000, 18000, 22000
    Branch 2, 17000, 14000, 13000, 15000
    Branch 3, 14000, 17000, 22000, 11000

You want to read this data into Table SALES and print the contents of the table. Figure C–47 shows this process.

Lines 250 through 290 fill the table in a row-by-row sequence (the first line of data fills the first row, the second line of data fills the second row, and so on). Lines 340 through 380 retrieve the table in a row-by-row sequence.

In line 350 we have put a semicolon after the name of the variable being printed. This semicolon keeps the carriage on the same line—the line on which the present value is being printed.

```
100   REM THIS PROGRAM GENERATES A 3 BY 4 TABLE OF SALES INFORMATION.
110   REM
120   REM ******* VARIABLE TABLE
130   REM          COUNT1 = FOR-NEXT LOOP CONTROL VARIABLE
140   REM          COUNT2 = FOR-NEXT LOOP CONTROL VARIABLE
150   REM
160   REM ******* ARRAY TABLE
170   REM          SALES(3,4) = A 3x4 SALES DATA ARRAY
180   REM
190   REM ******* INITIALIZATION SECTION
200   DIM SALES(3,4)
210   PRINT "SALES INFORMATION FOR FAN-FAN COMPANY"
220   REM
230   REM ******* PROCESS SECTION
240   REM THIS SECTION FILLS THE SALES ARRAY.
250   FOR COUNT1 = 1 TO 3
260     FOR COUNT2 = 1 TO 4
270       READ SALES(COUNT1,COUNT2)
280     NEXT COUNT2
290   NEXT COUNT1
300   REM
310   REM ******* OUTPUT SECTION
320   REM THIS SECTION DISPLAYS THE CONTENTS OF THE SALES ARRAY.
330   FOR COUNT1 = 1 TO 3
340     FOR COUNT2 = 1 TO 4
350       PRINT "   ";SALES(COUNT1,COUNT2);
360     NEXT COUNT2
370     PRINT
380   NEXT COUNT1
390   REM
400   REM ******* DATA SECTION
410   DATA 15000,20000,18000,22000
420   DATA 17000,14000,13000,15000
430   DATA 14000,17000,22000,11000
440   END
Ok
RUN
SALES INFORMATION FOR FAN-FAN COMPANY
    15000     20000     18000     22000
    17000     14000     13000     15000
    14000     17000     22000     11000
Ok
```

Figure C–47

Read Data into a Table and Print the Table

In line 370, by using a PRINT statement, we move the carriage to the next line. In line 200, we have dimensioned Table SALES. In many systems, a table as large as 10-by-10 does not need to be dimensioned. However, it is good programming practice to dimension all tables regardless of their size. The addresses and their contents are as follows:

SALES(1,1)=15000   SALES(2,1)=17000   SALES(3,1)=14000
SALES(1,2)=20000   SALES(2,2)=14000   SALES(3,2)=17000
SALES(1,3)=18000   SALES(2,3)=13000   SALES(3,3)=22000
SALES(1,4)=22000   SALES(2,4)=15000   SALES(3,4)=11000

C-36

DEFINING A SUBROUTINE

A subroutine is a series of instructions in a program. The subroutine can be called from anywhere in the program as many times as required.

There are two main reasons for using subroutines: saving time and making your program easier to write and debug.

Whenever a portion of a program must be used more than once, you can write it as a subroutine, and call it as many times as you want. Because you don't have to write the routine several times, you save time. Large programs can be divided into several small sections, and each section can be written as a subroutine. This is called modular programming. Modular programs are easier to write, maintain, run, and debug than non-modular programs.

C-37

ENTERING AND EXITING A SUBROUTINE

You use the GOSUB command to enter a subroutine and the RETURN command to exit a subroutine. The GOSUB command is very similar to the GOTO command as an unconditional branching technique.

C-38

A GENERAL CONFIGURATION OF A MAIN PROGRAM AND SUBROUTINES

A program with subroutines is divided into two major sections. The first section is called the main program, and the second section is called the subroutine section. A GOTO n command (n is the line number of the END statement) always separates the main program from its subroutines. As we mentioned earlier, the GOSUB command transfers control to the subroutine, and the RETURN command transfers control to the line immediately following the GOSUB command. Figure C-48 shows this configuration.

Lines 10 to 1995 are the main program, and lines 2000 to 3000 are the subroutine section of this program. The statements in this program are executed as follows:

10, 20, 30, . . ., 150, 2000, . . ., 3000, 160, . . ., 300, 2000, . . ., 3000, 310, . . ., 600, 2000, . . ., 3000, 610, . . ., 1995, 9999

Figure C-49 uses a subroutine to calculate the average of three numbers, the average of their squares, and the average of their cubes.

Figure C–48
A General Configuration of a
Main Program and Its Subrou-
tine

```
10  REM A PROGRAM WITH A SUBROUTINE.
20
30
  .
  .
150 GOSUB 2000
160
  .
  .
300 GOSUB 2000
310
  .
  .
600 GOSUB 2000
610
  .
  .
1995 GOTO 9999
2000 PRINT "SUBROUTINE STARTS HERE"
  .
  .
3000 RETURN
9999 END
```

Of course, this program could be written without using a subroutine; however, without it, lines 330 to 410 must be repeated three times. Using subroutines reduces the number of coding lines.

SUMMARY

This appendix provided a quick review of BASIC programming. We outlined the steps in the program-development life cycle and briefly discussed flowcharting. Different commands and statements were discussed, including the LIST, LLIST, RUN, SAVE, LOAD, CLS, DELETE, INPUT, PRINT, REM, END, GOTO, IF-THEN-ELSE, IF-THEN, READ DATA, DIM, TAB, and PRINT USING statements. We also provided a quick review of arrays, tables, and subroutines. This presentation should provide you with an introductory knowledge about programming in general and BASIC in particular.

```
100     REM THIS PROGRAM READS 3 NUMBERS FROM A DATA LINE AND
110     REM COMPUTES THEIR AVERAGE, THE AVERAGE OF THEIR
120     REM SQUARES, AND THE AVERAGE OF THEIR CUBES.
130     REM
140     REM ****** VARIABLE TABLE
150     REM          NUM1, NUM2, NUM3 = INPUT VARIABLES
160     REM          AVERAGE1 = AVERAGE OF NUM1, NUM2 AND NUM3
170     REM          AVERAGE2 = AVERAGE OF THE SQUARES OF NUM1, NUM2, NUM3
180     REM          AVERAGE3 = AVERAGE OF THE CUBES OF NUM1, NUM2, NUM3
190     REM
200     REM ****** INITIALIZATION SECTION
210     READ NUM1, NUM2, NUM3
220     REM
230     REM ****** DATA SECTION
240     DATA 1,2,3,4,5,6,7,8,9
250     REM
260     REM ****** PROCESS SECTION
270     GOSUB 330
280     READ NUM1, NUM2, NUM3
290     GOSUB 330
300     READ NUM1, NUM2, NUM3
310     GOSUB 330
320     GOTO 430
330     LET AVERAGE1 = (NUM1+NUM2+NUM3)/3
340     LET AVERAGE2 = (NUM1^2+NUM2^2+NUM3^2)/3
350     LET AVERAGE3 = (NUM1^3+NUM2^3+NUM3^3)/3
360     REM
370     REM ****** OUTPUT SECTION
380     PRINT "THE AVERAGE OF THE 3 NUMBERS =";AVERAGE1
390     PRINT "THE AVERAGE OF THEIR SQUARES =";AVERAGE2
400     PRINT "THE AVERAGE OF THEIR CUBES   =";AVERAGE3
410     PRINT
420     RETURN
430     END
Ok
RUN
THE AVERAGE OF THE 3 NUMBERS = 2
THE AVERAGE OF THEIR SQUARES = 4.666667
THE AVERAGE OF THEIR CUBES   = 12

THE AVERAGE OF THE 3 NUMBERS = 5
THE AVERAGE OF THEIR SQUARES = 25.66667
THE AVERAGE OF THEIR CUBES   = 135

THE AVERAGE OF THE 3 NUMBERS = 8
THE AVERAGE OF THEIR SQUARES = 64.66666
THE AVERAGE OF THEIR CUBES   = 528

Ok
```

Figure C–49
Using a Subroutine

REVIEW QUESTIONS

1. Why do you use flowcharts?
2. How do you load BASIC? What is the BASIC prompt?
3. Why should a program have line numbers?
4. What is the difference between the LIST command and the RUN command?
5. How do you erase a file from your disk?
6. What command provides you with a listing of all the files on your disk?
7. What are three methods of sending data to the computer?
8. What are numeric variables? String variables?
9. What command is used for interactive programming?
10. What are the differences between commas and semicolons when they are used with the PRINT command?
11. What are relational operations?
12. What command is used for unconditional branching? For conditional branching?
13. What is the difference between the END statement and the STOP statement?
14. What are the functions of PRINT USING statements? How many types of PRINT USING statements are there?
15. What are subscripted variables?
16. What are the major advantages of using arrays?
17. What are tables? How do you fill a table? How do you retrieve its contents?
18. What are the applications of sort operations? Of search operations?
19. What are the applications of subroutines? What is modular programming?
20. In the following program, how many data items are needed?

```
10 FOR A=1 TO 10
20    FOR B=1 TO 5
30       READ C
40    NEXT B
50 NEXT A
60 DATA
70 END
```

21. Read the following numbers into an array, and then sort the array in descending order:

   1, 10, 2, 29, 95

22. Write a payroll program that accepts a name, social security number, pay rate, and overtime rate and the number of hours worked from the keyboard, then prints a paycheck. The overtime rate is 50 percent more than the regular rate.
23. Write a program to print the following message as many times as the user requests: COMPUTERS ARE FUN!

Index